GOD'S DANGE

THE SURPRISING HISTORY OF THE
WORLD'S MOST RADICAL BOOK

GOD'S DANGEROUS BOOK

THE SURPRISING HISTORY OF THE WORLD'S MOST RADICAL BOOK

NICK PAGE

Authentic

First published 2011 by Authentic Media Limited
52 Presley Way, Crownhill, Milton Keynes, MK8 OES
www.authenticmedia.co.uk

Reprinted 2011

British Library Cataloguing in Publication Data

A catalogue record for this book is available from the British Library

ISBN: 978-1-85078-901-7

Internal design by Nick Page
Cover design by Phil Houghton
Printed and bound by CPI Group (UK) Ltd, Croydon, CR0 4YY

CONTENTS

THE FINGER OF GOD

In 1534 a group of German radicals evicted the leaders of the city of Münster and created a community which practised polygamy, outlawed private property and proclaimed non-violence.

In 1649 three political prisoners were executed, for demanding the right to vote, a written constitution, the right to a fair trial and the abolition of the death penalty for all crimes except murder.

In 1915, a young lawyer began a succession of political campaigns for Indian independence, based around the concept of peaceful non-cooperation and non-violent strikes.

All these people had one thing in common: they'd read the Bible.

***

I have just counted the number of Bibles on my bookshelves. There are 29 entire Bibles, five New Testaments, one Apocrypha, four Greek New Testaments, one Hebrew Old Testament. On my computer there are electronic texts of another twenty versions or so, plus more versions of the Greek and Hebrew. And I'm pretty sure that there are some other copies lurking elsewhere in the house.

You may think this is rather an excessive amount of Bibles.[*] But it illustrates just how common this most uncommon of books is. It's the biggest selling book in history; translated into hundreds of languages; widely available in all shapes and sizes; hardbacked, paperbacked, leather-bound; edited, annotated, illustrated; endlessly packaged and repackaged into every flavour under the sun.

Much as it might annoy Richard Dawkins, the Bible is part of the DNA of our society. It's not just the sheer number of copies knocking around, from the battered wrecks in the charity shops to the pristine white leather presentation editions to commemorate your christening/confirmation/wedding/imminent death; it's also

---

[*] You may have a point. Especially since I can't actually read Hebrew.

that the imagery, the stories, fill our culture. The English Bibles of the sixteenth and seventeenth centuries have shaped our language: viper, scapegoat, sea-shore, fisherman, broken-hearted, the apple of your eye, the powers that be, the signs of the times. Western art draws on biblical themes: its music, full of chorales and oratorios and requiems, is full of scripture verses and stories. Literature is crammed with allusions to the Bible, whether we're talking about Hobbes' *Leviathan*, or Shaw's *Back to Methuselah*. Film titles as well: *Pale Rider*, *Armageddon*, *Apocalypse Now*. Its iconography is on our buildings. Its subjects fill our art galleries: nearly one third of the paintings in the National Gallery are paintings of scenes in the Bible.

But more, even, than the words, the phrases and the pictures: the *ideas* of the Bible have shaped our society. The Bible, so often characterised as a 'Thou shalt not' text, is just as much a 'Have a go at this' text. It has inspired radical behaviour, behaviour which has led directly to ideas we take for granted today: democracy, equality, liberty. Even in the official, authorised versions, this book contains some dangerously unofficial ideas.

So how did that happen? How did words on parchment, in Hebrew, Aramaic and Greek, end up weighing down the shelves in my study? This book explores those questions. The first part deals with the Jewish and Christian texts and how they came together to form 'the Bible'. The second part is the story of how that Bible became the world's best-selling book; focusing in particular on the English Bible, and the fight to translate the Bible into the vernacular. We'll be looking at the origins of Scripture, how the Bible was compiled and by whom, and the many ways in which the Bible has changed those who encountered it.

The truth is that the Bible was not delivered whole, shrink-wrapped and jiffy-bagged onto the desk of St Paul by some heavenly Fed-Ex courier. The Bible, from the start, was the subject of discussion and argument, compromise and debate. The actual contents of the Old Testament were not finalised until some fifteen hundred years after Moses went up the mountain, and it was not until around four hundred years after the death of Jesus Christ that the Christian church finally came up with its official, approved list.

In fact, even today it has no final, fixed form: the Bible used in Protestant churches is different to that used by Catholic churches which is different again to that used by the Eastern Orthodox churches. And, of course, all three versions are significantly different to the Scriptures used by Jews.

Over the centuries, people have argued about it, studied, it, edited it, corrected it, lived for it and died for it. And they did so because the Bible is not like any other book ever made.

The Finger of God

In the first book of the Bible nobody writes anything. God speaks and the world is created, instructions are verbal, promises are unwritten, stories are told.

It is not until well into the next book that anything gets written down. 'Write this as a reminder in a book' God tells Moses, 'and recite it in the hearing of Joshua' (Exod. 17.14). The Hebrew word for 'book' here is *sefer*, which means document, or book, or scroll. Later, in chapters 20–23, God gives Moses the law: the ten commandments, the festivals, the social legislation. Moses writes down 'all the words of the Lord,' then reads them 'in the hearing of the people' (Exod. 24.3–8). Still later, God gives Moses more instructions – a kind of religious IKEA manual on how to build the Tabernacle, the Ark of the Covenant and other religious furniture. But these are different. This time it's not Moses taking dictation, but God doing the writing: the words are engraved on two 'tablets of stone, written with the finger of God'(Exod. 31.18). And when those tablets are destroyed, they are replaced, but this time it is Moses who does the engraving

> The LORD said to Moses: Write these words; in accordance with these words I have made a covenant with you and with Israel... And [Moses] wrote on the tablets the words of the covenant, the ten commandments (Exod. 34.27–28).

In Exodus, then, there are different kinds of writing. Ink on parchment *sefarim*, incised letters on tablets of stone. Words remembered and written and read out. Originals destroyed and new copies made. It is a varied, complex process.

Crucially, there are different kinds of writers as well: human and divine. What happens in these bits of Exodus is that we see how the Bible is made. We see the process in action. It starts with God speaking to hairy men on mountains, and after that there is a lot of copying involved; a lot of writing and rewriting. There are stone and paper and different materials. Things get added and things get taken away. Stuff goes missing and has to be rewritten. And through it all, somehow, the 'finger of God' is at work. This is what gives the Scriptures their power, their fizz, their subliminal crackle of electricity. It follows his voice pattern. It bears his fingerprints.

The Bible is a biometric record of God.

God's Dangerous Book

According to Jewish belief, those tablets written by Moses had to be kept in a special box, carried by trained handlers using very long poles. The box – the Ark of the Covenant – was a high-security container, a bomb-case for the word of God.

Its subsequent history shows why. When the Israelites cross the Jordan to take possession of the land, the Ark holds back the river. When the Philistines capture the Ark, their temple god is destroyed and they suffer from an outbreak of deadly tumours.[*] When the Ark returns to Israel and the people of Jeconiah do not rejoice, seventy of their number die.[†]

King David even delays bringing the Ark into the city because of its destructive power

> When they came to the threshing floor of Chidon, Uzzah put out his hand to hold the ark, for the oxen shook it. The anger of the LORD was kindled against Uzzah; he struck him down because he put out his hand to the ark; and he died there before God. David was angry because the LORD had burst out against Uzzah; so that place is called Perez-uzzah to this day. David was afraid of God that day; he said, "How can I bring the ark of God into my care?" (1 Chr. 13.9–12).

---

[*] Joshua 3.14–17; 1 Samuel 5.1–12. Scholars argue over whether this was bubonic plague or actually a really bad case of piles. I'm not sure which is worse, actually.

[†] 1 Samuel 6.19. An alternative translation implies they died because they dared to look in the Ark.

From the start the Scriptures were bafflingly dangerous. Poor Uzzah treated them carelessly and lost his life.

This sense of uncertainty persists. The Bible is a dangerous book. Used rightly, it has the power to change lives, to inspire and inform and educate and mobilise. Used wrongly, it has the power to unleash hatred and fear and even death. And the Bible certainly has been used wrongly; the Holy Bible has been used to justify some deeply unholy activities. In this book I have tried not to gloss over the evil, stupid ways in which the Scriptures have been perverted – often by those who should know better. But if the Bible has been used by tyrants and dictators, just as often it's been used against them. The Bible has certainly been co-opted by the powers of oppression, but the real story is how the oppressed keep taking it back. When slave owners in America justified their actions by pointing out the presence of slaves in the Bible, the slaves, far from rejecting the text, read it for themselves, and discovered in the stories of Exodus a powerful narrative that they could own. The Bible has been a weapon of radical opposition – to power, tyranny, ignorance, injustice, slavery, greed.

When you really start to read the thing, you realise that the Bible is brimming with danger and dissension. From God's advice to Israel not to have a king (1 Sam. 8) to James' warning that the rich will fade like flowers (Jas 1.9–11); from the opening truth that all people are made in the image of God, to the apocalyptic anti-imperialism of Revelation; the Bible has consistently offered encouragement to religious, political and social radicals alike. And central to the text of the Christian Bible is the figure of Jesus – a man who rejected wealth and power, hated hypocrisy, loved the outsiders and was convicted and executed by imperial forces.

The Bible is a book of the radical margins. Contrary to popular belief, it's a book which encourages free speech, equality and dissent, which shows that the godly are far more often persecuted than praised, and which talks of the duties of kings more than their rights. It shows God at work among outsiders and the excluded. It portrays the rich and powerful as being far from the kingdom of heaven. The Bible appeals to a higher authority. It says, bluntly, that human beings – all human beings, from commoner to king – are responsible to God, first and foremost. It promises a reward for those who have faith. It argues that the wicked will not ultimately prosper and that death is not the end.

All of which shows why access to the Bible has been restricted so often. The story of the transmission and translation of the Bible has often involved concerted attempts to stop people reading it. Only those with the training, only those who knew the language or had mastered the theology were allowed access, and then only under controlled conditions: in a church or in a monastery. The story of the Bible is, frequently, the story of unapproved, unauthorised access. Nor have those days disappeared. Possessing a Bible is currently illegal in many countries. It is not just because their state ideology is opposed to Judaism or Christianity. It is because their political ideas are opposed to the ideas found in this book.

The history of the Bible, then, is not some dry bibliographic exercise, it's a story about what happens when people get access to secret files; what happens when they start to read the truth for themselves. It's a story of heroes and villains and some who were a bit of both; and in the telling of that story we will travel from Assyria to Alexandria, from Rome to Russia. We see how the story of the Bible is bound up with technological innovation, with the creation of alphabets, the invention of the book, the expansion of printing. We will discuss democracy and literacy, learning and communication.

Above all, the story of the Bible is, like the stories within the Bible, about people finding freedom. 'The truth will make you free', said Jesus (John 8.32). And that is exactly what dictators and bigots and religious demagogues have always feared. Freedom is a drug. It can be used and it can be abused, but once you've sampled it, you're hooked for life. This is why reading the Bible is, so often, a heady experience. When people first read the Scriptures in their own tongue, it's a shock. What begins as a Bible study often can end in revolution, in a mad, amphetamine-rush of freedom. And if sometimes they took things too far, well, that's what happens when people who have been chained for so long suddenly experience the heady oxygen of freedom – it goes straight to their heads.

In 1534 the experiment in Münster ended in death, torture and defeat. The cages where the bodies of the revolutionaries were hung can still be seen hanging at St Lambert's Church, Münster.

In 1649 the calls from those political prisoners – known as 'the Levellers' – were eventually to form the basis of British democracy. Later political movements, including the Suffragettes and the Chartists, were all inspired by their reading of the Bible.

And the young Indian lawyer who began making a nuisance of himself in 1915 was called Gandhi. He read the Bible and he said this

> You Christians look after a document containing enough dynamite to blow all civilisation to pieces, turn the world upside down and bring peace to a battle-torn planet. But you treat it as though it is nothing more than a piece of literature.

He was right. The Bible is not just a 'piece of literature'.
It is God's dangerous book.

Torah Scrolls. Fourteenth Century.

PART ONE: THE MAKING OF THE BIBLE

THE BASIC BIBLE

Let's start with some basics.

The title comes from the Greek – *ta biblia* – the Books. We have turned a plural into a singular: Bible is not one book – it's a collection of many different kinds of book or writing, including history, poetry, stories, legal codes, proverbs and sayings, apocalyptic visionary descriptions, hymns, letters...

Throughout history, these have been arranged in different ways within the Bible. Broadly speaking, however, the Bible splits into two main sections and one main add-on:

- The Old Testament or Hebrew Scriptures – containing writings sacred to both Jews and Christians.
- The New Testament – containing only Christian Scriptures.
- The Apocrypha – consisting of disputed books which some traditions accept and others reject.

All Bibles are made up of varying arrangements of these works.

Hebrew Scriptures or Tanakh or Old Testament

The Jewish name for this is the Tanakh, an acronym which arises from the way that the Hebrew Scriptures are organised into three main sections: **T**orah (The Law), **N**evi'im (The Prophets) and **K**etuvim (The Writings).

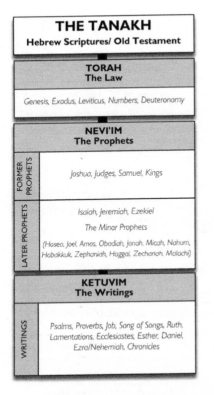

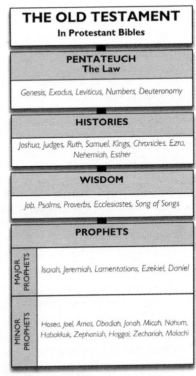

Christians call this section the Old Testament, a term which was invented at the end of the second century AD. The order of the books differs, not only between the Christian and the Jewish Bibles, but also between different versions of the Christian Bible.

Since the 'action' of the Old Testament covers a period of many thousands of years, dating the composition is tricky. The oldest parts of the Old Testament were written around 1100 BC; the youngest part is probably the second part of the book of Daniel, a lot of which was written not in Hebrew, but in Aramaic.[1]

Greek Scriptures

Unlike the Tanakh, the bulk of the New Testament covers a much more compressed timeframe – around a hundred years (although the book of Revelation takes us way into the future). We can date the composition of New Testament documents much more precisely. The earliest is probably Galatians, written in 49 AD, and the last Revelation, written around 93 AD.

Like the Old Testament, the New Testament is split into different types of writing: there are the Gospels and Acts, the letters of Paul, general letters*, and Revelation which is entirely in a class of its own.

The Apocrypha

The third section which appears in some Bibles is called the Apocrypha. These books were written in the 'gap years' between the end of the Old Testament and the beginning of the New, when Greek rulers sought to impose Greek culture onto the Jews. For reasons which we'll explore in due course, these appear in some Bibles – those of the Catholic and Eastern churches – but not in Jewish or modern Protestant Bibles. Jerome, who translated the Bible into Latin, gave them their name: 'Apocrypha' which means 'hidden things', because he believed that they had been hidden away, or that they had hidden meanings.

THE NEW TESTAMENT
Christian Scriptures
GOSPELS AND ACTS
Matthew, Mark, Luke, John, Acts
LETTERS

PAUL'S LETTERS	Romans, 1&2 Corinthians, Galatians, Ephesians, Philippians, Colossians, 1&2 Thessalonians, 1&2 Timothy, Titus, Philemon
GENERAL OR 'CATHOLIC' LETTERS	Hebrews, James, 1&2 Peter, 1,2&3 John, Jude

REVELATION
The Revelation of John

THE APOCRYPHA
Deuterocanonical Scriptures

CATHOLIC AND ORTHODOX	1&2 Esdras, Tobit, Judith, Wisdom of Solomon, Ecclesiasticus/Ben Sirach, Baruch, 1&2 Maccabees
ORTHODOX ONLY	3 Maccabees

---

* Also known as catholic letters, in that they were written for the wider or 'catholic' church

The language of the Bible

The Bible is written in two main languages – Hebrew and Greek – with bits of Aramaic and Latin.

The Old Testament is written almost entirely in Hebrew, with some small parts in Aramaic. The language is never referred to as 'Hebrew'; where it's referred to at all, it is called the 'language of Judah' or the language of Canaan.* By later Old Testament times most Jews spoke Aramaic; Hebrew was restricted to religious purposes. Between 605 and 586 BC, the Jews were taken into exile to Babylon, a place where everyone spoke Aramaic and, when they returned to Judah, they took the language with them.

Most of the Old Testament was written before that event, so the vast majority is in Hebrew, but there are some small bits of Aramaic. There is one Aramaic place name in Genesis: 'Jegar-sahadutha' or the cairn of witness – evidently Jacob's Uncle Laban spoke Aramaic – one verse in Jeremiah and some sections of Daniel and Ezra.† Jesus also spoke Aramaic, and many Aramaic names and words can be found in the gospels, some of which are usually left untranslated, such as *Abba* (Mark 14.36) and *Talitha cum* (Mark 5.41). Dying on the cross, Jesus cried out a verse from Psalm 22, and the language he spoke in was Aramaic.‡

Although Jesus and his disciples spoke Aramaic, the New Testament is written in Greek. Most people around the Mediterranean region spoke Greek and had done so since the time of Alexander the Great. The type of Greek they spoke – and which is found in the New Testament – has since been called *koine* or common Greek. This was the colloquial language of everyday folk: traders, housewives, shopkeepers. People like Paul and Luke and Mark wrote in Greek, the common language of the Roman empire.

Finally, there are also occasional Latin words in the New Testament, but these are mainly technical terms such as names (e.g. *kentyrion*, the Greek version of the Latin Centurion; *denarius,* the Roman coinage and *mille*, the Roman mile.)

---

*   2 Kings 18.28; Nehemiah 13.24; Isaiah 19.18. The term Isaiah uses is literally, the 'lip' of Canaan.

†   Genesis 31.47; Jeremiah 10.11; Daniel 2.4b–7.28; Ezra 4.8–6, 18; 7.12–26.

‡   '*Eloi, Eloi, lema sabachthani*' Mk 15.34. It's from Psalm 22.1

How was it written?

The first 'pens' were chisels and the first writing hieroglyphs or pictograms engraved on stone walls and pillars. Eventually the Babylonians developed what is known as cuneiform script, which consisted of wedge-shaped marks, pressed into wet clay with a stylus. The clay was then baked and dried, and hey presto, you've got something portable. At least more portable than a pillar. These clay tablets were collected by monarchs in huge libraries at places like Nineveh and Babylon – Ashurbanipal of Assyria had a library of some twenty thousand tablets.

Clay is a good medium for recording information in that it's cheap, widely available and durable (at least once it's been baked). However, carrying around lumps of clay isn't very practical, never mind the fact that you also need to pop it in the oven after you've written it. An alternative writing material was needed. Which is why, in the third millennium BC, in Egypt, some bright spark invented papyrus.

Papyrus and parchment

Papyrus was made from papyrus reeds, which were cut into long strips and the strips laid crisscross on top of each other. They were then soaked in water from the Nile and dried. The sap from the papyrus-reeds glued the sheets together. The result was a thin, light material, ideal for writing. Papyrus was expensive, however. Only Egypt produced the right kind of reeds, so they had a monopoly – they'd cornered the market in papyrus.

Enter parchment. Parchment was discovered in Pergamon, from which it derives its name (from the Latin *pergamentum*). Parchment is made from the skin of animals, such as deer or sheep, scraped and scraped until it forms a thin, almost translucent material. Parchment had several advantages over papyrus. First, it was widely available, because all you needed was a dead animal, and there were loads of them about. Second, it was extremely durable; get papyrus wet and you end up with a load of soggy reeds; but animal skin is *designed* to get wet. Third, parchment was reusable. You could 'rub out' previous writing by scraping the surface clean; the erased parchment could then be reused. This was a frequent practice in the Middle Ages, with the sad result that many ancient and precious works were scraped clean to provide room for the Abbey's household accounts or similar. However, it is possible to read the writing underneath; sometimes with the naked eye, nowadays by using infra-red scanners and photography. Writings where the original has been scraped clean and then written over are called palimpsests.

Clay tablets, parchment and papyrus were the main writing media of the ancient world, but there were alternatives. Some people – especially school pupils – used wax tablets, which could be wiped smooth and used again. For everyday, 'disposable' writing, people used old bits of pottery, called *ostraca*. If you had a pot, or a plate, which had been broken, then you could write on the flatter bits, a bit like using the back of an envelope.

Scroll and codex

The first writing was on stone or clay tablets, but from around the seventh or sixth century BC, the most popular form of media was the scroll. Scrolls were made of papyrus or parchment, sewn together to form long rolls. These were some eight to ten inches high and anything up to 35 feet long. You would usually write on one side of the paper only, since papyrus is not very opaque. You would write in columns – normally two – each two to four inches wide and containing around thirty to forty lines per column.

Around 600 BC, Jeremiah wrote in ink (probably soot mixed with water) on a two-column scroll. Ezekiel was given a scroll with writing on the front and on the back. (Typically, for Ezekiel, he had to eat it.) Isaiah talked of the sky, rolling up 'like a scroll'.[*] The books of the Old Testament were all scrolls. This is why the books of Kings, Samuel and Chronicles were split into two parts – they were too big to fit on one scroll.

Scrolls were the dominant form right up until the second and third century AD. But some time in the first century AD, a different medium began to emerge – the book, or codex. These were small parchment notebooks which people would carry around to make notes in, or draw up first drafts. Originally these notebooks were made out of two pieces of wood, joined together with leather strips. Later the wood

---

[*] Jeremiah 36; Ezekiel 2.9–10; Isaiah 34.4.

A man reading a scroll. From a fresco in Pompeii

was replaced by small sheets of parchment, loosely held by leather bands, a bit like a loose-leaf file.

Then, some time in the first century AD, someone invented the book. They took sheets of papyrus, folded them in half and then sewed through the spine and wrote on both sides of the page. These are called *codices* (plural) or a *codex* (singular) – and they are the same basic format as the book you have in your hand.* During the third century and into the fourth, the papyrus codex was superseded by a parchment codex. The great Bibles of the fourth and fifth centuries are all written on sheets of parchment or vellum.

The codex took time to catch on. For most writers in the Græco-Roman world, only scrolls were 'proper' books. As we shall see, the Christians, however, embraced this medium: early Christian literature from the second and third centuries is virtually all from codices. Everyone else used scrolls, but Christians used books.

Scribes and writers

Few people in the ancient world could either read or write. So, virtually all the Old and New Testament writings were written down by professional scribes.

In Judea these scribes worked in the villages and towns, where they were employed to write letters, contracts and wills. Over time their status rose. They became viewed as experts in the Law and played a significant role in copying and editing the Scriptures. By Jesus' day, the term 'scribe' is used not only of professional writers but of people learned in the Jewish law and able to give official interpretations.

---

* The name comes from *caudex* – the Latin name for the early wooden notebooks.

Paul used a number of 'ordinary' scribes such as Tertius and Silvanus.[*] Since writing materials were expensive, professional scribes used a concise hand which made the most of the space available. Paul is aware how 'unprofessional' his own writing is: 'See what large letters I make when I am writing in my own hand!' (Gal. 6.11)

The cost of writing materials also meant that you only put in what was absolutely necessary. In particular this meant cutting out the unnecessary items. Like vowels. Or punctuation.

The Hebrew Scriptures, for example, contain no vowels. This makes interprteation tricky at times. Take this phrase, for example: 'the bk ws rd'. Does that mean 'The book was read', or 'The book was red' or 'The book was rude'?[†] Tradition and context dictated most of the readings, but there was always the possibility of mistranslation. Later scholars produced a version of the Hebrew Scriptures with tiny marks – called vowel points – which indicated what the vowel sounds should be.

The Greek Scriptures on the other hand had lots of vowels, but, unfortunately, no punctuation. Ancient Greek writing is written in uppercase with no spaces between the words and no paragraphs.

SOYOUGETSENTENCESLIKETHISWHICHMEANT YOUHADTOBECAREFULREADINGTHEMOTHER WISETHEYMADENOSENSE.

This could be equally confusing. For instance, in the jumble above, did I write 'Them otherwise' or 'The mother wise'? Reading, then, required great care and attention.

And we should note that vowels and punctuation aren't the only thing missing in the ancient Scripture texts. There were no chapter and verse numbers either. The chapter numbers which we use today were not introduced until around 1231 AD and the verse numbers not for another three hundred years.

---

[*] Romans 16.22; 1 Thessalonians 1.1; 2 Thessalonians 1.1. These were part of a network of trusted Christian brothers: Silvanus worked with Peter as well (1 Peter 5.12).

[†] If you're talking about one of my books, the latter is more probable.

The books in the cupboard

All of this means that the ancient world thought about writing and publication in a very different way than we do. They had no mass-produced hardback or paperback books, printed on paper. Everything was handwritten; on scrolls, first, and later codices. This means we should be wary of talking about 'the Bible' of the Early Church or the ancient Israelites. When people in the Bible and in the Early Church talk about 'Scripture' they mean a collection of separate codices or scrolls. The Bible did not become a book – in the sense of a completed collection of lots of pages between two covers – until around 300 AD. But before that, if someone wanted to carry their Bible to church, they would have had to use a box. Or possibly a wheelbarrow.*

A book box, or capsa. These were cylindrical boxes, made of leather and used to transport scrolls.

This is important because it forms the background to the way in which the contents of the Bible were decided. Up until the fourth century, churches and synagogues stored their Scriptures in cupboards or chests. This, by its very nature, meant that the contents had a certain fluidity. To take a particular section out of a bound book is quite hard, but it's no problem, physically, to add or subtract a separate scroll or codex from the cupboard.

The first half of this book, therefore, is concerned with the contents of that cupboard. Who decided what constituted the Scriptures? How did they decide? What got left out? And how were the Scriptures gathered in the first place?

---

* Which they could have done, since the wheelbarrow or *hyperteria monokyklou* was invented as early as 400 BC. Although, after the collapse of the Roman Empire, it disappeared from Europe until the Middle Ages. Just thought you ought to know...

A Roman reader removing a scroll from its place in a library. The tags at the ends of the scrolls show the title and author.

The inspired Scriptures

The story of the Bible is more exciting, more fascinating, more perplexing than maybe we realise. But for Christians, the actual history raises some significant issues. For those of us who follow Jesus of Nazareth, the status of the Bible is of paramount importance. We talk about the Bible as the 'inspired' word of God. This is what makes it different from the works of ordinary mortals. But how, exactly, does it come from God? Did he dictate it? Did he 'plant' it into the minds of men? Was it some kind of magic writing, where he took over the hands of those who were wielding the pen? It is not my intention to question the idea of biblical inspiration in this book. But we might just take a moment to think about what it means.

At its simplest – one might say at its most simplistic – some Christians believe that the Bible is totally 100% inspired: that every word in it comes from God. In fundamentalist belief this means that the Bible is infallible and inerrant: it cannot be in error, and it contains no faults. Whatever, then, the Bible teaches is right. If the Bible says something is wrong, then it's wrong. Period. In this model, history and theology are inextricably linked. If the fundamentalist admits the presence of historical errors, then that opens the door for theological errors as well.

Inspiration is not a purely Protestant idea. Catholic theology teaches the inspiration of the Scriptures as well, although it teaches that church tradition and teaching are also inspired. The idea of literal inerrancy is really only a recent phenomenon, a result of attacks on the Bible in the Enlightenment. It was only towards the end of the nineteenth century that the Catholic Church adopted the theory of literal inspiration. The Catholic doctrine of inerrancy was first made explicit by Pope Leo XIII in *Providentissimus Deus* in 1893.

The Early Church clearly considered Scripture inspired. 'You have searched the holy Scriptures, which are true, which were given by the Holy Spirit,' wrote Clement of Rome in late first century AD. 'You know that nothing unrighteous or counterfeit is written in them.'[2] While Justin Martyr, writing about 150–160 AD, wrote

> I am entirely convinced that no Scripture contradicts another. I shall admit rather that I do not understand what is recorded, and shall strive to persuade those who imagine that the Scriptures are contradictory, to be rather of the same opinion as myself. [3]

But two things need considering here, before we can recruit Justin and Clement and their contemporaries into the fundamentalist cause. First, Justin admits that there are difficulties. The Scriptures might be perfect, but they're perfectly mysterious in some places.

Second, in neither case are they just talking about *our* Scriptures. Clement makes appeal to certain books of the Old Testament, in their Greek translation, but also to other unidentified sources. He also makes reference to traditions and words of Jesus, but not in the form in which they are found in the gospels in our Bibles.* While, for his gospels, Justin used not our versions, but a harmonised version, a synthesis of Matthew, Mark and Luke.† In other words, a text where all the contradictions and repetitions have been ironed out. He may even have used a now lost gospel called the *Gospel of the Ebionites*. So which of these is the 'perfect' version? Inerrancy is not a word which occurs in the lexicon of the Early Church. Inspiration, yes, perfection, yes. But are they the same thing as innerancy?

---

* For example 1 Clement 46.8, when Jesus is quoted as saying 'Woe to that person! Rather than cause one of my elect to sin, it would have been good for that one not to be born.' Compare with Matthew 26.24 and Luke 17.1.

† See page 85 below. Actually don't. Have patience. You'll get there in the end.

The great translator Jerome wrote that 'I am not, I repeat, so ignorant as to suppose that any of the Lord's words is either in need of correction or is not divinely inspired' but he, as much as anyone, knew that translation meant making choices.[4] And he spent his life correcting the errors which had crept into the translations.

Other Early Church figures, such as Tertullian, Origen and John Chrysostom, all acknowledged variation and differences in the different narratives. Tertullian, writing around 200 AD, said: 'Never mind if there does occur some variation in the order of their narratives, provided that there be agreement in the essential matter of the faith.'[5] While Chrysostom, in the fourth century AD, actually argued that 'the discord which seems to be present in little matters' was a sign of the trustworthiness of the gospels.[6]

The point of all this is to show that, right from the start, there were differences of opinion over the nature and the composition of the Scriptures. But all of these writers believed that the Scriptures were true. Whatever the method of inspiration, the Bible is, in some mysterious way, the word of God.

THE HEBREW BIBLE

It is September, 458 BC. The inhabitants of Jerusalem assemble in a large open space in the Kidron Valley, east of Jerusalem and near to the Water Gate. From there they can see Jerusalem; the ruined wall, burnt-out gates, piles of rubble, crumbling masonry. After the destruction of the city in 586 BC, the Jews had spent years in exile in Babylon. Although the first exiles returned almost a century before, the city still looks like a war zone.*

The scribe Ezra has called for this assembly. He arrived a month ago, to find a city and people on the edge of disintegration. They were being absorbed into the neighbouring provinces; their so-called Temple was little more than a shrine, the once great city of Jerusalem was still a rubble-strewn ruin.

This morning, he takes a stand. Literally, in fact. He climbs onto a raised wooden platform, sits down, opens some scrolls before him. And he begins to read...

A lot has been lost in the exile in Babylon. Language, for one thing: a lot of the people no longer understand Hebrew, only Aramaic, so Ezra's words have to be translated. From dawn till noon, he speaks, while interpreters explain every segment.

And what he reads is the Torah – the Law; the codified, authorised version of the first five books of the Bible.

It is September, 458 BC. And the Jews are listening to their law.

The earliest tales

The word *Torah* means 'Instruction' and, as we use it now, refers to the first five books of the Bible, also known as the Pentateuch. This was to become the core material of Judaism, containing not only their religious, social and criminal law, but the stories of their

---

* When Nehemiah returned in 445 BC he could not follow the course of the city walls on horseback because of the damage (Neh. 2.13–15).

origins and their divine right to the land. This material, however, had a long history before it was written down, before Ezra brought it to the assembled crowds in Jerusalem.

It began as stories – the oral tradition – tales of how they ended up in Canaan and why; tales from the deep past, of ancestors and heroes and encounters with their God, tales told among the different tribes, carefully learnt, repeated, remembered, handed on from generation to generation, until they acquired a solid shape and a form. One of the most ancient stories in the Bible is the tale of Noah's ark. The tale of a deluge which devastated the earth is a widespread tradition among the early civilisations of the East. There's a Phrygian story, a Babylonian account, an Assyrian version... they differ in the details but they agree on an event of unparalleled moistness. Events like that would have hung in the memories for a long time.

According to the Bible, the Law – the Torah – seems to have been recorded very early. After the slaughter at Ai, Joshua builds an altar and reads 'all that is written in the book of the Law' to the assembled Israelites (Josh. 8.30–35).* Samuel wrote a list of the rights and duties of kingship (1 Sam. 10.25).

But the rest of the material existed as spoken tales. And, unless they get written down, stories can easily get lost. It is the threat of loss which mainly leads to preservation. For example, when the northern kingdom of Israel was destroyed by the Assyrians in 722 BC, it sent shock waves through Judea, the kingdom in the south.† It must have encouraged scribes to make records, to preserve the stories and prophecies of the northern tribes, tales of prophets and kings, set in the now lost cities of Dan and Shechem and Samaria.[1]

Josiah reads the book

Even written versions could go AWOL. In 621 BC, during the reign of King Josiah of Judah, some workmen were repairing the Temple in Jerusalem when they found a book. The authorities rush to tell the king: 'The high priest Hilkiah said to Shaphan the secretary, "I have found the book of the law in the house of the LORD."'

---

* Joshua is recorded as writing words in 'the book of the law of God' (Josh. 24.26)

† After Solomon's death, the country split into two: Israel in the north and Judah in the south.

Josiah was a religious reformer, but clearly he never even suspected the existence of such a thing. When he listened to the book being read, he 'tore his clothes' and lamented that his ancestors had not obeyed 'the words of this book'. The book they had discovered was Deuteronomy. Josiah had it read out to the public and instituted a religious revival, including the observation of the feast of Passover (2 Kgs 22.8–13; 23.1–3).

The book had presumably been lost – or hidden – during the reign of Manasseh. And it's not the only lost text. The Bible lists several lost books:

- *The Book of Jashar* (2 Sam. 1.18).
- *The Book of the Acts of Solomon* (1 Kgs 11.41)
- *The Book of the Annals of the Kings of Israel* (e.g. 1 Kgs 14.19; 15.31; 16.5; 16.14, etc.).
- *The Book of the Annals of the Kings of Judah* (1 Kgs 14.29; 15.7; 15.23, etc.)
- *The Book of the Annals* (Neh. 12.23)[*]

There was also a *Book of the Wars of Yahweh*, from which we have one, obscure verse.[†]

Loss and destruction. No guarantees. And as in Israel, so in Judah; just thirty years after Josiah discovered the book of Deuteronomy, the Judean state itself was lost. It was the Babylonians this time; after a protracted, horrendous siege of Jerusalem, they conquered the city, destroyed the Temple and took the inhabitants into exile. The people had lost everything: their Temple, their homes, their nation. But it was to be the exile in Babylon which was to result in the Scriptures we have today.

By the canals of Babylon

Sitting on the banks of the Chebar Canal, in the heart of Babylonia, the exiles had to rethink everything they knew about their history and

---

[*] These are not alternative names for Chronicles, which was written much later than Kings.

[†] 'That is why it says in the Book of the Wars of Yahweh: "...Waheb near Suphah and the gorges of the Arnon and the slope of the ravine running down to the site of Ar and over against the frontier of Moab."' (Num 21.14–15 NJB). Shame it's lost. Sounds like a real page-turner.

their faith. How are they to live (Ezek. 33.10); how can they respond to the taunts of their captors, urging them to sing a song to their Lord, the Lord who has, it seems, let them down so badly (Ps. 137)? They found the answers in their history, their law, their stories.

When the Judeans went to Babylon, they took with them their stories and their source material, what books and writings they could recover from the disaster. It was in exile that they began the process of editing and compiling those stories, creating the 'definitive edition'. This process is known as redaction.

It was this material that Ezra eventually took back and read out in Jerusalem. Josiah had read out Deuteronomy, but Ezra's book is different. It takes longer to read, for one thing. The reading, according to the account in Nehemiah, took some seven days. And it contains things which are not found in Deuteronomy. On the second day, the people discovered a festival that was completely new to them – the Feast of Booths or Tabernacles. This festival seems to have been new to large portions of the crowd. The people had not celebrated it since the days of Joshua (Neh. 8.17).*

Why had they never heard of this festival before? Either it had been forgotten, or it had never actually been part of their stories. But during the time in exile it had been rediscovered, recorded, and, crucially, placed into a larger document, the document which Ezra read to the crowd in 458 BC, the document which had, perhaps, been finally gathered together in exile.

As to how the final version was compiled, there are lots of competing arguments. Fundamentalists would argue that no real redaction took place, that these books weren't 'edited' in that sense at all, they already existed as one document. Some also argue that the five books were written by Moses and that references elsewhere in the Bible assume Mosaic authorship. However, even in ancient times, this idea was by no means universally accepted. Rabbis and scholars pointed out that Moses would have had to describe his own death (Deut 34:5–8), not to mention predicting the Israelite monarchy, and providing a list of the Kings of Edom many centuries before any of them were born (Gen. 36.31–43).

---

* The festival appears in Leviticus 23.39–43. It may be the celebration mentioned in Judges 21.19 and 1 Samuel 1.3

Since the nineteenth century, the most widely accepted theory is that the final version of the Torah was edited together from various texts. Two early sources which make up the bulk of Genesis are identified by the name they use for God: the Yahwist or Jahwist source (known as J) uses the word *Yahweh*; the Elohist source (E) uses the word *Elohim*. Then there is the Deuteronomist source (known as D) – which provides, unsurprisingly, the book of Deuteronomy. There is also a lot of material which has a fascination with the priestly matters, known as the Priestly source (P).[*] This material was combined, at different times, to form one, coherent, definitive version, arrived at some time during the fifth century BC.[2]

Despite its popularity, this hypothesis has been challenged. Opponents argue that it's a bit too neat. And it doesn't explain why there is still duplication; if the job is to create coherent accounts, then why do we still get repeated events and stories? Why are so many stories told twice or even three times?[†]

The Torah clearly contains different stories and traditions. But whatever view we take of its origin, we should remember that compilation is not the same as invention: an anthology of medieval literature published in the 21st century doesn't suddenly make all that material modern. Wherever and however it took place, this was a matter of combining texts which were already in existence and which had been passed on for a long time. Few of the events described in the Torah can be confirmed by archaeology, but its description of settings and customs reflects life in the second century BC. The story of Abraham might have been finally compiled in 600 BC, but the man himself clearly comes from twelve hundred years earlier.

In fact, a reading of the text shows that the redactors have been inclusive rather than exclusive; they *haven't* cut things out, they *haven't* smoothed out the wrinkles and created a single narrative with no inconsistencies. They have, in fact, taken pains to record all

---

[*] Scholars, who are rarely content with the simple explanation, have also suggested other minor sources such as 'The Book of Generations' which is a genealogy list and 'The Stations list' which describes the places where the Israelites stopped on their journey through the wilderness (Num. 33.5–37, 33.41–49).

[†] For example, there are two accounts of the creation story (Gen. 1.1–2:3 and Gen. 2.4b–25) and the covenant with Abraham (Gen. 15 and 17), and three accounts of the wife/sister saga (Gen. 12.10–20 ; 20.1–18; 26.6–11–14).

the stories, to make sure that
they did not exclude different
traditions and groups. This,
is a process which we will see
again in the creation of the

TORAH The Law
Genesis, Exodus, Leviticus, Numbers, Deuteronomy

Bible: the inclusion of material which doesn't fit neatly, but which
the redactors believe has to be recorded because it is authentic.

Amidst the battleground of hypotheses, rebuttal and arguments,
what remains true is that these are the important stories of ancient
Israel. These are their traditions, from different viewpoints and
different places. This was the Law, the Torah, the book which Ezra
read out on that cold and rainy day in 458 BC. And it came to form
the first – and most important – section of the Hebrew Scriptures.

The Prophets

So the Torah is the first of the Jewish Scriptures. But other writings
were also collected together during the Exile – histories and
prophecies and poetry. These were eventually to form the other two
sections of the Hebrew Scriptures: the Nevi'im or Prophets, and the
Ketuvim, or writings.

A late Jewish tradition records that, during the time of Ezra and
Nehemiah, a 'great synagogue' met to decide on the status of the
various Hebrew Scriptures. The exile and return was a period when
the Torah was agreed upon and the prophets collected, but the
'great synagogue' is a myth; the process of approving the Scriptures
actually went on for centuries.

First, around the same time as the redaction of the Torah, a
collection which has been termed the 'Former' or 'Early' prophets
was brought together. This might not strike us as particularly
'prophetic' since it consisted of the rest of the history of Israel,
starting with the book of Joshua and continuing through Judges,
Samuel and Kings. After the exile, other writings made a claim for
inclusion, most obviously the works of those who had foretold the
Babylonian captivity and the works of those who had been active
during the time in Babylon. So the prophets – the Nevi'im – grew to
accommodate Isaiah, Jeremiah and Ezekiel, and a section known as
'The Twelve' aka the minor prophets.

This was not entirely comfortable, though, because the prophets are some of the most exciting, baffling and even dangerous books of the Bible. People like Jeremiah and Ezekiel offer extreme, even bizarre behaviour. Not only that, they challenge some of the most cherished parts of later Jewish worship. The finger of God prods Amos to say 'I hate, I despise your festivals, and I take no delight in your solemn assemblies' and concludes 'But let justice roll down like waters, and righteousness like an ever flowing stream' (Amos 5.21–24). This is a serious challenge for a culture where the Torah-enshrined religious festivals were so important and where the Temple was the centre of religious life.

Ezekiel, in particular, always caused problems, particularly at the beginning and end of his book. In the concluding chapters, some of the legal rulings in Ezekiel's vision of the new Israel appeared to contradict laws in the Torah (Ezek. 40–48). The rabbinic tales tell how this almost led to the book's exclusion from the Hebrew Scriptures. The first-century AD scholar Hananiah ben Hezekiah decided to resolve the matter by shutting himself away in his study and refusing to emerge until he'd reconciled Ezekiel with the Torah. He eventually concluded that Ezekiel was a true prophet – but he burnt through three hundred lamps-worth of oil before he could do it.[3]

The intense mysticism of Ezekiel was powerful and even threatening. Public discussion and reading of the first chapter was prohibited, because it dealt with the secrets of God's throne.[4] Another rabbinic tale tells of R. Yohanan ben Zakkai (again, from the first century AD) riding along on his donkey. His disciple, Eleazar ben Arakh, asked Yohanan to teach him about Ezekiel's vision of the chariot. Initially, Yohanan replied that only a fully qualified sage was fit to listen to such teachings, but when Eleazar himself began talking about the chariot, fire rained from heaven, consuming the trees around, and Yohanan had to leap from the donkey and shelter under an olive tree.[5] These were fiery teachings in every sense of the word and access to them was restricted. In the fourth century AD, the Christian scholar Jerome reported that some rabbis prohibited the reading of the beginning and end of the book by anyone under the age of thirty.

Despite their difficult and
outspoken polemic, the
prophets were accepted as
being scriptural – at least
prophets up to the time
of Ezra, after which it was
decided that the age of
prophecy had ended. By the
third century BC, the list of
the books contained within
the prophets was pretty

NEVI'IM The Prophets	
FORMER PROPHETS	Joshua, Judges, Samuel, Kings
LATER PROPHETS	Isaiah, Jeremiah, Ezekiel The Minor Prophets (Hosea, Joel, Amos, Obadiah, Jonah, Micah, Nahum, Habakkuk, Zephaniah, Haggai, Zechariah, Malachi)

much accepted. In *The Wisdom of Jesus Ben Sirach*, a work written
around 190 BC, there is a list of heroes, and one part gives us the
official list, as it were, of the Nevi'im, as the writer praises Isaiah,
Ezekiel, Jeremiah and 'the Twelve Prophets'.[6]

The Writings
The final section of the Tanakh to be decided was the Ketuvim or
Writings, which brought together books of wisdom, history and
stuff that just didn't seem to fit anywhere else. It's a particularly
diverse collection of material, which includes books of history such
as Chronicles, Ezra, and Nehemiah; the stories of Ruth, Esther and
Job; poetry such as Lamentations and Song of Songs; and the wisdom
books of Ecclesiastes and Proverbs. Finally there was Daniel – part
narrative history, part apocalyptic prophecy.

The real star of this collection, however, was the book of Psalms,
which held something of an exalted space. Both the Jewish writer
Philo, and Luke in the New Testament, separate it off from the rest.*
Philo talked about 'laws and words prophesied by prophets and
psalms and the other writings...'[7] The core list of which poems to
include in the Psalms was probably in place quite soon after the
exile, but even so, the official list of 150 Psalms was not finalised
until after 70 AD.

The Ketuvim were the final set of books to be admitted into the
canon of the Hebrew Scriptures. Evidence from the Dead Sea

---

* See Luke 24.44 for example: 'everything written about me in the law of Moses, the
prophets, and the psalms must be fulfilled.'

Scrolls indicates that the
Torah and the Nevi'im were
standardised by the fourth
century BC, and most of the
Ketuvim was also in place.
But it was to be a further
three hundred years before

KETUVIM The Writings
WRITINGS	Psalms, Proverbs, Job, Song of Songs, Ruth, Lamentations, Ecclesiastes, Esther, Daniel, Ezra/Nehemiah, Chronicles

the list was finally agreed. Once again, the catalyst was going to be
exile and destruction.

Meanwhile in Samaria

During the exile in Babylon, the Samaritans had established
themselves in the region, and they also used the Torah, only in their
own language. Known as the Samaritan Pentateuch, the text dates
from the fourth century BC and is written in the Samaritan alphabet.

It differs from the Hebrew Torah in a number of ways. There
are some four thousand orthographic differences – that is simply
different ways of writing the same words. An equivalent for us might
be the difference between American and proper spelling.* However,
there are some more significant differences. The Samaritan version
of the Ten Commandments, for example, commands them to build
the altar on Mount Gerizim, which became the most important
Samaritan religious site. But there are also other instances where
the Samaritan Pentateuch reading differs from the Hebrew version
which we have today, and the interesting thing is that sometimes the
Samaritan text agrees with other ancient Hebrew versions, such as
those found at Qumran among the Dead Sea Scrolls.

This means that, back in the fourth century BC, there was more
than one text version around. The text preserved for us by Jewish
scholars was not the only version being read. Take, for instance, this
text, from Exodus 12:40. The Hebrew version reads

> Now the sojourning of the children of Israel, who dwelt in Egypt,
> was four hundred and thirty years.

Whereas the Samaritan Pentateuch version has

---

* Sorry, American and *English* spelling.

> Now the sojourning of the children of Israel and of their fathers
> which they had dwelt in the land of Canaan and in Egypt was four
> hundred and thirty years.

The Samaritan version is not found in any ancient Hebrew text.
But it – along with another 1900 variants from the Hebrew – is found
in another ancient version of the Torah, one written not in Hebrew,
nor in Aramaic, or Samaritan, but in Greek.

Meanwhile in Alexandria
Alexander the Great conquered Egypt in 333 BC and, as he did
throughout his empire, he instituted a policy of imposing Greek
culture – a policy which has been called Hellenisation, from the
Greek word for Greece, Hellas.*

Alexander also founded around twenty cities, built on Greek lines,
thirteen of which were called Alexandria.† The most famous of these
Alexandrias was in Egypt. It was situated in the fertile arable land
of Egypt which supplied grain to most of the Mediterranean world.
This not only made it wealthy, but also a natural place for traders to
come and establish businesses. It soon became the cultural centre
of the southern world. Alexandria grew to become home to some
150,000 people including Greeks, Egyptians, Africans – and Jews.
There had been Jews in Egypt since the time of the exile, and they,
like many others, gravitated towards Alexandria, making the Jewish
colony one of the biggest outside Palestine.

The Jewish leaders in Alexandria soon realised that there was a
problem: their Scriptures were in Hebrew. But the Jewish colony, like
the rest of the Hellenised world, spoke Greek. Just as the people back
in Judah needed a translation in Aramaic, the Jews in Alexandria
needed the Torah in their own language. So, some three hundred
years before the time of Christ, the Torah was translated into Greek.

Going to the library
After Alexander's death, Egypt was taken over by one of his generals,
Ptolemy I. Ptolemy founded the 'museum' – a kind of ancient

---

* The term was coined in the nineteenth century. Ironically, Alexander wasn't
  actually Greek: he was a Macedonian. But you try saying Macedonianisation.

† Or its local equivalent, such as Iskandariya in Iraq.

think-tank full of poets, scientists and philosophers – and a magnificent library, which soon became the greatest in the world. Partly this was due to its acquisition process which, according to one – probably apocryphal – story, was an early form of literary piracy. Any boat docking at Alexandria with books aboard had the books taken away and copied.* The originals were then stored in the library, while the owner took away the copies.

Founded around 300 BC, the library at Alexandria was the first to order its collection alphabetically. Its first librarian, Zenodotus, also introduced a method for establishing the 'proper' text of Homer, which involved obtaining as many different copies as he could and comparing the differences. This basic process has been followed by scholars ever since to establish authoritative texts of the Old and New Testaments.†

According to a Jew called Aristeas, it was a subsequent librarian, Demetrius of Phaleron, who observed that the library lacked a significant document – the Law of the Jews. The king – by now Ptolemy II – decided that a translation should be made.

> King Ptolemy at once gathered 72 Elders. He placed them in 72 chambers, each of them in a separate one, without revealing to them why they were summoned. He entered each one's room and said: 'Write for me the Torah of Moshe, your teacher.' God put it in the heart of each one to translate identically as all the others did.‡

It was a miracle! The 72 translators had, independently, each come up with an identical translation. This, then, was not just a translation: it was *God's* translation. It is from this story that the Greek version gets its name. It's known as the Septuagint, from the Latin phrase *Interpretatio septuaginta virorum* – 'translation of the seventy interpreters'. It's often given the abbreviation LXX, the Latin numerals for seventy. This comes from its Hebrew name: *Targum Shiv'im* – 'the translation of the seventy'.

---

* I suppose that's *literally* literary piracy.
† Eventually, the library burned down. When this happened is not known. Plutarch put it at 50 BC, but it was still going in 30 BC and probably struggled on till 270 AD.
‡ Josephus, *Antiquities* 12.11–16.

It's an unlikely story. For a start, Demetrius of Phaleron was sent into exile by Ptolemy II for supporting the claim to the throne of his elder brother, so it's hardly likely he'd have been appointed as librarian. Well, not unless the pay and working conditions were seriously awful. It's much more likely that the impetus behind the translation was provided by Jewish emigrés, keen to preserve their religion. The Septuagint could, of course, be read by Greeks interested in what Jews believed, but its main initial readership were Greek-speaking Jews in Egypt. Translating it into Greek meant that Judaism could survive, even in the Hebrew-starved atmosphere of Alexandria.

The myth may not be true, but it reveals a core anxiety about Bible translation – and one which persists to this day: we are not just dealing here with any old text. This is not the latest comedy by some local playwright; it's not even poetry as exalted as Homer. This is the Law of God. Some ultra-conservative Jews thought the translation a sin.[8] So making it the world's first divinely inspired translation was a way to show that God's fingerprints were on the translation as well.

There were other imperatives. For the religious leaders in Jerusalem it was an economic necessity that diaspora Jews stay true to their faith, because it was how they made an income: every male Jew of a certain age had to pay a tax to the temple, it was the richest religious institution in the world. The myth of the divinely inspired Septuagint, therefore, was the perfect solution: it kept the Greek-speaking Jewish diaspora attached to the homeland, while comforting the traditionalists.

The translation of the Torah was only the start. Over subsequent years the other books of the Tanakh were translated. It wasn't long before the Septuagint spread out from Alexandria and into the Mediterranean world.

There were differences. The Septuagint uses a different version of the Tanakh than the Hebrew version which later became the authoritative text. Not only that, but it has more books in it. There are thirteen books in the Septuagint which are not in the Hebrew canon, as well as additional chapters to Esther and Daniel, and an extra Psalm. Some of this material originated in Judea and was originally in Hebrew; other parts, like the Wisdom of Solomon and

2 Maccabees were originally written in Greek. Together, they form what we know now as the Apocrypha. They are also known as Deuterocanonical – secondary canonical – books, a term coined in the sixteenth century by a man with the rather super-villain name of Sixtus Senensis. For reasons which we'll explore in due course, these appear in some Bibles – those of the Catholic and Eastern churches – but not in modern Protestant Bibles. We don't know exactly when these books became part of the Septuagint. But we do know that they were included in it by the first century AD, because they were known to the writers of the Early Church.

Because it was in Greek, the Septuagint was the most widely read version of the Hebrew Scriptures of its day. Even in Palestine the Septuagint was probably widely used. We know

THE SEPTUAGINT
Greek Translation of Old Testament

TORAH
The Law

Genesis, Exodus, Leviticus, Numbers, Deuteronomy

HISTORY

Joshua, Judges, Ruth, 1 &2 Samuel, 1 & 2 Kings, 1 & 2 Chronicles, 1 Esdras, Ezra/Nehemiah, Esther (with additions), Judith, Tobit, 1, 2, 3 Maccabees

WISDOM

Psalms (with Psalm 151), Prayer of Manasseh, Job, , Proverbs, Ecclesiastes, Song of Songs, Wisdom of Solomon, Sirach, Psalms of Solomon

PROPHETS

MINOR PROPHETS

Hosea, Amos, Micah, Joel, Obadiah, Jonah, Nahum, Habakkuk, Zephaniah, Haggai, Zechariah, Malachi

Isaiah, Jeremiah, Baruch, Lamentations, Epistle of Jeremiah, Ezekiel, Daniel (with additions)

APPENDIX

4 Maccabees

that in Jerusalem there were Greek-speaking synagogues (Acts 6) as well as a synagogue of the Freedmen (Acts 6.9). Jesus appears to quote *Ben Sirach*.[*] The Septuagint was to become the Old Testament version used by the first Christians and, along with the Apocrypha, it was used as the basis of the Latin Old Testament used by the church for over a thousand years.

---

[*] Matthew 11.28, which seems to draw on Sira 51.23–27.

The Apocryphal Old Testament: A brief guide

You will not find these books in either the Tanakh or in most Protestant Bibles. And in those Bibles which do include them – Bibles of the Catholic and Orthodox churches – they are separated off from the other text. They are termed Apocryphal or Deuterocanonical and are viewed by the Catholic Church as authoritative, but at a lower level than the other books of the Hebrew Scripture.

1 Maccabees

1 Maccabees is a reliable history of the Maccabean wars, where the Jews revolted against their Greek rulers who were trying to impose Greek religion and culture. It also tells the story of the Jewish festival of *Hanukkah*.

Composed: The book was originally composed in Hebrew, probably around 130–100 BC.

2 Maccabees

2 Maccabees is a summary of a five-volume work by someone called Jason of Cyrene (the original is now lost) which tells of the events leading up to the outbreak of revolt under Judas Maccabeus, and the subsequent battles up to 161 BC. It's a separate work to 1 Maccabees, not a sequel. Less concerned with the historical order of events than 1 Maccabees, the book emphasises the role and importance of the Jerusalem Temple.

Composed: The book was written between 124 BC and the arrival of the Romans in 63 BC.

1 Esdras

1 Esdras is a retelling of various portions of Jewish history, drawing heavily on Chronicles and Ezra. (Indeed, Esdras is the Greek form of the Hebrew name, Ezra.) The only original material is a curious contest between three bodyguards of King Darius where they answer the question 'What one thing is the strongest?' Each writes his own answer and puts it under the pillow of King Darius. When the king wakes up he reads the answers and decides the winner.*

Composed: Who knows? Probably 1st century BC to 1st century AD, but it's hard to tell.

---

* It turns out to be truth, with women a strong second. Drunken, drug-crazed elephants (see 3 Maccabees) don't get a look in.

2 Esdras

A piece of apocalyptic writing which tries to explain why God allowed the Romans to destroy the Jewish Temple in AD 70. The book contains seven purported visions of Ezra who, in the end, is taken up to heaven without dying. It's a hotch-potch of writing from different times, with Chapters 1, 2, 15 and 16 generally recognised as later Christian interpolations.

Composed: The bulk (chapters 3–14) were written late 1st century AD, after the fall of Jerusalem. Chapters 1–2 probably comes from 2nd century AD and chapters 15–16 from even later.

3 Maccabees

A somewhat romantic account of God's miraculous interventions on behalf of persecuted Jews in Alexandria, Egypt. The highlight comes when the Jews are saved from being trampled by a herd of elephants. Drunken elephants. Drunken *drugged* elephants.* Since the book deals with events (a) 50 years before the Maccabeans began fighting in Palestine and (b) in Egypt, the title is somewhat misleading.

Composed: Between the late 2nd century BC and early 1st century AD.

4 Maccabees

This is a philosophical discussion about the superiority of reason over emotions, which attempts to reconcile reason with the observance of Jewish law. Surprsingly, however, it also includes several gratuitously gory stories, including the torture of the elderly priest Eleazar, and a ridiculously detailed account of the torture of an aged mother and her seven sons.†

Composed: It was certainly written by a Jew living outside of Palestine – perhaps in Antioch in Syria, or Asia Minor. It probably dates from the mid-first to second century AD.

---

* No, really: 'Then the king, completely inflexible, was filled with overpowering anger and wrath; so he summoned Hermon, keeper of the elephants, and ordered him on the following day to drug all the elephants—five hundred in number—with large handfuls of frankincense and plenty of unmixed wine, and to drive them in, maddened by the lavish abundance of drink, so that the Jews might meet their doom' (3 Macc 5.1–3).

† Here's a sample verse: 'The wheel was completely smeared with blood, and the heap of coals was being quenched by the drippings of gore, and pieces of flesh were falling off the axles of the machine.' (4 Macc 9.20).

Baruch

The book claims to be a letter from Baruch, Jeremiah's scribe. Baruch writes from exile in Babylon to the priests and people of Jerusalem. The book is a combination of three sections which originally were separate: a prose prayer and two poems.

Composed: Since it's composed of three different parts, it's hard to date. Probably during the second century BC.

Judith

Judith tells of a Jewish woman living in Jerusalem when the city is under attack by the Assyrians. She sneaks into the enemy camp, seduces the Assyrian general and cuts off his head, leading to an amazing victory. Job done.

Composed: Written by a Palestinian Jew, possibly during the reign of John Hyrcanus (134–104 BC) when Jerusalem was besieged for a year by the Seleucids.

Letter of Jeremiah

Claims to be a copy of a letter sent by Jeremiah to those Judeans about to be exiled to Babylon. It's similar to the letter in Jeremiah 29.1–23 and mainly attacks idolatry.

Composed: Very hard to say. Any time between the late fourth and late second century BC.

Prayer of Manasseh

The Prayer of Manasseh is based on a reference in 2 Chronicles 33, where Manasseh, Judah's most sinful king, is taken to Babylon (2 Chr 33.10–19). There, after a lifetime of wickedness, he repents of his sins before he dies.

Composed: Probably late first century BC.

Wisdom of Ben Sirach/Ecclesiasticus

Ecclesiasticus, also known as The Wisdom of Jesus ben Sirach, is a wisdom book. It includes a famous passage which begins, 'Let us now praise famous men' (Sirach 44.1–50.31) in which the author modestly includes himself.

Composed: c. 200–180 BC. Ben Sirach was a rabbi in Jerusalem.

Psalm 151

An extra Psalm, consisting of just seven verses and celebrating the defeat of Goliath by David.

Composed: Probably in the Hellenistic period (332–63 BC) but it's impossible to be precise.

Tobit

A piece of historical fiction, probably written by a Diaspora Jew. Tobit is a blind, poor Jew living in Nineveh, Assyria, whose fortunes are restored through the actions of his son, Tobias, and the angel Raphael, disguised as a relative called Azariah. The book expounds the simple moral that piety will be rewarded.

Composed: Late 3rd to 2nd century BC

Wisdom of Solomon

A wisdom book, which seems to be a kind of positive reply to Ecclesiastes. It talks a lot about the uses of wisdom, particularly in preparing a soul for life after death. It's not, of course, by Solomon, since it was originally composed in Greek.

Composed: Probably in Egypt, between 30 BC and 70 AD, although the lack of any allusions to events makes it difficult to date.

Additions to the Book of Daniel

There are four extra parts of the Book of Daniel. 'The Prayer of Azariah' and 'The Song of the Three Children' are inserted into Daniel, chapter 3, where the young men are thrown into the fiery furnace. 'The History of Susanna' is perhaps the earliest detective story in the world and tells of a woman unjustly accused of adultery, whose innocence is revealed by Daniel. It usually becomes Daniel chapter 13. 'Bel and the Dragon' (which becomes Daniel chapter 14) tells how Daniel escapes from a plot to put him to death.

Composed: They were probably inserted into Daniel sometime between the third and first century BC.

Additions to Esther

There is a different version of the Book of Esther, with extra material, including a new prologue, Mordecai's dream, letters from the emperor and various prayers. Significantly, these extra bits mention God, something absent from the version in the Hebrew Bible.

Composed: Late second or early first century BC. A postscript in the Septuagint records that this version was brought to Egypt sometime in the mid-first century BC, 'during the reign of Ptolemy and Cleopatra' (Esth 11.1).

The Hebrew canon

By Jesus' day, the main Scriptures of the Old Testament were in place. The synagogues of Palestine had their Hebrew Tanakh, the Samaritans around Mount Gerizim had their version of the Torah, while Jews in the rest of the Græco-Roman world had the Septuagint – with all those extra books – in Greek.

However, the arguments persisted. Torah, Nevi'im and Ketuvim were all scriptural, but some bits were more scriptural than others. Nobody doubted the supremacy of the Torah: that was direct revelation, it was given by God to Moses, and that was that. The Torah was the ultimate authority.

Yet, clearly the boundaries were fuzzy. During a visit to Jerusalem, Jesus is embroiled in a religious argument which threatens to turn nasty. During the dispute, he quotes Scriptures at his attackers – 'Is it not written in your law...' he begins. But then he proceeds to quote from Psalm 82.6, which is not part of the Torah. The idea of what constituted the Law, then, was fluid.[9] Probably, different groups accepted different Scriptures as authoritative. Although evidence is scanty – since we don't have any complete collections from this time – the absence of Esther from the Dead Sea manuscripts found at Qumran indicates that community, at least, had decided to leave Esther out.

These arguments over the status of Scripture are fundamental to the long-running row between the Sadducees and the Pharisees. The Sadducees believed that only the Torah was 'Scripture'. They dismissed anything not found in there as 'unscriptural'. Thus, they rejected the resurrection of the dead because there was no precedent for it in the Torah. The Pharisees had a wider view of what constituted Scripture. More than the Torah, more than even the Tanakh, their 'Scripture' also included the oral tradition, the many rules and regulations which the rabbis had developed to help people live the Jewish faith in their everyday situations. In modern terms, therefore, the Pharisees were the Catholics, citing both written Scripture and tradition as authoritative; the Sadducees were the Protestant *sola scriptura* party, the biblical fundamentalists.

Even at the level of the ordinary synagogue worshipper, the different sections of the Tanakh were afforded different status. In

Luke chapter 4, Jesus visits his home town

> When he came to Nazareth, where he had been brought up, he went
> to the synagogue on the Sabbath day, as was his custom. He stood
> up to read, and the scroll of the prophet Isaiah was given to him...
> (Luke 4.16–17).

Jesus chooses a text from Isaiah (Isa. 61.1–2), then gives a very
brief exposition, the nucleus of which lies in a single statement:
'Today this Scripture has been fulfilled in your hearing' (Luke 4.21).
But when we look closely at what Jesus does with the passage from
Isaiah, we can see how flexibly first-century Jews viewed and used
their sacred writings. Although Jesus reads a section from Isaiah,
he misses out an entire line (omitting a phrase about binding up
the brokenhearted), compresses two lines into one (the statement
about providing liberty to the captives) and, most surprising of all,
he introduces a phrase from an entirely different bit of Isaiah (Isa.
58.6 – 'to let the oppressed go free').

This scriptural mash-up may lead us to think that Luke has
misquoted, but in fact, he is faithfully reflecting synagogue practice
with regard to Scripture in first-century Judea. The Torah had to be
read from the text, it could not be recited from memory, and anyone
reading from the Torah had the synagogue attendant standing right
by them to check that what they were reading was correct. The same
level of scrupulous accuracy was not, however, required when it
came to the prophets. When reading the Prophets you were allowed
to move things about a bit. Rabbinic law stated that 'They may leave
out verses in the Prophets but not in the Law. How much may they
leave out? Only so much that he leaves no time for the interpreter to
make a pause.'[10] So the Prophets could be treated in a different way to
the Law. The reader could skip verses, or select other verses, while the
translator was translating the verse before! Jesus' teaching at Nazareth
is, then, a graphic demonstration of the different status of the Old
Testament texts. The Torah was authoritative for everyone. But the
Prophets could be altered and adapted within certain guidelines.

Targum

The 'interpreter' in the synagogue was a translator, who would translate the Hebrew into Aramaic. Over the next few centuries, a considerable body of these Aramaic translations were written down and eventually they were codified into a form known as Targum. There are various Targums: the Jerusalem Targum, the Palestinian Targum (originally discovered in Cairo) and versions produced in Babylon, dating from the sixth and seventh centuries AD. They are not straight translations into Aramaic, the text was also expanded, interpreted and even altered.

Dead Sea discoveries

In 1947, two young Bedouin went looking for a goat which had strayed into one of many small caves which dot the limestone cliffs overlooking the Dead Sea at the Wadi Qumran. One of the boys threw a rock into the cave to try to drive the goat out, but instead of the sound he expected to hear (i.e. pained goat) he heard the sound of pottery breaking. When they investigated, they found a cache of seven ancient scrolls which had been hidden in pottery jars. Subsequent expeditions to the caves around the area produced an astonishing number of scrolls and papyrus fragments dating back to the first century BC. The scrolls fell into three main categories: the Hebrew Scriptures, Jewish apocryphal writings (such as Tobit and Jubilees) and other previously unknown Jewish writings, including the community's own rules and literature. It is widely supposed that the community who put this library together were a religious group called the Essenes, although scholars are by no means united on this, and recent evidence indicates that the Qumran community itself was actually a pottery. The library was probably hidden in the desert during the first Jewish revolt of 66–70 AD and represented, therefore, the kind of religious writings that were being read in the time of Herod the Great. It was one of the greatest archaeological finds in history.

The Scriptures in the Dead Sea collection include two near complete scrolls of Isaiah, a commentary on Habakkuk and fragments of all the other books of the Hebrew Scriptures, except Esther. The fragments show they had multiple manuscripts of biblical texts, including twelve different copies of Isaiah, fourteen of Deuteronomy, ten copies of the Psalms and eight copies of the Scroll of the Twelve Prophets.[11]

These scrolls were significant for a number of reasons. For a start, they were a thousand years older than the oldest known manuscripts of the Hebrew Scriptures.[*] The reason for this lies in the way Hebrew scribes copied their Scriptures during the first nine centuries AD. Synagogue scrolls were regarded with great veneration by the rabbis. Old and worn scrolls were buried, because the rabbis wanted to make sure that texts which bore the sacred name of God were never destroyed, or used for profane purposes. So the old scrolls were copied and then put in a temporary storage place, known as a *genizah* – a small, secret storage area attached to the synagogue.[†]

The Cairo Genizah

In the second half of the nineteenth century, one such *genizah* was discovered in the synagogue at Fustat in Cairo. Inside were two hundred thousand fragments of scrolls, which had been deposited in it in the ninth and tenth centuries AD. As well as biblical texts, they included bits from the Mishnah, the Talmud, Targums, hymns, prayers and even private documents. These scrolls had been hidden and then forgotten for hundreds of years. Among the treasures were pages of the Apocryphal book Ecclesiasticus in Hebrew. Previously it was only known in translation.

So the Dead Sea Scriptures were old. Very old. But they were also different; they showed some differences between the accepted Hebrew text as it had come down to us and the texts found in the scrolls. The commentary on Habakkuk, for example, included excerpts from previously unknown versions of Habakkuk. The two complete scrolls of Isaiah were different from each other: one is very close to the accepted Hebrew text, the other differs more widely. None of these variants were very significant – they are mostly what is called haplography – when the scribe copying has missed a word – or grammatical differences. But sometimes the fragments revealed bits which are missing from the traditional Hebrew Scriptures. For example, at the end of 1 Samuel 10, the Dead Sea version has an extra paragraph:

---

[*] The previous oldest manuscript copy was the Leningrad Codex in St Petersburg which dates from 1008. Admittedly the fragments represent a much smaller portion of the text – the Codex contains the entire Tanakh.

[†] *Genizah* means 'hiding place'.

Now Nahash, king of the Ammonites, had been grievously oppressing the Gadites and the Reubenites. He would gouge out the right eye of each of them and would not grant Israel a deliverer. No one was left of the Israelites across the Jordan whose right eye Nahash, king of the Ammonites, had not gouged out. But there were seven thousand men who had escaped from the Ammonites and had entered Jabesh-gilead.

OK, it's not earth-shatteringly important. It has no effect on theology or traditional belief. It's just a bit about a king with a tendency towards blinding people.* But what it demonstrates is that different groups had their set of Scriptures and that many of the copies of Scriptures had minor differences between them.

A bit about haplography

Up until the invention of printing, all copies of the Scriptures were made by hand. When a scribe is working fast the eye can play tricks, and sometimes, when two identical words were close together in the text, the scribe hopped a word or two. This is known as haplography. Most examples, reasonably enough, take place when the scribe is copying big lists of names or places. Perhaps the most notorious case of haplography, though, is in a printed Bible, the so-called Wicked Bible of 1631, where, in the seventh commandment – 'Thou shalt not commit adultery' – the typesetter missed out the tiny, but crucial word, 'not'.

Jamnia 90 AD

The event that caused the Dead Sea community to hide their scrolls took place in 66 AD when the Jews rose in revolt against the Roman occupiers. Years of brutal and corrupt government, combined with a growing sense of nationalism, led to Jewish rebels massacring the Roman garrison and taking charge of Jerusalem. Inevitably, the revolt was crushed. Four years later, the Romans recaptured Jerusalem and destroyed the Temple. According to the traditional story, some time before this destruction the rabbinical scholars had already left the city and settled in Jamnia or Jabneh, a town some twelve miles south

---

* Most modern Bibles don't include it. But it is added to the NRSV, the Message and the NLT. For any rugby fans, it does give a biblical precedent for banning anyone for eye-gouging.

of Jaffa. This was to become the centre of Jewish theological thought up until the Second Jewish revolt of 135 AD. They were, in a way, in exile again – an exile from the old ways of doing things. No more Temple meant no more sacrifice. Once again the very identity of the Jewish nation was under threat.

In Jamnia, the Pharisees began to codify the huge collection of oral law, the teachings which helped people to live their lives as Jews in the towns and villages of Palestine. Without the Temple, this became more important than ever. Eventually it was to be collected together as the Mishnah, around 200 AD.

Before that, they addressed the thorny question of what writings should be allowed in the official Hebrew Scriptures. They drew up the first canon list. When we talk of 'the canon' of Scripture, we mean the official, standard list. The word, appropriately enough, comes from a Greek word *kanon*, which in turn comes from the Hebrew *qaneh*. The root meaning of the word is 'reed' (we borrow it for the word 'cane'). These straight reeds were used as measuring rods, so the word *kanon* can be used to imply a kind of rule of faith. I suppose we might say it is those books which measure up. More specifically, the word came to be used of a list or an index. The term – in the sense of meaning a precise list of sacred writings – was only really applied to the Scriptures in the late fourth century AD.[12] So when we talk of canonicity, or the canon of Scripture, we mean those books which conform to a certain standard, a certain set of rules.

The fact that a book is in the official canon confers on it a sense of authority. But it's important to note that the authority of the book came first. From now on in this history, we'll encounter different canon lists, but in all these lists, people didn't just bung the book in the canon list and then claim that made it authoritative: it was because the book was considered authoritative that it made it into the list in the first place.

As the rabbis at Jamnia tried to rebuild Judaism from the wreckage of the failed Jewish revolt, they tried to clarify once and for all what constituted their sacred Scriptures. There were arguments about many of the books – the story about Hananiah ben Hezekiah studying Ezekiel comes from this period – but four, in particular, gave them real problems: Proverbs, Ecclesiastes, Song of Solomon and Esther. It's not really hard to see why: Proverbs is a collection of... well... proverbs; Esther doesn't once mention God; the Song of Songs is hot and steamy and Ecclesiastes sometimes reads like the work of a particularly depressed art student.

It helped its case if a book was linked with a Jewish festival. Esther was the story which was celebrated in Purim; Ruth's story was recited at the feast of Weeks or Pentecost; Ecclesiastes at Sukkoth; Lamentations at the late summer feast on the ninth of Ab; Song of Songs at Passover.[13] The debate took many years, and was not properly decided until around the last decade of the first century AD. The list which emerged was the list of Scriptures we find in our Old Testaments today.

Whether everyone stuck to this list is uncertain. Certainly in the Greek-speaking world, the Septuagint still ruled, with its extra books. But there is evidence that other regions also made their own list. Melito, the Christian bishop of Sardis, drew up a list of the Old Testament books about 170 AD, based on enquiries he had made while travelling in Syria. His list doesn't contain Esther.* Either he has missed it out by accident, or not everyone thought that Jamnia was the ultimate authority when it came to authoritative Scriptures.

The order of the Tanakh is different from that of the Christian Old Testament, especially with the inclusion of historical works such as Samuel and Kings in the 'prophets' group. Jamnia probably didn't decide this order, but confirmed an existing arrangement. We know from the gospels that Jesus knew of this way of ordering the Scriptures: Jesus talks of the prophets who have been martyred 'from the blood of Abel to the blood of Zechariah' (Luke 11.51; Matt. 23.35). Of course to our ears this has a nice A to Z ring to it, but that's not why Jesus chose these two names. Abel is the first 'martyr' in Genesis (Gen. 4.8) and Zechariah is the last martyr in Chronicles (2 Chr. 24.21). And those, in the order set out above, were the first and last books of the Tanakh. So Jesus clearly knew this arrangement of books and this 'Palestinian canon' was the one which was to become traditional within Judaism.

---

* Nehemiah and Lamentations were also missing, but they may have been included with Ezra and Jeremiah, as was common.

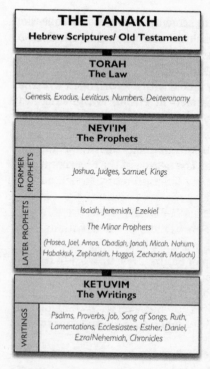

THE TANAKH
Hebrew Scriptures/ Old Testament

TORAH
The Law

Genesis, Exodus, Leviticus, Numbers, Deuteronomy

NEVI'IM
The Prophets

FORMER PROPHETS

Joshua, Judges, Samuel, Kings

LATER PROPHETS

Isaiah, Jeremiah, Ezekiel
The Minor Prophets
(Hosea, Joel, Amos, Obadiah, Jonah, Micah, Nahum, Habakkuk, Zephaniah, Haggai, Zechariah, Malachi)

KETUVIM
The Writings

WRITINGS

Psalms, Proverbs, Job, Song of Songs, Ruth, Lamentations, Ecclesiastes, Esther, Daniel, Ezra/Nehemiah, Chronicles

Of course, that raises the question of why Chronicles was chosen to be the last book – especially since, chronologically, Ezra and Nehemiah come after it. It may be to do with the ending, since Chronicles ends on a positive note with the Jews being allowed to return home by Cyrus. Certainly it has none of the slightly downbeat realism of their return as recorded in Ezra-Nehemiah.[*] Elsewhere the order of the various books could vary: apart from the Torah and the Former Prophets, whose order is always the same, later manuscripts and printed editions have different arrangements of the books, especially in the Writings. Anyway, 'order' here refers to the method of storing and cataloguing the scrolls in the various synagogues and libraries of Palestine around 200 AD. Each section – Law, Writings and Prophets – would have been stored in their own *armarium* – a cupboard for storing scrolls.

Masoretes

Storing the texts was one thing, reading them was another matter entirely. Because as time went by, the difficulties of deciphering the ancient, vowel-less Hebrew became acute. And, no matter how carefully the scribes worked, over the centuries of copying some errors and corruptions had inevitably crept in.

Thus, around the ninth century AD a group known as the Masoretes decided to safeguard the authentic text. Their name comes from the

---

[*] Christians, of course, end their Old Testament with Malachi, which is not only the last of the minor prophets, but which also contains prophecies pointing to Jesus.

Hebrew word *masorah*, meaning 'tradition' and that's what they were doing: preserving the traditional readings and interpretation. They invented a system of dots and dashes – known as pointing – which they placed above each word, to indicate which vowel should go where and how the word should be read. They added marginal notes known as *masora*, to indicate where there was uncertainty, and offered alternative readings. They also indicated what should be said when the Scriptures were being read, if the written word was not allowed (a good example is that the divine name YHWH should never be pronounced, so the Masoretic text indicated that 'Adonai' – Lord – should be spoken instead.) They also reorganised the text, breaking it into paragraphs and verses and ordering it into weekly readings for either a yearly or annual cycle.

The earliest Masoretic manuscript dates from 895 AD, but this contains only the Prophets. The earliest complete copies of the Tanakh – the Aleppo and Leningrad Codices – are from the tenth century and it is on the Leningrad Codex that the standard Hebrew edition – the *Biblia Hebraica* – is based.[14]

Sometimes, however, tradition was a way of falsifying the reading, not clarifying it. Judges contains a story about the tribe of Dan worshipping idols. And one of those involved in this practice was 'Jonathan son of Gershom, son of Moses' (Judges 18.30). The scribes thought it too shocking

A manuscript of the Hebrew Bible, with the vowel points and accents. The text shows the end of Genesis and the start of Exodus.

that the grandson of Moses should have been involved in such an impious practice, so in the pointing above the word 'Moses', the synagogue reader was directed to say the word 'Manasseh' instead. Did they wish to mislead people? Or were they implying that Jonathan's behaviour was more like to the wicked king Manasseh than the great patriarch Moses? Whatever the case, it was an attempt to tone down the Bible, to make it safe.

The strange tale of Jehovah

The lack of vowels has led to some strange consequences. For example, the word 'Jehovah' is widely used as a name for God, appearing in many worship songs for example. But you won't find it in the Bible, because it wasn't invented until the thirteenth century AD.

The Hebrew name for 'God' is YHWH – usually transliterated as Yahweh. However, no Jew would utter the sacred name out loud, so those reading the text out would substitute a different phrase – either 'Adonai' (Lord) or 'Elohim' (God). In later manuscripts, Jewish scribes put the vowels of these words in tiny letters above YHWH, indicating which substitute was to be used. But Western translators thought these marks were the missing vowels from YHWH. So they combined Adonai and Yahweh to get 'Jehovah'. Although translations such as the King James version use the word occasionally, and we sing 'Guide me oh thou great Jehovah,' we are using a name that no ancient Jew ever used. And all because they left the vowels out.

Otherwise the care with which the text was copied was extreme. We might feel that a text which has been so copied would be bound to be corrupted at the end of a thousand years – like the literary version of Chinese whispers. But although there were variants and errors, evidence from the fragments of earlier texts which have been found – in the *genizah*, in quotes from early Christian writers and from the Mishnah – show that the Masoretes did their work well. Their work is used in synagogues throughout the world and in the Bibles which Christians use today.

And that's where we have to head next. Because by the time that the Jamnia rabbis were deciding on the official list, their Scriptures had already been appropriated by a group of heretics, many of whose members were not even Jews: the followers of Joshua ben Joseph, Jesus of Nazareth – the Christians.

THE CHRISTIAN BIBLE

In 1 Timothy chapter 4, Paul advises his protégé to 'give attention to the public reading of Scripture, to exhorting, to teaching' (1 Tim. 4.13–14). In another letter he says that 'all Scripture is inspired by God' – literally, all Scripture is 'breathed out' by God (2 Tim. 3.16). These verses are often used by Christians when talking about the Bible, but they forget that Paul wasn't talking about the New Testament at all. At the time Paul was writing – in the AD 60s – there was no such thing as the New Testament. What Paul means by the 'Scriptures' is the Old Testament, and in particular he means the Septuagint.

The Septuagint was the first Bible of the church; at least eighty per cent of the Old Testament quotations in the New Testament come from the Septuagint. The reason is simple: the vast majority of Christians spoke Greek. And not just outside Judea: the seven deacons appointed in Acts chapter 6 were Greek-speaking Jews: when Stephen, one of them, is about to be stoned, he quotes from the Septuagint. Paul, as a trained Pharisee, could certainly read Hebrew, but he wrote in Greek and he visited synagogues through the Græco-Roman world, where only a minority spoke Hebrew. Greek was the common language of the empire. The Septuagint was, therefore, the perfect missionary Bible.

The Catenae among the pigeons

It's unlikely that many ordinary Christians would have had copies of the Septuagint. More likely is that they had small copies of selected Scriptures – ones which they thought important for explaining who Jesus was and what he did. These are known as *catenae* and we can see some excerpts from them in action in the New Testament when Paul quotes what appear to be well-known excerpts from the Tanakh (e.g. Rom. 9.25–29; 10.18–21).

To tree or not to tree

As Christianity expanded, the use of the Septuagint caused some problems, particularly between Christian and Jew. First, the Septuagint had the Apocryphal books – which were not acknowledged by the Jews. But there were other examples of extra material. For example, the Septuagint text of Psalm 96.10, has the phrase 'the Lord reigns from the tree', which became a favourite Christian proof text in debates, showing how the Psalms predicted Jesus' crucifixion. But the Hebrew text never mentions a tree – it has simply 'the Lord reigns'.

Then there was the problem of mistranslation because, while the Septuagint is very accurate for the most part, sometimes the translation into Greek is very different. For modern readers this can lead to real confusion, because the Old Testament of modern Bibles isn't based on the Septuagint, but on the Masoretic text.* The result is that the Old Testament used by Christians today is different to that used by the Early Church. Look up virtually any bit of the Old Testament that is quoted in the New and you will find some significant differences between the two versions.† It's a curious irony that the quest for the authentic, accurate Hebrew Scriptures has actually taken us away from the Scriptures used by those who founded the church. The people who created Christianity, people like Peter, Paul, Timothy and Luke were, by implication, using a less accurate translation.

Perhaps the best example of the difference between the Hebrew and Greek Old Testaments is Matthew's interpretation of Isaiah 7.14. The Septuagint uses the Greek word *parthenos* (virgin) to translate the Hebrew word *almah* (young woman). Matthew, of course, read this, and saw in it a prophecy of the virgin birth. This doesn't mean that Matthew made it up. Clearly, he viewed the virgin birth as a historical event which was confirmed by the prophecy in Isaiah. But it explains why, when you look up Isaiah 7.14 in many versions, there is no virgin mentioned. It also faces modern translators with

---

* Only the Orthodox church uses the same Old Testament as the first Christians. Their liturgy preserves the Greek version of the Hebrew Scriptures.

† For example, compare Amos 9.11–12, with Paul's quotation of the same passage in Acts 15.15–19.

an issue. Do they go for the woman or the virgin? The result is that you can generally classify the theological stance of a Bible by which word they use. The more conservative translations tend to keep the word 'virgin' in, arguing that *almah* means 'maiden' – that is, to a young woman who is unmarried and sexually chaste, and thus has 'virginity as one of her characteristics'.*

The Apocrypha and the Discovery of America

Up until the sixteenth century, the church used as its Old Testament a Latin translation of the Septuagint which, of course, included the Apocrypha. Rather curiously, this led to the discovery of America. In an account of creation, 2 Esdras has:

'On the third day you commanded the waters to be gathered together in a seventh part of the earth; six parts you dried up and kept so that some of them might be planted and cultivated and be of service before you' (2 Esd. 6.42–43)

Columbus, who read this in his Latin Bible, figured that if the water only covered a seventh of the world, then the distance between western Europe and – as he thought – the east coast of Asia couldn't be that far. So he used this text as part of his argument to King Ferdinand and Queen Isabella to supply him with funding.[1]

The Revised Standard Septuagint

In using the Septuagint, Christians had one important argument: the Septuagint was inspired. It could not, therefore, be outgunned by quotes from the Hebrew original. The result was that Jews began wondering if the legend about the divine inspiration of the Septuagint was all it was cracked up to be. Gradually, Jewish use of the Septuagint declined. If Christians used it, there must be something suspect about it. And Christians had a tendency to claim it for their own. In Justin's *Dialogue with Trypho*, the earliest recorded Jewish-Christian dialogue, Justin quotes many texts from the Septuagint and challenges his opponent on whether he has really understood them.

---

* ESV Study Bible Note on Isaiah 7.14. Of the main modern versions, NIV, TNIV, ESV, CEV have 'virgin'. NRSV, NJB and NET have 'young woman'. See page 263 ff. for more examples.

Are you acquainted with [these passages], Trypho? They are contained in your Scriptures, or rather not yours, but ours. For we believe them; but you, though you read them, do not catch the spirit that is in them.[2]

'Yours, not ours': no wonder Jews retreated from the use of the Septuagint. If the Christians wanted the Greek version, let them have it. For Jews who needed a Greek translation, other, more accurate, Greek versions were produced. The most significant of these was by Aquila, a Gentile Christian who converted to orthodox Judaism. His translation, produced about 140 AD, slavishly replicated the Hebrew text, even down to the order of the words. The result was both incredibly accurate, and also clunkingly unreadable. It actually proved really useful to Christian scholars, who wanted to see what the Hebrew word meant and who weren't much worried by fancy written style. A translator called Theodotion went the other way, with a kind of revised Septuagint, which aimed for readability rather than word-for-word accuracy. This dilemma – accuracy versus readability – has been faced by every Bible translator ever since.

Hymns and creeds

The Scripture of the Early Church was the Septuagint. But they also added to that their hymns or creeds, which told the story of Jesus of Nazareth, the Son of God. These can be found in passages like Philippians 2.5–11, which is a hymn or poem, telling the story of who Jesus was and what he did.

Paul's letters also contain what you might call 'official stories'

For I received from the Lord what I also handed on to you, that the Lord Jesus on the night when he was betrayed took a loaf of bread, and when he had given thanks, he broke it and said, "This is my body that is for you. Do this in remembrance of me." In the same way he took the cup also, after supper, saying, "This cup is the new covenant in my blood. Do this, as often as you drink it, in remembrance of me." (1 Corinthians 11.23–26)

'Here's the story. Pass it on.' Paul and the other converts memorised the key stories and passed them on to others. Their stories included Jesus' trial before Pontius Pilate (1 Tim. 6.13) and the 'rulers' role in crucifying Jesus (1 Cor. 2.8). Paul passes on a tradition about the list of people who saw the resurrected Jesus. He recounts a range of Jesus' teachings on a variety of subjects, while James is full of allusions to Jesus' teaching.*

These stories are the base layer of what would become the New Testament. Just as the Old Testament originated in stories about Yahweh, the New Testament originated in stories about Jesus, with eye-witnesses travelling from church to church, making sure that the stories were remembered accurately. We know who some of these storytellers were. Paul tells us that the brothers of Jesus, Peter and their wives travelled (1 Cor. 9.4–7). There were others as well: Aristion and John the Elder. The core group of twelve, the members of the seventy-two he sent out, the women and children whose lives he touched, itinerant story-tellers, peddlers of truth, trudging the roads of the Græco-Roman world, passing it on.

Most Christians could neither read nor write. But what they could do, and what they did very well, was remember. Non-literate cultures tend to have very good ways of learning and recalling stories, sayings and history. In a world where you can't write down a reminder, remembering things accurately is crucial, and there is good evidence that shows this process in action.

Papias takes note
Papias was a respected leader of the church in Asia Minor, best known for his five volume work entitled *Expositions of the Sayings of the Lord*. Only fragments of this work survive, quoted in the works of other, later writers. Papias, like other Christians, must have learned the stories which were passed on, but he did more than that. When a Christian VIP was in town, when someone who actually *knew* the disciples came his way, he made notes

> I will not hesitate to set down for you, along with my interpretations, everything I carefully learned then from the elders and carefully

---

* See for example Romans 13–15, Galatians 5–6, 1 Thessalonians 4–5, James 2.1–13.

remembered, guaranteeing their truth... And if by chance someone who had been a follower of the elders should come my way, I inquired about the words of the elders – what Andrew or Peter said, or Philip or Thomas or James or John or Matthew or any other of the Lord's disciples, and whatever Aristion and the elder John, the Lord's disciples, were saying. For I did not think that information from books would profit me as much as information from a living and abiding voice.[3]

According to Eusebius, Papias also passed along other 'accounts of sayings of the Lord belonging to Aristion... and the traditions of John the Elder'.[*] Clearly Papias was concerned with authenticity: he wanted to hear from the source.

The important thing is that these stories would have been learnt, *and also written down*. You'll often read how the gospels were written thirty or forty years after the events they describe – but it is frankly inconceivable that the first Christians waited decades before committing anything about Jesus to paper. Or papyrus.

Taking notes from speakers was quite common in antiquity. It was not unusual for unauthorised editions of famous authors to appear, based on notes taken at their lectures. Quintillian prefaces his textbook on oratory with a warning about two books, apparently by him, which are merely notes taken at lectures. They were written by students who published them in an act of misguided homage. Quite clearly the words of Jesus, stories of his actions, and accounts of particular events could easily have been collected and circulated in this way. Indeed, at one point, Tertullian calls the gospels *commentarii* or notes. These accounts and traditions formed the scraps of what would become the gospels.

Indeed we *know* that Christians wrote things down. Because they wrote each other letters.

The Letters
The earliest Christian documents we have are the New Testament letters. Dating these is a tricky business – especially with letters like

---

[*] Papias mentions two Johns. This second John – John the Elder – may well be the author of John's gospel and was a disciple of Jesus based in Jerusalem.

James and Hebrews which contain little chronological information. The earliest of Paul's letters is probably Galatians, assuming it was written after his visit to the region in AD 48/49 and before the Jerusalem council of AD 49. The rest of his letters were written between AD 50 and his death in the mid 60s AD. Of the non-Pauline letters, James is probably the earliest.

Physically, these letters would have been very similar – each written with a reed pen on papyrus or sometimes parchment. This would have been rolled and put in a container and then taken by hand to its destination via a messenger. Paul dictated his letters to a scribe, occasionally adding a greeting in his own hand.

The normal procedure with letter-writing was to make two copies: one kept by the writer and the other sent to the recipient. You made your own arrangements for delivery, usually using a servant, friend or business associate as a messenger. Christians would have only trusted their letters to other Christians. The majority of letters, of course, were written to specific recipients, such as the church at Corinth or Rome. However, once the letter had reached and been read to its intended recipient, it would have been copied and passed on. As Papias shows us, words from the actual apostles were highly valued among the first Christian communities. Bootlegging texts was not only rife, it was the commonest way to get hold of them. If someone had a text in which you were interested, you simply asked them to copy it. This was the way that Paul's letters were distributed: officially copied, first-century filesharing.

There are thirteen letters by Paul in the New Testament, although scholars argue as to whether all of them are really by Paul, or whether some of them are merely attributed to him. Not all of Paul's letters survived. We have two letters to the Corinthians, but we know that he wrote at least four. It's possible that the text of one of these missing letters has actually been merged with 2 Corinthians. But the other letter has been lost completely. Which may not be that surprising since it was, by all accounts, a harsh letter which they may not have wanted to make public. There is also a reference to a letter to the church at Laodicea (Col. 4.16). And there must, no doubt, have been many other letters – perhaps more personal notes, such as that sent to Philemon – which did not survive.

Paul's letters were radical, counter-cultural documents. In a world where the family unit, the kinship group, was a rigid fixture, he claimed that all Christians were brothers and sisters. His claim that there was no real difference between Jew and Gentile would have caused outrage among devout Jews, while his claim that there was no real difference between slave and free would have outraged everyone else. These were dangerously radical and inflammatory ideas.

Another recurring theme in Paul's letters is the imminence of Jesus' return. And it was that event – or rather non-event – that made for the next stage of the development of the New Testament. The Early Church lived in the eager expectation of the return of Jesus. So while they took notes and passed on the stories, there was no pressure to create any detailed account. But as the years went by and the first witnesses died the eyewitness accounts became more important. Once again, the stories could be lost. So they decided to write down the accounts. They created, in fact, the gospels.

The memoirs

'I in my turn, after carefully going over the whole story from the beginning, have decided to write an ordered account' writes Luke at the beginning of his gospel.[*] But it's not clear what form his investigations took or what materials he had at his disposal. By the time the gospels came to be written – probably in the 60s AD – a number of written resources may have been available, including

- An Aramaic collection of the sayings of Jesus.
- A collection of miracle stories.
- An earlier 'gospel' in Aramaic.
- An account of the last week of Jesus' life.
- A collection of Jesus' teachings, which scholars call Q.

Matthew, Mark and Luke are usually grouped together as the 'synoptic' gospels, from the Latin *syn*=one and *optic*=seeing. They see events, broadly speaking, from one perspective and follow the same overall scheme. Mark is generally assumed to be the earliest of the four gospels and one which provided much of the source material for Matthew and Luke.

---

[*] Luke 1.3. New Jerusalem Bible.

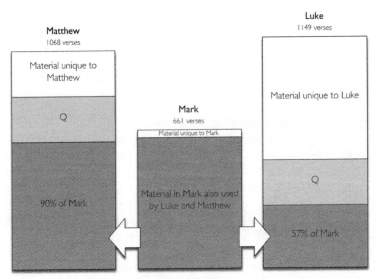

The Ingredients of the Synoptic Gospels.

Matthew uses 97% of Mark; Luke use 57%. There is other material – some 230 sayings of Jesus – which is shared between Matthew and Luke, but which is not present in Mark. This, scholars suggest, is from another document, a collection of Jesus' sayings, which they call 'Q'. The initial comes from the German word *Quelle*, meaning source.

Scholars make great claims for Q; they end up talking about 'the Q community' and even attempt to make subdivisions within Q itself, but we should bear in mind that it is a hypothetical document. No-one has ever seen a copy of Q. No fragments of it have ever been found, and several well-known scholars believe that its case has been overstated. However, it seems reasonable that a collection of Jesus' sayings and stories was compiled. And there may well have been other collections – a parable collection, perhaps, such as the group which fills Mark 4, or the three parables of the lost coin, lost sheep and lost son in Luke 15.

The fourth gospel – the gospel of John – is very different to the other three and is generally assumed to have been written later. John's style is different to the other gospels. It is more voluble, more wordy, but much of that wordiness tends to be restricted to Jesus's speech. When it comes to describing events he is careful and clear. The author is only identified in the text as 'the beloved disciple', however the Early Church almost unanimously agreed it was written by 'John'. Whether it was John son of Zebedee, or another apostle called John is the subject of some debate.

When were they written?

The dating of the gospels, and the order and manner of their composition, are matters over which there is fierce debate. Many scholars place Mark, Matthew and Luke in the 70s AD, with John significantly later. Others argue for an earlier dating, with Mark and Luke in the early 60s AD, Matthew shortly after and John in the 80s.*
The usual factor in the dating is the destruction of the Temple in 70 AD. Since Jesus is recorded as predicting the destruction of the Temple (Mark 13) the argument runs like this

1. Jesus predicts the destruction of the Temple and the siege of Jerusalem by the Romans.
2. But we know that prediction is impossible...
3. Therefore the Christian writers made up these predictions after the event...
4. Therefore the gospels must be written after 70 AD.

There are some problems with this kind of reasoning. First, it assumes that prediction of the sort that Jesus was doing in Mark 13 is impossible. But Judea in the time of Christ was a hotbed of political intrigue and unrest, and it did not take someone with divine powers to see that revolution and disaster was always a possibility. Jesus grew up in Nazareth, a place which had suffered under the Romans: just after Herod the Great died, a revolt broke out and the city of Sepphoris – just three miles from Nazareth – was razed to the ground by the Roman forces. So, you did not have to be a great prophet to know that, when the Romans moved in, it resulted in death and utter destruction. That was what the Romans *did*. Indeed, they were renowned for utterly destroying the cities they besieged.

---

* Frankly, whatever variation you want there is bound to have been a scholar who will argue for it. Although John is agreed to be the 'youngest' gospel, a fragment from it is the oldest known manuscript copy of any New Testament work. A fragment of papyrus found in 1934, containing a small portion from John chapter 18, has been dated to 100 AD.

And, if the 'prediction' was created by Christian writers after the siege of Jerusalem, it's odd that they missed out on some of the more impressive features. The first-century Jewish historian Josephus includes many more historical details which would have been meat and drink to anyone creating a prophetic, apocalyptic vision: he talks of sickness, cannibalism and the fire that destroyed the buildings.

Finally, if you want to be picky, then you can see that the details *do not* fit the event perfectly. Jesus says 'not one stone will be left standing', but quite a lot of stones were. (The huge stones in the Western Wall are still upright.) He talks of people running to the hills, but if those in Jerusalem had fled to the hills during the siege, they would have run straight into the Roman army, which was stationed on the Mount of Olives and Mount Scopus. And according to early-church tradition, the Christians in Jerusalem fled to Pella, in Perea, which is some 285 feet below sea level!

Further evidence for a pre-70 date can be found in the book of Acts. Acts ends in a most abrupt way. The latter half of the book builds up to a climactic confrontation between Paul and the Roman authorities, yet it finishes before the climax is reached. It ends, not with an explosion but with a whimper. Why doesn't Luke mention the trial? Or the fall of Jerusalem – the most significant, climactic event of the first century for both Jews and Christians alike? If Luke was writing Luke-Acts after 70 AD, it's bizarre that he makes no mention of the Roman destruction of Jerusalem – especially when you consider he was writing his book for Theophilus, a Roman patron.

These reasons seem to indicate an earlier date of composition for the gospels. It seems to me much more likely that the first gospels – Mark and Luke-Acts – date from before 70 AD.

Who, then, wrote the gospels? None of the gospels are attributed within the text (with the exception of John, although he calls himself 'the beloved disciple') but the Early Church believed them to be by people who had known Jesus or known someone close to Jesus. Here's an account of the origin of Mark's gospel, as recorded by Eusebius, quoting Papias

> And the elder [Papias] used to say this: 'Mark, having become Peter's interpreter, wrote down accurately everything he remembered,

though not in order, of the things either said or done by Christ. For he neither heard the Lord nor followed him, but afterward, as I said, followed Peter who adapted his teachings as needed but had no intention of giving an ordered account of the Lord's sayings.[4]

This statement illustrates why these four gospels were considered authoritative: they claimed a direct link with those who had witnessed events. They were eye-witness accounts. In Mark's case, Peter is obviously the prime source, but within the gospels themselves, there are moments when we enter into someone's story, where a detail comes from a specific source. Mark records the incident where Simon of Cyrene is compelled to carry Jesus' cross-beam

> They compelled a passer-by, who was coming in from the country, to carry his cross; it was Simon of Cyrene, the father of Alexander and Rufus (Mark 15.21).

Why does he mention Alexander and Rufus? They're not mentioned anywhere else in the text. The answer must be that they were well-known in the Christian community. Indeed, Rufus may well be the Rufus whom Paul greets in Rome (Rom. 16.13). This story was *their* story, the tale they told among the Christian communities. Their Dad carried Jesus' cross on that day.

This apostolic link is important. Indeed, the term 'the Apostles' came to be a catch-all term for the writings of the New Testament. In Ephesians, Paul claims that their faith is built on the foundation of the Apostles and the Prophets – the two most important types of literature for the Early Church (Eph. 2.20). Ignatius of Antioch (c.115) urges the church in Magnesia to remain firm in the teachings of the 'Saviour and the Apostles.'

Additional Gospels

Go back a moment. To those stories, the ones memorised by Paul, for example. Writing in 54 AD to that fractious congregation at Corinth, he reminds them of Jesus' words about the wine: 'Do this, as often as you drink it, in remembrance of me.' Three years later, in his farewell speech at Miletus, he reminded leaders from Ephesus of Jesus' words:

'It is more blessed to give than to receive.' And the interesting thing is that neither of these sayings of Jesus appear in the four gospels. They are part of a different tradition, a different set of stories and sayings which never made it into the gospels. The gospels themselves acknowledge that there was another lode of material to be mined. John writes that 'Jesus did many other signs in the presence of his disciples, which are not written in this book' (John 20.30). Even after the gospels were written, stories continued circulating. A fragment of papyrus found in Egypt, for example, records an incident between Jesus and a Pharisaical priest in the Temple.[5] Eusebius says that Papias had 'recorded other accounts as having come to him from unwritten tradition, certain strange parables of the Lord and teachings of his and some other statements of a more mythical character.'

There was an expanded version of Matthew's gospel, which is known today as the *Gospel of the Nazoreans*, used from the second century AD by a group of Jewish Christians in West Syria. It probably originated in Egypt some time in the first century. Epiphanius (writing late in the fourth century) preserves a few lines from the *Gospel of the Ebionites* – the name is a modern invention – which was a harmonised gospel, created from episodes in Matthew, Luke and Mark.* There was the *Gospel of the Egyptians*, probably a life of Jesus written in the first half of the second century and used in Egypt.

The most frequently mentioned extra 'gospel' however, was the *Gospel of the Hebrews*. Originally written in Greek, and aimed at the Jewish-Christian community, it's the only lost gospel whose actual title is mentioned by contemporary writers. The earliest quotations from the text come from the writings of people who lived in Alexandria, so it probably originated amongst the Jewish Christians in that region. It's an early gospel – certainly it was known to Papias who died around 130 AD. A copy was recorded as being at Caesarea, but it is long lost. Jerome quotes several verses from this Gospel, including an account of Jesus' resurrection appearance to his brother James, and a slightly different version of the Lord's prayer.

These versions did not make it into our New Testament, with one possible exception. According to Eusebius, Papias' works included 'a

---

* The Ebionites were a Judaistic sect which rejected Paul's teaching and believed in a purely human Jesus. For this reason they seem to have omitted the nativity stories and genealogies.

story about a woman accused falsely of many sins before the Lord, which the Gospel of [the] Hebrews contains.'[6] This is the story of the woman caught in adultery – or a version of it anyhow – which is included today in most Bibles as part of the gospel of John. This story is absent from the earliest manuscripts of John's gospel and the style is different to the style of John as well. It's possible, then, that this story comes not from John, but from the lost *Gospel of the Hebrews*.

There were other Christian writings as well, which in some places had a special status. These include letters from Early Church leaders like Clement and Ignatius, a letter attributed to Barnabas, a vision called the *Shepherd of Hermas* and the *Didache* – a kind of Early Church discipleship manual.

Then there was Revelation...

Other Christian writing

Other Christian writings were also passed around the Early Church and proved very popular. Some of these even ended up in some of the earliest complete Bibles.

1 Clement

1 Clement is a letter from Christians in Rome to their fellow Christians in Corinth, where the young men of the church had deposed the established leaders. The Roman church wrote to Corinth and sent a delegation to sort out this breach of discipline. Clement was part of the leadership of the church at Rome. It is possible he was the Clement mentioned in Philippians 4.3. The document was written during a time of persecution, probably around 95–97 AD. It tells us about things like the tradition that Peter and Paul died during the Neronian persecutions, between 64–68 AD. Clement also indicates that leaders from the apostolic times are still living in Rome. Many people in the Early Church viewed 1 Clement as scriptural, and it turns up in the earliest Bibles as part of the New Testament writings.[*]

The Didache

The *Didache* – which means 'the teaching' – is an early Christian discipleship manual, containing the do's and don'ts of the Christian life.[†] It is difficult to date precisely, since it was altered and added to over time, but its core probably dates from the 60s or even earlier; the church it describes, with

---

[*] Clement of Alexandria viewed the letter as scriptural. A late fourth-century document known as the *Apostolic Constitutions* puts 1 Clement as part of the New Testament. And in the *Codex Alexandrinus* which was copied in the fifth century AD, it follows Revelation. Didymus the Blind also includes it in his canon.

[†] Similar teaching is found in 1 Peter 2.11–5.11, Ephesians 4.1–6.20 and 1 Timothy.

travelling apostles and a simple, two-layer structure of elders and deacons, reflect the times of Paul and James. It was designed to show new Gentile followers how to be a Christian. 'There are two ways,' it begins, 'one of life and one of death and there is a great difference between these two ways.'[7]

The Letters of Ignatius

A collection of letters written by Ignatius of Antioch, probably during the reign of Trajan (98–117 AD). The letters were written during the last seven weeks of his life, when Ignatius was being taken to Rome to be martyred for his faith. They reflect a situation where there were problems with false teaching, and contain much about the need for unity. Not unnaturally, they also contain a lot of material about Ignatius' forthcoming death.

The Letter of Barnabas

The Letter of Barnabas was another letter which was highly regarded among some parts of the Early Church. Despite the title, there is no claim to authorship in the text. The letter is concerned with the understanding of Jewish Scriptures; indeed, the writer seems to have had access to various old Greek versions of the Hebrew Scriptures. The letter may have been written in Alexandria, but it's not certain. There is more certainty about the date, however: the letter refers to the destruction of the Temple, so it must be post AD 70, but it also expects the Temple to be rebuilt, which means it must have been written before 135 AD, since in that year the Roman emperor Hadrian constructed a Roman shrine on the site of the old Temple, rendering any rebuilding project impossible.

The Shepherd of Hermas

The Shepherd of Hermas is a curious book, which contains a series of visions given to Hermas, a former slave living in Rome, who became, evidently, a leader of some standing in the church.[*] The theme of the book is the need for pious observance of the divine commandments and for self-control, and the need for repentance. It also talks about wealth and riches, and the obligations of the wealthy to help the poor – a concern which reflects, perhaps, the author's constituency among the lower-class slaves and freedmen, with a lower social standing. The book was widely read in the second and third centuries AD. Various church leaders at that time accepted it as Scripture, and it's even included at the end of the *Codex Sinaiticus* – the fourth century biblical manuscript.[†]

---

[*] According to the Muratorian Canon, Hermas was the brother of Pius, Bishop of Rome around 140–154 AD. It may well be a composite document, with the early part (Visions 1–4) dating from 90–110 AD, and the later visions coming from the mid-second century AD.

[†] Irenaeus and Clement of Alexandria accepted it as Scripture, as did Origen and Tertullian for a while. Didymus the Blind included it in his canon of Scripture.

Beauty and the Beast

On February 28 1993, the United States Bureau of Alcohol, Tobacco, and Firearms attempted to execute a search warrant at the HQ of a religious sect called the Branch Davidians. They believed that the group were stockpiling weapons. They were right. In the ensuing gunfight, four agents and six members of the cult were shot and killed. The FBI were called in and a siege began, ending 51 days later with the compound in flames and seventy-six people dead.

There were many causes of this disaster, not least the paranoid personality of the cult leader, David Koresh, and the ham-fisted tactics of the FBI. But one key factor was that the Branch Davidians were a cult with deep roots in the book of Revelation.

Chapter 13 of that unearthly book depicts a beast which spoke like a dragon but looked like a lamb, which could bring down fire from heaven, which would mark the earth's inhabitants with a number – 666 – and which would deceive everyone. It was this image which the Branch Davidians applied to the US Government. And when those FBI agents surrounded their compound, with their tear gas and their semi-automatics and their smooth-talking hostage negotiators, it only confirmed what their leaders had told them: this was not a war against the US Government: this was a battle against the beast.

The book of Revelation was written almost exactly 1900 years earlier than the events in Texas, but the events of 1993 illustrate perfectly why the book took so long to gain acceptance. Of all the books in God's dangerous book, the vision, seen by John in his incarceration, was one of the most dangerous. Unlike some of the other books, we know where the book was written, and who wrote it. The author – John – is mentioned five times in the book.* He wrote it on the prison island of Patmos – a kind of first-century Alcatraz or Robbens Island – just off the coast of modern Turkey. And he most likely wrote it during the persecution by Diocletian, sometime around 95 AD.

Revelation is, first and foremost, a work of apocalyptic literature – a type of religious writing which flourished from around 200 BC to 100 AD. Indeed, Revelation is only one of many apocalypses

---

* Revelation 1.1–2, 4, 9; 22.8.

from that time. There are Jewish apocalypses like the latter part of Daniel, much of Ezekiel and books like *The Apocalypse of Baruch*, *The Apocalypse of Zephaniah*, *The Wisdom of Solomon* and *The Book of Enoch*. There are later Christian apocalypses attributed to figures such as Peter, Paul, James and even one attributed to Adam.

As a type of writing, apocalyptic literature is characterised by extensive use of symbolism, and by its depiction of past, present and future events leading up to a decisive intervention by God. But its key characteristic is that it claims to reveal the truth. Not the apparent truth. Not the obvious, on-the-surface truth of the official documents, or the Roman Empire press releases. No, apocalyptic literature lifts the covers of reality and shows you what's underneath. That's what the name means. 'Apocalypse' doesn't mean 'end of the world' as we commonly use it. It means, in fact, 'revelation'. It comes from the Greek word *apokalupso* – to reveal.

Apocalyptic literature, therefore, is not necessarily concerned with the end of the world; it claims to reveal what is hidden – to show what is really going on. This makes it the medium of choice for the oppressed, the persecuted, the misunderstood. It's an avowedly political genre and the Book of Revelation is no exception.

In Revelation, this protest has a specific focus in the figure of Babylon – depicted as a dangerously beautiful and alluring whore. The whore represents not the actual Babylon, but the city of Rome, the centre of the evil empire, the source of the persecution and violence which was attacking the church.

The political stance of Revelation is one of the prime reasons why it nearly didn't make it into the Bible. Because at the time when the final canon of the New Testament was being put together, Christianity's relationship with the empire had changed; it had become the official religion of the empire.

Revelation did not sit comfortably in this new cosy relationship. It was a reminder of a different time, a time when John was imprisoned because he refused to worship the emperor, when the empire's soldiers were attacking the church, rather than joining it. Revelation is an avowedly anti-Imperialist book.

And it's been inspiring protesters and radicals ever since.

Christians and the book

Towards the end of his life, while under house arrest in Rome, Paul wrote to his friend and protégé Timothy. He asks Timothy for a favour: 'When you come, bring the cloak that I left with Carpus at Troas, also the books, and above all the parchments' (2 Tim. 4.13).

Those two words – books and parchments, *biblia* and *membranae* in the original – actually mean different kinds of writing materials. *Biblia*, as we have seen, literally means 'books', but in Paul's day it meant scrolls – secular, civil documents, religious documents such as the Hebrew Scriptures, or historical books – anything written on a long, rolled piece of papyrus.

Membranae, however, is a Latin word which means 'parchment'. In particular, the word means small parchment notebooks which people carried around with them to write everyday notes in, or to draw up the first drafts of important documents. Some time in the first century, someone had the idea of making these notebooks out of papyrus, by simply folding sheets of papyrus and sewing through the spine. These codices – or codex in the singular – are the same basic format as the book you have in your hand.* In other words, sometime in the first century, someone invented the book.

They did not catch on for a long time. For most writers in the Græco-Roman world, only scrolls were 'proper' books. Codices or *membranae* were relegated to the status of informal, unimportant documents. Except among Christians. Because, remarkably, virtually all the fragments of Christian literature from the second and third centuries comes from codices. In the Graeco-Roman and Jewish traditions, the scroll was ubiquitous; everything was written on a scroll, but Christians used books. The figures tell the story: all of the fourteen fragments of Christian literature from AD 100–150 came from codices. Of the remains of Greek books that can be dated earlier than AD 200, over 98 percent are scrolls; in the same period the surviving Christian books are almost all codices. It wasn't until the fourth century that the codex use equalled that of the scroll in the wider Graeco-Roman world. But the Christians, for some reason, had been using the codex exclusively for centuries. Some scholars have even argued that, given its popularity among Christians, it was a Christian who first folded papyrus and 'invented' the book.[8]

---

* See page 21

A Roman reading a scroll. There are more in the cupboard behind him.

Why did Christians opt for this 'inferior' medium to record their most important writings? Several reasons have been offered: codices could be more easily hidden, they offered easier access to the contents; they were often bound with wooden covers, giving the contents more protection. But the key reason, I think, was familiarity. *Membranae* were common among craftsmen and traders, who used them as everyday notebooks. Christianity – written in the kind of Greek spoken by the common tradesman – used a vernacular medium: the *membranae* of the trading and commercial classes, of dyers of purple and makers of tents.[9]

For the first time with these codices, the Bible is actually a book.

Spreading it around

It was expected from the start that these documents would be shared around. The Early Church had a highly developed communication network along which the writings could travel. By the end of the first century, Christianity had its major centres in cosmopolitan, well-connected cities. Ephesus, Corinth, Rome, Alexandria, Jerusalem

– all received visitors from around the world. We've already seen prominent Apostles like Peter and Paul traversing the Empire, but beyond the New Testament, we know of other Christian leaders on the move: Polycarp, Bishop of Smyrna, travelled to Rome; the tombstone of Abercius, Bishop of Hierapolis, tells how he travelled west to Rome and east to Syria, even crossing the Euphrates to Nisibis, meeting Christians everywhere.[10]

Ignatius, in his prison escort towards Rome, is visited by many church representatives, and he constantly sends and receives letters, and passes on news. Messengers and messages ping back and forth from Ephesus, Magnesia, Tralles, Troas, Philadelphia, Philippi, Smyrna, Antioch.[11] It's an Early Church intranet, an internal communications system, delegates, messengers and church leaders constantly on the move. And we know that texts were already widely circulated. Writing around 115 AD, Ignatius includes quotes from Matthew, 1 Corinthians, Ephesians, and 1 and 2 Timothy as well as echoes of Ephesians, Romans, Galatians, Philippians, Colossians and 1 Thessalonians.*

Once a letter or text reached a congregation, it would be read out, for the simple reason that most people in the congregation could neither read nor write. (Estimates vary, but the maximum would have been something like 10 per cent.) Dionysus, Bishop of Corinth around 150 AD, writes to Rome

> This day, therefore, we spent as a holy Lord's day in which we read your epistle, from the reading of which we shall always be able to obtain admonition, as also from the former epistle written to us through Clement.[12]

Having been read out, the letter would also be copied and passed on. And a fascinating nugget in the *Shepherd of Hermas* shows how the text was actually transmitted. In the book, Hermas has a vision, while walking on the road to Cumae, in which he sees an elderly woman, with a book in her hands, sitting on a chair made from 'snow-white wool'. A year later, in the same place, he sees her again,

---

* It is notable, however, that Ignatius makes no use of Mark or John, and only minimal use of Luke, and even that is debated.

and this time she asks him to report what he sees to 'God's elect'. Hermas replies 'Lady, I cannot remember so many things, but give me the little book, so that I can copy it.' She gives him the book and he copies it out 'letter by letter'.

Later, in yet another vision, the lady visits him again and tells him to 'write two little books, and you will send one to Clement and one to Grapte.' Grapte – evidently the deacon responsible for the church's charitable work – is to use it to instruct the widows and orphans. Hermas is to read it to 'this city [Rome] along with the elders who preside over the church.' Clement, however, is to 'send it to the cities abroad, because that is his job.'[13]

Clement, it seems, had the official role as a kind of communication officer for Rome. It was his job to send letters and documents to other parts of the church. He was the nearest the Early Church got to a fax machine. And what was true of Rome must have been true of other places: each church probably had its own 'Papias', someone who received information, wrote it down and passed it on.

Like most documents in the ancient world, both the originals and the copies would have been written by professional scribes. Although in the case of the New Testament writings, the relationship between the scribe and the author of the book was far from formal. The people who wrote the letters for Paul and Peter were not detached professionals, but fellow believers, fellow citizens of the underground, trustworthy, part of the team. (And not all the documents would have needed a scribe: people like doctors, engineers, tradesmen and craftsmen were often literate. As a doctor, someone like Luke would have had no difficulty doing his own writing.)

Nomina Sacra

Christian scribes also invented a way of abbreviating certain words – the so-called *nomina sacra*. Words or phrases with divine associations, such as 'God', 'Lord', 'Father', 'Jesus', etc. were differentiated from the surrounding text by using an abbreviated form with a line drawn above them. In Greek, for example, Jesus is spelt *Iesous*, or, in uppercase, *IHSOUI*. This was contracted to IH or IHS. Even today it is not unusual to go into a church and see the letters IHS on a banner or the pulpit. It's simply an Early Church abbreviation.

Church Libraries

So we have the different writings of the church – Paul's letters, the memoirs of the apostles, discipleship training such as the *Didache* – travelling throughout the empire, being copied and recopied, read out and remembered. Gradually, the New Testament was coming into being.

But it wasn't a book. For the first three hundred years, at least, of its life, there was no 'Bible' as such. There were codices, of course, and scrolls and manuscripts, but no single volume, for the simple reason that the technology did not exist to combine them. People could make books, but they couldn't make books big enough. So the 'Bible' of the Early Church is not a single volume, but a cupboard full of codices. It's not a book, it's a bookcase.

In New Testament times, only the rich would have been able to afford a private library. However, since most Christian churches met in people's homes, no doubt the wealthier Christians would have been able to provide a library of some sort. They might have had a copy of the Septuagint – or more likely a part of it, since the entire Septuagint ran to some forty rolls. The 'church library' would also have contained copies of letters from church leaders.

But there was no single volume and, more importantly, no official list. The memoirs and the letters, the discipleship manuals and the mystical visions were not 'Scripture' at this point. There was no list of which books were in and which were out.

That was still to be decided.

THE EARLY CHURCH BIBLE

By around 150 years after the birth of Christ, there were plenty of holy Scriptures, but no New Testament. Different groups in different places had their own favourite set of Christian writings. Visit the church in an Antioch apartment block, or a house in Alexandria, or an old warehouse in Rome, and you would be taught using different blends of letters and gospels.

We can see this by examining the Second Letter of Clement – which, confusingly, is neither by Clement, nor is it a letter – it's actually a sermon: the first Christian sermon that we have.* Based on Isaiah 54.1, the sermon either quotes or makes reference to Isaiah, Genesis, Jeremiah, Ezekiel, Proverbs Daniel, Malachi, and Tobit (all from the Septuagint, of course). From what the writer calls the 'apostles' – the Christian writings – he quotes or refers to Matthew, Luke, Acts, 1 & 2 Corinthians, 1 & 2 Peter, 1 Timothy, Ephesians, James, Hebrews, and Philemon. So far, so Christian. But the sermon also includes quotes from unknown works, including several sayings of Jesus that are not found in the four gospels and a quote from the *Gospel of the Egyptians*.[1] Clearly the idea of what constitutes Christian Scripture is still in formation.

Significantly, 2 Clement contains twice as many quotes from the gospels as all the other sources put together. Clearly these were the key writings. Although some people thought differently...

Enter Marcion

100 AD: Ignatius has been arrested and taken to martyrdom; it's ten years since John had his Sunday morning shock on Patmos; and a boy called Marcion is born in Sinope, in the Roman province of Pontus, on the south shore of the Black Sea.

---

* Scholarly consensus seems to be that it's from the church at Corinth, who preserved it with a letter written to them by Clement of Rome – hence the mix up.

He was always a handful, this boy. As a young man he was thrown out of his church for heretical opinions, which might not be so surprising were it not for the fact that the person who threw him out him was his father, the local bishop.* Marcion made good use of his exile, amassing a fortune as a ship-owner. Then he made his way to Rome, took the first century equivalent of early retirement, donated all his money to the Christian community, and devoted himself to study and writing and promoting his ideas.

His big idea was one which has, sadly, struck a lot of people over the years. He believed that Christianity was just too Jewish. That God of the Old Testament? How can he be the loving heavenly father of Jesus? So, out went the Hebrew Scriptures with their Jewish Yahweh, but that didn't really solve the problem, because a lot of the Christian writings were rather irritatingly Jewish as well. So Marcion drew up a new list. Only Luke's Gospel was allowed to stay (that was the only gospel written by a Gentile) and even then only in a heavily edited version. Marcion added to that ten Pauline Epistles and... well, that was it actually. Except for the addition of a work of his own, called the *Antitheses*.

The church leaders in Rome listened carefully to Marcion's arguments, before throwing him out. But Marcion's heresy raised, for the first time, the issue of which Christian writings were actually canonical. His anti-Semitic, racially pure catalogue was the first suggested canon of the New Testament Scriptures. And the church leaders had nothing to counter it with, because they didn't actually have a list of their own. Indeed, they didn't seem to want one. What the church leaders found particularly offensive was that he *reduced* the accepted list. It was the narrowness of Marcion's canon that caused offence.

Marcion's heresy took a long time to die away. The church in those times had not yet developed its patented method of dealing with heretics (i.e. burning, garrotting, etc.) It just expelled them. Marcion, indeed, set up his own church, which he called the 'true church' and which in many ways resembled the church which had rejected him: they baptised people, they celebrated the Lord's supper (albeit with

---

* Some care has to be taken with the accounts of Marcion's life, which were all written by his enemies. They are not what you'd call 'unbiased'.

water instead of wine), they prayed and worshipped. Justin Martyr stated that Marcion's followers could be found throughout the empire and some scholars believe that Marcionites even outnumbered non-Marcionites in the 160s and 170s.[2] In the third century, Marcionism began to decline in the West, but it persevered in the East into the fifth century, with Marcionite congregations and churches existing side by side with their orthodox brethren.[*]

Enter Montanus

Marcion was not the only heretic on the block. Around 160 AD, in Ardoban, a small village in Phrygia, a man called Montanus fell into a trance and began to speak in tongues.[†] He declared himself an instrument of a new outpouring of the Holy Spirit and attracted two female followers who left their husbands to join him. They relocated to the little town of Pepuza, some twenty miles north-east of Hierapolis. They had been reading that most tricky of Christian books, Revelation, and they believed that it was here that the New Jerusalem was going to descend to earth.

Montanus attracted many new followers, who entered similarly spirit-filled states and whose pronouncements were recorded and treated as Scripture. One leader, Themiso, even wrote a general epistle to the church.[‡] The bishops of Asia Minor declared this new prophecy to be the work of demons, a decision which was upheld by the bishops of Rome, Carthage and elsewhere in North Africa. For them, the Montanists presented the opposite problem to Marcion. Marcion had reduced Scripture, but the Montanists, with their new 'divinely-inspired' documents, added to it. And this raised an uncomfortable issue: if anyone could claim spiritual inspiration for their writings, then how could the church combat false teaching?

With their emphasis on the end times and their belief in the new Jerusalem, the activities of the Montanists made orthodox church

---

[*] It could get confusing – Cyril of Jerusalem felt the need to warn Christians not to enter a Marcionite church by accident.

[†] Epiphanius dates it 156, Eusebius 172.

[‡] A feature of the Montanists' activities was that women were appointed to leadership: a direct challenge to the increasingly institutionalised church elsewhere.

leaders very suspicious of apocalyptic literature in general – and Revelation in particular. Several apocalypses, which were widely used by some churches and which might have become canonical, were effectively dead in the water.[3]

Enter the Gnostics

As Christianity expanded, strange teachings began to emerge, mutant Christianities taught by people claiming exclusive access to secret knowledge. These were the Gnostics – the word comes from the Greek word *gnosis*, meaning hidden knowledge. Gnosticism was not a coherent movement – the term covers a fuzzy mass of attitudes and beliefs. One strand of Gnosticism believed, for example, that Christ wouldn't have had something as messy as a human body. Either he was a spirit who just appeared as a human, or else the 'spirit' Jesus joined the 'man' at his baptism, but conveniently left before the crucifixion.* Other forms of Gnosticism taught that the world wasn't made by God but by some lesser being. The Gnostics were conspiracy theologians; a spiritual elite who believed that their understanding was greater than the common herd.

But the Gnostics had a problem: Jesus had never said any of the things which they taught. And the gospels, rather inconveniently, portrayed Jesus as a living, breathing, sweating, bleeding human being. The Gnostics decided that the only way to solve this problem was to produce their own 'gospels'.

Gnostic groupies around the world – and there are many – are keen to claim an early date for their composition, but the earliest Gnostic gospel was compiled around 150 and most of them date from considerably later. They were not eye-witness accounts. There has never been anyone who seriously believes that *The Gospel of Philip* was written by Philip, or that Paul had anything to do with *The Apocalypse of Paul*.

Nevertheless, these 'gospels' have since become a kind of touchstone for disaffected Christians, who see the Gnostics as mystical outsiders, second century theological vegans, preaching

---

* The idea of the 'spiritual' Jesus is called Docetism, from the Greek word *dokeo* which means 'to seem': Jesus only 'seemed' to be human. The idea that the 'spirit' Jesus left Jesus' body before the crucifixion is called Cerinthianism after Cerinthus, its most prominent spokesman.

Nag Hammadi

In 1945, in Upper Egypt, two peasants went hunting for *sabakh*, a soft soil used as a fertiliser. Instead they found a red earthenware jar with thirteen leather-bound papyrus books containing some 52 texts. The Nag Hammadi library, as the find became known, gave a unique insight into the lost world of the Gnostics. There were gospels attributed to Philip, to Thomas and Mary; there were apocalyptic visions attributed to John, Paul, Adam, and three to James. Some of these writings had been known of for many centuries, and fragments of Gnostic gospels were recorded in the works of other writers. But until Nag Hammadi, no primary texts – complete versions – had ever been discovered.

The manuscripts themselves date from 350–400 AD. Strangely, for such heretical books, the library probably originally belonged to the nearby monastery of St. Pachomius. Perhaps during a purge of heretical books, a monk chose to bury them in the ground rather than see them destroyed.

proto-feminism and free love, man. Frankly, those who see a kind of liberating theology in the Gnostic writings are seeing what they want to see. Far from being liberated, Gnostic texts abound in anti-Semitism and misogyny. Here's a little cracker from the *Gospel of Thomas*, for example

> Simon Peter said to them, "Let Mary leave us, for women are not worthy of life." Jesus said "I myself shall lead her in order to make her male, so that she too may become a living spirit resembling you males. For every woman who will make herself male will enter the kingdom of heaven." (*Thomas*, Logion 114)

This is not to say that the writings do not contain nuggets of truth, or genuine memories, or even (as may be the case with Thomas) some genuine sayings of Jesus. But they were never seriously considered as contenders for the New Testament. Gnosticism is big business today. Scholars, mystics and journalists routinely claim that the church somehow suppressed these books because they contained 'hidden truths'. The church certainly did suppress Gnostic writings, but they did so because they were such palpable forgeries. Gnosticism gained some traction but by the mid-second century it had been rejected, its teachers ostracised, and over the next few centuries, its sacred books were destroyed. Or interred, until, centuries later, they were dug up by people looking for fertiliser.

Pious forgeries

Not all forged Christian Scriptures were done for heretical reasons. Some were done to give Christianity a bit more historical clout, or simply because the authors wanted to tell more of the stories of various apostles. Just as today, when loyal fans of Star Wars or Star Trek create their own original tales based on the characters from the show, so many Christians created their own

A leaf from a sixth century manuscript of The Gospel of Peter

theological fan fiction. Of these, the most famous was the *Acts of Paul and Thecla*, which is a kind of early Christian romantic novel, telling of the relationship between the apostle Paul and a female convert called Thecla. It was written, according to Tertullian, by an elder in Asia who claimed that he wrote it in honour of Paul.

Another popular type of Christian fan fiction was the infancy gospels, which tried to fill in the rather frustrating gap in the gospel accounts between Jesus' birth and the start of his ministry. In them we find Jesus as a schoolboy, playing frequent miraculous tricks on errant schoolmates or nasty teachers, turning them into birds, or killing them and then bringing them back to life. The most influential of these was the *Protevangelium of James*, written sometime in the late second century.

These gospels had a wide circulation and became extremely popular in medieval times, due largely to their espousal of the emerging Catholic theology and the fact that they contained highly dramatic, visual and vivid fairy tales.

Famous Fakes

There are many fake 'Gospels' and Christian writings, which every now and then surface in the press. Here are some of the more well-known – if not notorious – ones.

The Gospel of Judas

According to the National Geographic Society, who published the first translation with much hype in 2006, this rediscovered gospel offers 'new insights into the disciple who betrayed Jesus'. In fact all it really offers is an insight into what Archibishop Rowan Williams has called 'the more eccentric fringes of the early century Church'. The manuscript – which emerged from Egypt in the 1980s, via the black market – actually dates from around the late third century. It tells us something about third century Gnosticism, and just as much about twenty-first century marketing and PR.

Gospel of Thomas

The most famous Gnostic gospel, this is a collection of some 114 sayings of Jesus. Around half of these bear a similarity to sayings found in the synoptic gospels. A text was found at Nag Hammadi, but fragments have also been found at Oxyrhynchus in Egypt (dating from c.200 AD). Although it has been called the 'fifth gospel' it was probably composed in Syria, in the late-second century AD.[4] The first mention of it isn't until 220, or 230 AD, when it is mentioned by Hippolytus of Rome in a work called *Refutation of all Heresies*. Certainly it comes way after the orthodox gospels – there's a fascinating section where it appears to contrast itself to the gospels of Matthew and Mark.[5]

The Edessa Letters

These are letters which Jesus supposedly wrote to Abgar Uchomo, King of Edessa. The King writes asking Jesus to come to Edessa and cure the king of a terrible illness. Edessa – in what is now southern Turkey – was the first ever Christian state. Christianity was widespread within Edessa before 190 AD and, just a few years later, the royal family converted and Christianity became the official religion of the kingdom. The letters were probably written in the third century, and were a pious attempt to show that the relationship between Christianity and Edessa went back a lot further.

Gospel of Peter

The Gospel of Peter comes from around 200 AD (it's not mentioned before around 190). Only a fragment of this work exists, starting at the end of the trial and showing Jesus's mockery, crucifixion and burial and resurrection. Full of historical inaccuracies, it's an attempt to rewrite history, mainly by exonerating Pilate and blaming the Jews. Jesus is condemned, not by Pilate, but by Herod Antipas, (who had no jurisdiction in Jerusalem at the time). Actions which, in the other gospels, are done by Roman soldiers, are attributed to Jewish soldiers. Some scholars claim that *The Gospel of Peter* contains fragments of a much earlier Passion narrative. But there is virtually no support for this theory.

The Acts of Paul and Thecla

A piece of fan fiction written by a elder in Asia. Thecla is a young woman who is converted through hearing Paul speak. She follows Paul around, but undergoes a series of terrible trials, including being thrown to the wild animals in the circus where she is attacked by carnivorous seals. Thecla became hugely popular in parts of the Christian world. The story may reflect a tradition of an early female Christian martyr. It also contains a portrait of Paul which is so unflattering that it very well may be original: 'And he saw Paul coming, a man small in size, bald-headed, bandy-legged, well-built, with eyebrows meeting, rather long-nosed, full of grace. For sometimes he seemed like a man, and sometimes he had the countenance of an angel.'

The Acts of Peter

Another work with a long influence is the *Acts of Peter*, which contained a detailed account of the martyrdom of the apostle, including the famous Quo Vadis episode, and the tradition that Peter was crucified upside down. Intriguingly, the final chapters are also found preserved separately as the Martyrdom of Peter in three Greek manuscripts and in other languages. So it may well have originated with an original account of Peter's death, which was then heavily added to and embroidered.

The Infancy Gospel – or Protevangelium – of James

Written sometime in the late second century, this is one of the earliest acts of homage to Mary. It is to this gospel that we owe the tradition that Joseph was old when he married Mary; and it also contains the idea of the perpetual virginity of Mary – an idea which is still current in Catholic theology. Despite its claims to be by Jesus' brother, the gospel shows no knowledge of contemporary Jewish culture and customs, while all its references are from the Greek Septuagint. It's mentioned by Origen, early in the third century, but there's no evidence he thought it – and *The Gospel of Peter* which he mentions alongside it – as anything more than recent inventions.

The Fourfold Gospel

So, by the end of the second century, the churches' sacred Scriptures were facing three different kinds of challenge: Marcion wanted them restricted to Luke and Paul, the Montanists wanted to add their inspired prophecies, while the Gnostics and well-meaning Christians were simply making things up. One might have thought, in the face of these challenges, that the church would react quickly to create their own official list, but the process was to take another two hundred years at least. Nevertheless, some ideas came into currency which we take for granted today, in particular the primacy of the four gospels and the idea of an 'Old' and a 'New' testament.

Justin Martyr (c.100–c.165) emphasised the primacy of the 'memoirs of the apostles'

> For the apostles, in the memoirs composed by them, which are called Gospels, have thus delivered unto us what was enjoined upon them; that Jesus took bread, and when He had given thanks, said, "This do ye in remembrance of Me, this is My body;" and that, after the same manner, having taken the cup and given thanks, He said, "This is My blood;" and gave it to them alone.[6]

Curiously, though, the gospel text actually used by Justin was what is called a gospel harmony – an account which synthesises different gospels – in Justin's case Matthew, Mark and Luke – into one coherent narrative. He also uses the phrase 'It is written...' to refer to the words of Jesus, which might not seem a big deal, but it's exactly the same terms which Jesus and the gospel writers used when referring to the Tanakh.[*]

> In the Gospel it is written that He said: All things are delivered unto me by My Father...[7]

---

[*] e.g., Matthew 4.4–10, 21.13, Mark 1.2, Mark 14.27, Luke 19.46, John 10.34. Justin was born at Nablus in Samaria, the site of the Old Testament city of Shechem. For a time he taught at Ephesus, before moving to Rome, where he opened a kind of Christian college. He was denounced by the Cynic philosopher Crescens: arrested, beaten and eventually beheaded, hence the soubriquet 'Martyr'.

So by the early second century the 'memoirs' are becoming sacred and were given pride of place in the Sunday worship. Justin gives us the first description of an Early Church service

> ...on the day called Sunday, all who live in cities or in the country gather together to one place, and the memoirs of the apostles or the writings of the prophets are read, as long as time permits; then, when the reader has ceased, the president verbally instructs, and exhorts to the imitation of these good things.[8]

A book press containing the four gospels. From a Byzantine mosaic in Ravenna.

Irenaeus of Lyons (writing c. 170–180) was the first writer to promote the four separate gospels as canonical, arguing that only Matthew, Mark, Luke and John were 'true and reliable'. It is also around this time that the Scriptures of the church are described as the 'New' and 'Old' Testaments – although whether it was Irenaeus or Melito of Sardis who did this first is uncertain.[9]

Irenaeus' view was not necessarily followed by others. Justin used a harmonised document; others used extra, different gospels. Clement of Alexandria, or Titus Flavius Clemens, to give him his proper name, was born around 150 and died in 215. One work of his, written about 180 AD, uses the 'It is written...' formula when quoting from a gospel, but the gospel he's quoting from is our old chum the *Gospel of the Hebrews*. He also mentions the *Gospel of the Egyptians* and a book called *The Traditions of Matthias*. He is, however, aware that these are not 'traditional' gospels. Quoting from the *Gospel of the Egyptians*, he writes

> When Salome inquired how long death should have power the Lord
> (not meaning that life is evil and the creation bad) said: "As long
> as you women give birth to children"... We do not have this saying
> in the four traditional gospels but in the Gospel According to the
> Egyptians.[10]

Clement also viewed the *Epistle of Barnabas* as authoritative,
as well as other books such as *1 Clement, Hermas, Sirach, The
Apocalypse of Peter* and others.

Sometimes even the church leaders weren't fully aware of what
was being used in their churches. In 200 AD the Bishop Serapion of
Antioch agreed that Christians in his diocese could read *The Gospel
of Peter* in church. He changed his mind when he actually read it and
found out that it denied the humanity of Jesus.[11]

Four (or five) into one

Justin, as we've seen, used a gospel harmony, and it was a pupil of his
who created the most famous of these: the *Diatesseron*.

The *Diatesseron* – a Greek word meaning 'according to four' or 'one
through four' – was created around 170 AD by a Syrian scholar called
Tatian. As the name implies, he wove the four strands of the gospels
into one coherent story, removing any repetitions, harmonising
discrepancies, and even 'correcting' what he considered omissions.*
It was hugely popular, partly for practical reasons – a synopsis was
much more portable and easier to use than four separate codices –
but also because it was simpler for people to grasp one story.

It was also probably the first ever gospel translation, since it was
written in Syriac. It was so popular in Syria that it became the official
Syriac Gospel for some three hundred years until, in 423, Theodoret,
Bishop of Cyrrhus on the Euphrates in upper Syria, impounded
some two hundred copies and introduced instead the use of the four
separate Gospels.

No actual copy of the original Syriac *Diatesseron* has survived (only
one fragment of the actual text has ever been found) but scholars
have been able to reconstruct it from other ancient translations and

---

* Other gospel harmonies were created by Ammonius of Alexandria and Theophilus
of Antioch.

commentaries.* The name implies that the *Diatesseron* was concerned only with the four gospels, but some readings within it come from the *Gospel of the Hebrews*. Once again, other gospel sources were being used, even if the basic framework was 'the four'.

The *Diatesseron* shows that, at the end of the second century, the Christian Scriptures were still in a state of flux. Despite the conflicts, there was no fixed list. In fact, nobody – apart from that heretic Marcion – had even suggested one. Even those who bitterly opposed Marcion, used gospels which later were considered 'uncanonical'. Christian worship services might include readings from both canonical and non-canonical gospels. Sunday morning in Alexandria might contain readings from Mark and Matthew, but also from the *Gospel of the Egyptians*. Go to the east and you'd hear the *Diatesseron*. Go to Rome and you might hear John, but also *Hermas*.

At this time Christianity was thriving in the East, in Syria and beyond, while in the West it was about to enter a time of persecution. If that situation had persisted, there's a chance that, today, each morning in church, we would have been reading not Matthew, Mark, Luke or John, but Tatian's *Diatesseron*.

Danger and dialogue

While Christians were thinking about the canon of the New Testament, they were also rethinking their position on the Old Testament. As Christians engaged more and more with Jewish teachers over the nature of their beliefs, they began to realise that the Jews, with their knowledge of Hebrew, had better ammunition than they did.

So, Christians did their homework. They began to study the texts, to learn Hebrew and to compare the different editions of the Scriptures to establish the authentic readings. The leader of this approach was Origen, one of the greatest biblical scholars of all time. Origen studied first in Alexandria and then later moved to Caesarea where he created the *Hexapla* – the first parallel Bible. This amazing book was a Tanakh in six columns, containing

---

* The *Diatesseron* was translated from Syrian into Arabic, Greek, Latin, Georgian, Armenian, Old Saxon, and there are even adaptations in Middle Dutch and Italian from the thirteenth and fourteenth centuries. There is even a Middle English version, once owned by Samuel Pepys.

1. The Hebrew Text
2. The Hebrew text, but in Greek letters (i.e. a transliteration)
3. Aquila's Greek Translation
4. Symmachus' Greek translation
5. The Septuagint
6. Theodotion's Greek version

It was begun in Alexandria, either in 230 or in 238, and finished some fifteen years and 350 miles away in Caesarea. The *Hexapla* was enormous: it ran to over 6,500 pages, in fifteen volumes.[*] For this reason, it stayed in Caesarea and was never copied in its entirety and only a few fragments of it survive.[†]

As well as the *Hexapla*, Origen left a large collection of sermons, and wrote commentaries on nearly all the books of the Bible. He divided the Christian Scriptures into two main parts: the Gospels and the Apostles and called the whole the New Testament, showing that the phrase had, by now come into common currency. Towards the end of his life, he stated that the four gospels were 'the only indisputable ones in the church of God under heaven'.[12] But he occasionally quoted from gospels outside the four 'which the church approves' and his list includes quotes from *The Gospel of Peter*, the *Protevangelium of James* and the *Gospel of the Hebrews*. He also uses sayings of Jesus which are not recorded elsewhere. One such beatitude is 'Blessed is he who even fasts in order that he may feed a poor man.'[13] Another is similar to a saying from the *Gospel of Thomas*: 'Whoever is near me is near to the fire.'[14]

The nearest Origen comes to a canon list is in his *Homily on Joshua*, written around 240. The order is different, with the gospels at the beginning, followed by the general epistles, Acts and Revelation, and then Paul's letters, but it is undoubtedly the familiar 27 books – it is the first time that anyone actually described the content of the New Testament.[‡]

---

[*] He also used other translations at some points, known as Quinta, Sexta, and Septima, which turned six columns into seven or even eight. Origen further used a series of symbols to show the differences and similarities between the versions.

[†] The original was probably destroyed in the seventh century, when the library of Caesarea was burned during the Arab invasion.

[‡] This is only preserved in a Latin translation by a man called Rufinus (c. AD 345–410) so we can't be sure that Rufinus hasn't added in his own opinions.

Origen is the forerunner of today's textual scholars, who labour over the manuscripts and fragments to establish an authentic, reliable Greek and Hebrew text.* The column of the *Hexapla* which contained the Septuagint was copied and widely circulated. It assumed a kind of authorised status; not only was it the oldest and most reliable version, it was also the most readable. Scholars even published their own, revised versions of Origen's Septuagint. There was a version edited in Antioch by Lucian and another by Hesychius. Little is known of Hesychius – he was probably an Egyptian bishop who was martyred under Diocletian.[15] Lucian also died under persecution – starved to death in a jail in Nicomedia in 312, after nine years of imprisonment and torture. And Origen himself died as a result of the brutal treatment he received at the hands of the authorities. The Christian Scriptures by now were dangerous: translating them, revising them, studying them – even owning them – was to risk imprisonment, torture and death.

---

*   Origen was not a fundamentalist. 'Who is so silly,' Origen wrote, 'as to believe that God, after the manner of a farmer, planted a paradise eastward in Eden, and set in it a visible and palpable tree of life, or such a sort that anyone who tasted its fruit with his bodily teeth would gain life?'

THE IMPERIAL BIBLE

It's February 23rd, AD 303, and in Nicomedia[*] – capital of the
Eastern Empire – the Imperial troops start knocking on the doors of
Christians. They are searching for copies of the Christian Scriptures,
following the posting of an edict which ordered all copies of Christian
books and liturgy to be surrendered and burnt.

The edict soon affects other parts of the empire. In Cirta, capital
of Numidia, the 'Mayor' – a man called Munatius Felix – leads the
search. He goes first to the house where the Christians usually meet.
The library there is empty, so they move on, to the houses of the
church leaders. One of these, Catullinus, a subdeacon, brings out a
large volume.

> Mayor: Why have you given one volume only? Produce the Scriptures
> that you have.
> Marcuclius and Catullinus: We haven't any more because we are
> subdeacons. The readers have the books.

When the two subdeacons refuse to give the names and addresses
of the leaders, they are arrested and the search moves on. At the house
of Eugenius, they find four codices; at Felix's, five; at Victorinus'
eight; at Projectus' five large codices and two small ones; at the house
of Victor the Schoolmaster, two codices and four sets of gatherings
that have not yet been sewn into a book form. Coddeo is out when
they call, but his wife, helpfully, gives the officers six codices.[1]

So, a single grab-raid in this provincial city has raised thirty-three
codices, plus some which were waiting to be bound.

Not all places were as accommodating to the police raids. In
many other places, Christians protected the Scriptures with their
lives. In the same year – 303 AD – in the African town of Tibiuca,

---

[*] Modern Izmit in Turkey.

soldiers ordered the Bishop, Felix, to hand over whatever 'books and parchments' he held on behalf of the church. He refused. He was sent to the Proconsul in Carthage who repeated the request. Again, he refused. This time he was beheaded.[2]

The following year, books belonging to Christian women in Thessalonica were confiscated. A further investigation revealed that one of them – a woman called Irene – had kept back many 'parchments, books, tablets, small codices and pages' which were hidden in cupboards and chests in her house. 'We chose to be burned alive,' she said, 'or to suffer anything else that might happen to us, rather than betray them [i.e. the writings].' Her punishment was brutally Roman: she was placed naked in the public brothel and the writings which she protected so fiercely were publicly burned. Eventually Irene and two companions were burned at the stake in the spring of AD 304.[3]

What was in the cupboard? We don't know in Irene's case, but elsewhere a fragment of a Christian library list survives, showing that it held:

- *The Shepherd of Hermas*
- several works of Origen
- Various biblical books, including Job, Leviticus, Acts, Song of Songs, Exodus and possibly Numbers
- A large book – described as a *mega biblion* – probably a bound codex of the four gospels.[4]

These writings were not the preserve of the church officials. Ordinary people had them, or excerpts from them. Studying and reading the Scriptures was something you did as a Christian. You had them in your house: even if that led to arrest, humiliation and, ultimately, death.

Enter Constantine

All that changed in 312 AD. In that year, Christianity moved from a marginal faith to one at the heart of the empire. The evening before a crucial battle, a Roman general called Constantine saw a vision – a cross of light which shone amidst the rays of the sun, and with it the

The Chi-Rho sign

words 'In this sign, conquer.'* Later that same night, he dreamt he saw Christ himself carrying the same sign: a combination of two Greek letters - Chi and Rho – the first two letters of the word *Christos*, formed into the shape of a cross. It was an omen, a command. The next day his troops destroyed their old pagan imagery and marched to battle under this new, Christian symbol. Constantine was victorious and duly established himself as the Emperor of the West. He halted the persecution of Christians and ordered the return of any confiscated property. The following year, along with Licinius, Emperor of the East, he issued the Edict of Milan, which proclaimed toleration for all faiths.

How far Constantine himself ever really embraced Christianity is debatable. But after becoming sole emperor in 324 AD, he did much to establish Christianity as the official religion of the empire. He built magnificent churches; he oversaw the first ecumenical Church Council at Nicea in 325; he tried to resolve disputes. And he gave Christianity power.

The Emperor Constantine

For the first time, the church could call on the state for support. It wasn't long before things turned nasty, and the business about the Christian writings was at the heart of it.

In North Africa, there was a dispute over who should be the Bishop of Carthage. The chosen candidate was Caecilianus who, much to the anger of his opponents, had handed over copies of the sacred

---

* He claimed that all his soldiers saw this vision as well. Although, strangely, not one of the forty thousand said anything about it at the time.

Scriptures to the pagan magistrates. His opponents – known as Donatists after their support of Donatus, the other candidate – saw such people as collaborators. In November 316 AD, Constantine confirmed the decision and actually confiscated the churches of the opposing supporters. An argument between the two factions turned into rioting, and several opposition Christians were killed by a mixture of soldiers and an angry mob.

A sign again, but of a different kind. A sign of worse to come.

The canon of Eusebius

In the first three centuries after Jesus' death and resurrection, Christians had responded to power by either keeping their heads down or by forthright opposition. But suddenly they were in power. At the turn of the century Christians were being executed for possessing the Scriptures: twenty years later those same Scriptures were to become foundational documents of empire.

This is the background to the work of Eusebius of Caesarea who, between 300 and 325 AD, wrote a monumental *Ecclesiastical History*. In the book, Eusebius talks a lot about the development of the Bible: when writing about authors of the past, he often mentions their opinions or use of alternative or uncanonical books. But even in Eusebius' *History,* there is still no 'official' list of Christian Scriptures. He does provide a kind of list, but it is one based on the way these Scriptures had been viewed by Christian writers and scholars of the past. Eusebius classes the Christian writings into four main groups:

1. Undisputed – books agreed to be orthodox and canonical. This group contains 21 books: four gospels, Acts, Paul's letters (13), 1 John, 1 Peter. But then Eusebius adds the curious phrase, 'After this we must place, if it really seem right, the Apocalypse of John...'

2. Disputed – orthodox, but only considered canonical by some parts of the church. They 'are nevertheless familiar to the majority'. This includes James, Jude, 2 Peter, 2 and 3 John.

3. Spurious (the word he uses also means 'illegitimate') – books with orthodox teaching, but Eusebius considers them uncanonical. The list includes *The Acts of Paul*, *The Shepherd of Hermas*, *Apocalypse of Peter*, *Letter of Barnabas*, *Teachings of the Apostles* (i.e. the *Didache*). Surprisingly, he puts Revelation in here as well,

arguing that it 'is rejected by some, but others give it a place among the acknowledged writings.' He also includes the *Gospel of the Hebrews*, 'a work which is especially acceptable to such Hebrews as received the Christ.'

4. Heretical – books which are both unorthodox and uncanonical. He specifically mentions *The Gospel of Peter*, *The Gospel of Thomas*, *The Gospel of Matthias*, and *The Acts of Andrew and John*. He dismisses these completely

> None of these have been deemed worthy of any kind of mention...
> by a single member of successive generations of churchmen; and the
> character and the manner is far removed from the apostolic manner...
> they are certainly the forgeries of heretics.[5]

There are still areas of disagreement. James, Jude, 2 Peter, 2 and 3 John are all still being fought over, while the *Gospel of the Hebrews* is found helpful by some parts of the church. The curious point, of course, is his treatment of Revelation, which gets into both groups 1 and 3. Eusebius didn't like apocalyptic writing and you get the feeling that his hand is being forced: he has to put it in the green group, because by the time he is writing it is widely accepted, but if it were left to him, it would be firmly removed. (There is also no mention of the Letter to Hebrews; the most likely explanation is that Eusebius grouped it with the letters of Paul.)

There was another pressing reason why Eusebius needed to clarify the official list of New Testament writings, because in AD 332, he turned from church historian to Bible publisher. Emperor Constantine ordered him to supply fifty copies of the sacred Scriptures by professional scribes, on specially prepared vellum. He was given two carriages to send back the manuscripts to Constantinople, where they would be placed in the churches that were busily being built.

According to Eusebius, 'Such were the emperor's commands which were followed by the immediate execution of the work itself, which we sent him in magnificent and elaborately bound volumes of threefold and fourfold form.' The exact meaning of the final sentence is unclear. Unhelpfully, Eusebius does not tell us what books he selected to go in these volumes. Nevertheless, this must have been a huge publishing venture: and fifty copies in the capital, at the heart of the Empire, must have played a huge part in deciding the future shape of the Christian Bible.

Eusebius has become known as the father of church history. He was also the father of Bible publishing.

THE CANON LIST OF EUSEBIUS c.325 AD			
UNDISPUTED Orthodox and canonical in all churches	DISPUTED Orthodox and canonical in some churches	SPURIOUS Orthodox but not canonical	HERETICAL Unorthodox and not canonical
Matthew Mark Luke John Acts Romans 'The letters of Paul' I John I Peter Revelation ◄- - -	James Jude 2 Peter 2 & 3 John - - - - - - - - - - - - -	The Acts of Paul The Shepherd [of Hermas] Apocalypse of Peter Letter of Barnabas Teachings of the Apostles [Didache] Gospel of Hebrews - - ► Revelation	Gospel of Peter Gospel of Thomas Gospel of Matthias Acts of Andrew and John

Muratorian Fragment

Eusebius' list is largely echoed by the other main canon list from this time, a list known as the Muratorian Fragment. I say 'from this time' but there is enormous argument over whether the list actually comes from a great deal earlier.

It gets its name from the man who discovered it – Lodovico Antonio Muratori – who found it in the Ambrosian Library in Milan in 1740.[*] For a long time this was assumed to be a very early list – around 170 AD. Some scholars still argue this, but the latest thinking is that it dates from the fourth century AD and comes from Syria or Palestine. We don't really know.

Although Matthew and Mark are not mentioned, the fragment begins mid sentence, then states that the 'third book of the gospel is that according to Luke' before moving on to say that 'the fourth of the

---

[*] Small portions of the same list have also been discovered in four Latin manuscripts from the eleventh or twelfth century.

THE MURATORIAN CANON c.350? AD		
ORTHODOX Allowed to be read in church	ORTHODOX But should not be read in church	HERETICAL
[Matthew Mark] Luke John Acts I & 2 Corinthians Ephesians Philippians Colossians Galatians I & 2 Thessalonians Romans Philemon Titus I & 2 Timothy Jude I & 2 John Wisdom of Solomon Apocalypse of John (i.e Revelation)	Apocalypse of Peter The Shepherd of Hermas	Letter of Paul to the Laodiceans Letter of Paul to the Alexandrians Anything written by Arsinous or Valentinus or Miltiades Anything by Basilides

Gospels is that of John.' So it's perfectly reasonable to assume that the missing first two were Matthew and Mark. Indeed, the sentence with which the fragment begins runs '. . at which nevertheless he was present, and so he placed [them in his narrative]' which is reminiscent of Papias' account of the origins of Mark's Gospel. It then explicitly lists as orthodox seventeen books which are in our New Testament, plus the Wisdom of Solomon from the apocrypha.[*] He also lists some non-canonical works, including *The Apocalypse of Peter* (although he admits that 'some of us are not willing that the latter be read in church') and *The Shepherd of Hermas* (again, denying that it should be read in church since it was written after the time of the apostles.)

He also gives a list of books which he says are forged: two letters purporting to be from Paul – to the Laodiceans, and to

---

* See p.44

the Alexandrians. And he refuses to accept anything written by 'Arsinous or Valentinus or Miltiades, who also composed a new book of psalms for Marcion, together with Basilides, the Asian founder of the Cataphrygians'.

So, what's missing? Hebrews, James, 1 and 2 Peter and 3 John are passed over in silence. Clearly whoever wrote the Muratorian fragment, like Eusebius, had not yet made up his mind.

After Eusebius, there were further attempts by the Greek-speaking church in East and the Latin-speaking church in the West, to tidy things up. But for all its new found power, the church was still in no rush to come to a definitive conclusion. The Council of Nicea in 325 AD was occupied with church government issues and, mainly, with doctrinal disputes over the nature of Christ. The official list of the Bible was not high on their list of priorities.

Where it was discussed, the sticking points remained the same: the status of 'non-apostolic' books, like *Hermas* and *Barnabas* and *Clement*, and the nature of the general epistles (the various letters of James, Peter, John and Jude) and Revelation. Cyril of Jerusalem (c.315–386) wrote a series of lectures for catechumens – apprentice Christians – which he delivered around 350 AD in Jerusalem. One lecture contained a list of New Testament books, which includes all the books, except Revelation.

When the church did get round to discussing it, at the Synod of Laodicea in 363 AD, it concluded that 'The Gospels are to be read on the Sabbath, with the other Scriptures' and that 'No psalms composed by private individuals nor any uncanonical books may be read in the church, but only the Canonical Books of the Old and New Testaments.'[6] Later manuscripts attach a list of the Scriptures. And guess what? The list does not include Revelation.

Athanasius and the list

And then along came Athanasius. Athanasius was a churchman with clout. The most influential theologian of his day, he was Bishop of Alexandria, one of the four great centres of Christendom. For six centuries, Alexandria had maintained its reputation as a centre for learning. It was home to the *Didascalium*, or the Christian Cathechetical School – the first Christian theological college,

founded c. 190 AD, whose staff and alumni included Clement of
Alexandria, Origen and Dionysius 'the Great'.*

It was usual for the Bishop of Alexandria to issue a letter each spring
giving the dates of Easter – from which every other church festival was
calculated. In the letter released in spring AD 367, Athanasius included
a list of the canonical books of the Old and New testaments.

For the Old Testament, Athanasius excluded the Apocryphal
books, although he called them devotional reading. And in his list of
the 27 books of the New Testament, he included all those with which
we are now familiar. It was the first time that the twenty-seven books
we find in modern Bibles were listed as a definitive canon.

Athanasius' list is often referred to as the document wot did it –
the list which finished the argument and decided on the official list,
but in fact it made no difference whatsoever. It didn't even decide
things in Alexandria, the Bishop's home territory.

In 1941 in a grotto near Toura, Egypt, archaeologists discovered two
thousand pages of papyrus manuscripts containing commentaries
on the Old Testament by Didymus the Blind. Didymus was the
head of the Catechetical School: a position to which he had been
appointed by Athanasius. Blind since the age of five, he never even
learned the alphabet, yet Jerome, who was no dunce himself, called
him 'the most erudite man of his time'.[7]

Didymus' work doesn't give us a canon list as such, but from his use
of Scriptures in his commentary, and his description of certain books
as 'divinely authored', or part of the divine Scriptures, we can draw
up a list. It includes most of Anathasius' list, but in all his writings,
Didymus never once mentions 2 and 3 John. When he talks about 1
John he simply refers to it as 'the epistle according to John'. Nor does
he mention Philemon.†

But, significantly, there are other books, which he clearly views as
canonical, including the *Shepherd of Hermas*, *Barnabas*, the *Didache*,
and *1 Clement*. He also quotes Ignatius' *Letter to the Romans*, but it is
not certain how he views this.

---

* It gets its name from the fact that the catechetical method – the idea of question
   and answer – began there.

† Although a statement claiming that 2 Peter was a forgery has been attributed to
   him, this comes from an entirely different writer – writing in Latin – and conflicts
   with the view in his commentaries.

ATHANASIUS AND DIDYMUS c.367 AD

ATHANASIAN CANON LIST	BOOKS USED BY DIDYMUS
Matthew	Matthew
Mark	Mark
Luke	Luke
John	John
Acts of the Apostles	Acts of the Apostles
James	James
1 & 2 Peter,	1 & 2 Peter,
1, 2 & 3 John	1 John
Jude	Jude
Romans	Romans
1 & 2 Corinthians	1 & 2 Corinthians
Galatians	Galatians
Ephesians	Ephesians
Philippians	Philippians
Colossians	Colossians
1 & 2 Thessalonians	1 & 2 Thessalonians
Hebrews	Hebrews
1 & 2 Timothy	1 & 2 Timothy
Titus	Titus
Philemon	Revelation of John
Revelation of John	*The Shepherd of Hermas*
	Letter of Barnabas
	Didache
	1 Clement

Clearly, Didymus the Blind – appointed, remember, by Athanasius himself – had a different view of what constituted Scripture to the list suggested by his Bishop. So the implication is that Athanasius wasn't issuing a definitive list of all the books of the New Testament; instead he was offering a list which the entire church – or the vast majority of it at any rate – could sign up to.

We find more evidence in a much more substantial form. Because Alexandria didn't just produce lists, it also produced Bibles.

The great codices

In the basement of the British Library, parchment pages glowing in the dim light, are two of the oldest Bibles in the world: *Codex Sinaiticus* and *Codex Alexandrinus*.

Alexandrinus is the youngest. As the name implies, it comes from Alexandria and dates from the late fourth to early fifth century. The two-column text is written in capitals (known as uncial script), and consists of the entire Greek Bible (although most of Matthew is missing, along with some bits of John and 2 Corinthians). Its origins are obscure. It arrived in England in 1627, a gift to King James I from Cyril Lucar, Eastern Orthodox Bishop of Alexandria.[*]

Next to it is, perhaps, the most valuable book that the library owns: *Codex Sinaiticus*. And its story is also one of survival against the odds. Not to mention skullduggery, adventure and even communism.

It was discovered by Constantine Tischendorf (1815–1873) – the Indiana Jones of Bible manuscripts. Tischendorf was a genius who had published a new edition of the Greek New Testament aged just 27, and who managed to decipher the mysterious palimpsest *Codex Ephræmi* using nothing but his naked eye.[†] He was acclaimed as the world's greatest paleographer.

Around the time he was working on *Codex Ephræmi*, he began travelling to Egypt, Sinai and the Levant, hunting for manuscripts. In 1844 he paid his first visit to the remote monastery of Saint Catherine on Mount Sinai. There he entered what is probably the oldest of the Coptic-built monasteries in the world. When Islam conquered all around it, the monastery survived by building a mosque on the roof, thus protecting all the buildings underneath it (the mosque was used by the servants of the monastery). Its high, surrounding wall had no door – just an opening some thirty feet up, through which Tischendorf was hoisted, in a chair attached to a rope.

Inside, the monastery was a time capsule of faith, a living survivor of the ancient monastic practices of the desert monks. There were twenty-two chapels; there were Byzantine mosaics; there was a

---

[*] James died before the manuscript arrived so it was given to his son, Charles I, instead.

[†] The original fifth century manuscript had been erased by a monk in the 12th century and replaced with the writings of Ephraim of Syria. Today special imaging techniques and infra-red make reading palimpsests somewhat easier.

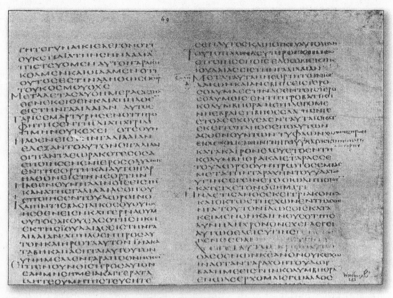

Codex Alexandrinus

charnel house guarded by the skeleton of Stephanos, the monastery caretaker. (The fact that he had died some 1,100 years before was seen as no reason to remove him from his post.) Eventually, after much dogged, determined searching, Tischendorf came across what he thought was a waste basket. Inside, were pages from a very old Bible. He asked to purchase it, but the monks only allowed him to leave with 43 leaves. Returning to Germany, he deposited the fragments at the University of Leipzig. They were published in 1846, but the place of origin was kept a secret.

Tischendorf was not able to return to Egypt until 1853, but by then the monks had become suspicious and refused to let him see the manuscript he had seen before. It had, apparently, disappeared. He returned a third time in January 1859, this time with some heavy backers, most notably the Tsar of Russia. And yet, once again, he failed to find the manuscript. Then, on February 4, the last day of his visit, he was invited to have a drink with a young monk. He began talking about the Greek New Testament. 'I have a Greek Testament in my cell,' said the monk. 'You're welcome to have a look at it.'

The monk lifted down a bundle wrapped in red cloth, which was kept behind the spare coffee cups. He cut the string, unwrapped the cloth. And out tumbled not only the missing leaves of the parchment which he had seen in 1844, but many more. Loads more. In all there were 346 leaves, heaped on the table in front of him.

The next day, the negotiations began. The monks were not keen but, in the end, Tischendorf was allowed to take the manuscript to Cairo and copy it. Eventually, after months of negotiation, and some Russian power politics, Tischendorf was allowed to leave with the manuscript, and the full *Codex Sinaiticus* was published in a lavish facsimile edition in 1862. The Codex remained in Russia, eventually winding up in the Imperial Library. To the monks, it was a loan; to the Russians, it was a gift.

Then, in 1917, revolution swept Russia. The Tsar and his family were executed and the Bolsheviks took over. They had no interest in ancient Bibles, but a lot of interest in not going bankrupt, and in 1933, Stalin's government sold the manuscript to the British Museum for £100,000.

It's an amazing object. Its pages are made of sheepskin and goatskin parchment, with the text arranged in four columns on each page. Some 360 animals gave their lives to make this book – it was an enormously expensive operation.* The text, for the most part, follows what is known as the Alexandrian text-type – that is the Bible text is of a version which originated in Alexandria. It is full of corrections and amendments – between the fourth and twelfth centuries, seven or more correctors worked on this codex, making it one of the most corrected manuscripts in existence. Along with *Codex Vaticanus*, the *Codex Sinaiticus* has proven to be one of the most valuable manuscripts for establishing the original text of the Greek New Testament, as well as the Septuagint. Its actual date is a matter of dispute. It was probably written between AD 325 and 360.

Actually that's not the only thing that is disputed about it. Because ever since it left Egypt, there have been many complaints about cultural robbery and nefarious dealings. Tischendorf did rescue

---

* It has been suggested that *Codex Sinaiticus* was one of the special fifty copies of the Bible that Emperor Constantine commissioned from Eusebius of Caesarea; but since the manuscript appears to originate from Alexandria, this is unlikely.

many manuscripts: it is rather romantic revisionism to assume that they would have survived, had they been left where they were. To this day, however, the monks complain that they wuz robbed. The year after it arrived in London, Archbishop Porphyrios of Sinai sent a telegram claiming ownership, but the British weren't playing. They'd paid for this thing in good faith and, since the Soviet archives were inaccessible, no one could prove that the monks hadn't actually given it away. The fall of communism, however, opened up the Soviet archives and there researchers found an official receipt, a document donating the Codex to the Tsar, signed by the then Archbishop of Sinai, Kallistratos, and by the Synax of the Monastery of Saint Catherine's itself. It does seem, rightly or wrongly, willingly or unwillingly, that the monks gave it away.*

Since then, other parts of the manuscript have been found. In 1975, reconstruction works in the monastery revealed a forgotten store-room, under the north-western wall of the St. Gregory Chapel. This room appeared to be the monastic equivalent of a *genizah*, storing damaged and decrepit books. Among the gems uncovered there were a further twelve leaves and 24 fragments of the *Codex Sinaiticus*.

Most recently, on 3 September 3 2009, Nicholas Sarris, a member the *Codex Sinaiticus* Project, noticed a previously unseen piece of the manuscript glued to the binding of a book, when he was looking through photographs of manuscript bindings in the library of St Catherine's Monastery. The text has been confirmed as the beginning of the Book of Joshua, chapter 1, verse 10.

Today, *Codex Sinaiticus* is held across four sites – St Catherine's Monastery on Mount Sinai, the British Library, Leipzig University Library, and the National Library of Russia in St Petersburg. But the good news is that you can see it in one place – on the internet. The manuscript has been digitised and can be viewed online. And so the world's oldest complete Bible can be explored today in the world's newest medium.

---

* The dispute has still not been resolved. The official, diplomatic statement issued by the four institutions which hold pages of Sinaiticus recognises that 'events concerning the history of the *Codex Sinaiticus*, from 1844 to this very day, are not fully known; hence, they are susceptible to widely divergent interpretations and recountings that are evaluated differently as to their form and essence.' In other words, your guess is as good as mine.

Codex Sinaiticus

Codex Vaticanus

Codex Vaticanus

Codex Sinaiticus and *Codex Alexandrinus* come from Alexandria. And they are joined by a third, which vies with *Sinaiticus* as the oldest complete Bible in the world: the *Codex Vaticanus*.

It gets its name from its present home – the Vatican Library – where it has been since the fifteenth century. The manuscript remained largely hidden until the nineteenth century. Unlike *Sinaiticus*, this was not due to the ignorance of monks, but to the Vatican's time-honoured policy of Not Allowing Anyone To Look At Anything Important Unless They're The Pope. Scholars knew it was there: they just weren't allowed to go near it.

In 1845, for example, a scholar called Tregelles spent six months trying to get access. Although he had been given permission to study the manuscript by Cardinal Lambruschini, who held the rather important-sounding office of 'Apostolic Librarian', he was refused access by Monsignor Laureani, the main custodian who, it seemed, had been given secret orders not to allow anyone near the thing. Tregelles managed to get permission from the Pope, but even that didn't seem to get him past Mgr. Laureani. He could only look at it under ridiculously strict controls

> They would not let me open it without searching my pockets, and depriving me of pen, ink, and paper; and at the same time two prelati kept me in constant conversation in Latin, and if I looked at a passage too long, they would snatch the book out of my hand. So foolishly and meaninglessly did the papal authorities seek to keep this precious MS. to themselves.[8]

Tregelles left Rome after five months without having been able to really study the manuscript. And throughout the nineteenth century the library continued its policy of obstruction.

Once scholars were allowed access to it, however, they realised that it was extremely early. It's missing most of Genesis, some of Hebrews, the Pastoral Epistles, and the book of Revelation. (These were the bits at the front and back of the volume which is the part most likely to be lost or damaged.) The loss of these sections means that we don't know if it originally included extra New Testament books, or even if Revelation was actually in it.

There are some interesting features about the volume. For a start, like *Sinaiticus* and other early codices, much of the text has numbered sections, kind of proto-chapter numbers. But 2 Peter has no numbers, indicating that perhaps the system of numeration dates back to a time before 2 Peter was accepted as canonical.* Also, it has the older ending of Mark. The gospel stops at 16.8. Most modern Bibles indicate that the longer ending (16.9–20) is a later addition. However, in *Vaticanus*, the scribe leaves an empty column after the end – the only empty column in the entire codex. Did he know that something was missing?

The unfixed canon

Back to that canon list of Athanasius. These magnificent codices demonstrate not only the sophistication of the Bible production that was going on in and around Alexandria, they also demonstrate clearly that, despite Athanasius' letter, the canon was still open.

Codex Sinaiticus includes the *Epistle of Barnabas* and the *Shepherd of Hermas*, which follow Revelation, while in *Codex Alexandrinus*, Revelation is followed by 1 Clement and 2 Clement (although the final pages of this are missing). In neither case are the books distinguished in any way from those preceding them. These books were, it seems, literally and theoretically considered to be part of the Bible. There were also variations in the Old Testament as well. Different Bibles contain different selections from the Apocrypha. None of the great codices – *Sinaiticus*, *Alexandrinus* and *Vaticanus* has the same contents or sequence.

And what was true in Alexandria was true further afield. Several canon lists survive from the later fourth and early fifth centuries, and they also show some significant differences.

Around 385, another distinguished contemporary of Athanasius, Gregory of Nazianzus, produced a list of the canonical books in verse – presumably as a memory aid. His Old Testament list agreed with Athanasius, but his New Testament list was in a different order and omitted Revelation. Around a decade later, a list attributed to a man called Amphilochis rejects 2 Peter, 2 and 3 John, Jude and, yes, Revelation again.

---

* The 'chapters' in Paul's letters are numbered continuously as his letters were considered to be one, huge book.

This distaste for certain books can be found throughout the Christian world. In Antioch, only James, 1 Peter and 1 John were accepted as canonical among the Catholic epistles. Indeed, the illustrious scholar Theodore of Mopsuestia rejected all of the Catholic epistles.[9] While in Constantinople, the greatest preacher of his day, John Chrysostom (c.347–407) left hundreds of sermons containing some 11,000 verse references, none of which come from 2 Peter, 2 and 3 John, Jude or Revelation.* Chrysostom, incidentally, was probably the person who gave the Bible its name. It was he who first explicitly used the term *ta biblia* – the Books – to describe the collection of sacred Scriptures.[10]

Meanwhile, in the Latin-speaking church of the West, two old Latin lists show some variants. One, from about 300, contains all 27 books from the Athanasian list, but also *Barnabas*, *Hermas*, the *Acts of Paul* and the *Apocalypse of Peter*. The second Latin list, which probably originated in North Africa, around 360, omits Hebrews, Jude and James, and seems to express reservations about 2 and 3 John and 2 Peter. But Revelation gets in this time!

The fact is that there never was a point when 'the church' sat down and decided what constituted the New Testament. The story of the creation of the New Testament canon shows just how fluid, open and even elastic the process was. This was, above all, an inclusive process. It was a process which attempted to bring together a list of books on which everyone could agree. This is why the New Testament actually includes books which, in some ways, do not fit well alongside each other. The church Fathers could, for example, have easily gone along with the *Diatesseron* idea; it would have smoothed out the differences between the gospels and formed everything into one tidy, organised line. But they didn't. Instead they chose – deliberately – to embrace a diversity of opinions and traditions.

It was the production of one-volume Bibles, as much as anything else, which fixed the contents. Codices like *Sinaiticus* and *Vaticanus* must have changed the way in which people viewed the Bible. Up until

---

* Revelation was, in the end, to make it into the Bible of the Greeks, but it's fair to say that it has never been fully accepted. It has never, for example, become part of the official lectionary of the Greek church, either in Chrysostom's day or in ours.

then, the Bible had truly been *ta Biblia* – 'the Books' – collections of scrolls, or individual codices. Now, these were gathered together in one volume, a kind of third-century scriptural boxed set. It is much easier to shift the order about when talking about separate books or scrolls, but these one volume editions – the technical term for them is 'pandects' – could not be rearranged. For the first time, the books have been gathered together in a book; *ta Biblia* becomes the Bible.

Tests of canonicity

The canon of the New Testament is rather glorious in its diversity. The process by which it came together may seem to our eyes rather messy, but it was driven by a desire to get things right. So how did they decide? How did they 'get it right'? Broadly speaking, there were three ways in which a book might be eligible for inclusion in the New Testament.

- Orthodoxy

  This was a basic prerequisite: did it agree with the teachings of the church? Any work which was subsequently ruled to be the work of a heretic was rejected.

- Apostolic connections

  A work had to be shown to be traced to the apostles. Mark and Luke weren't apostles, but their works were connected to Peter and Paul, respectively. There was an emphasis on the importance of eyewitness testimony.

- Use by the church

  Was the book used and accepted by the church at large, over a long period of time? A book which had been valued and used by a range of churches across generations was more likely to be accepted than one with only local currency.

Modern Christians, used to the idea of 'divine inspiration', might note that this wasn't really a key criterion. It's not that the ancient church didn't think the Scriptures were divinely inspired – Clement of Rome, for example, talked about the sacred Scriptures as 'true and given through the Holy Spirit' – but they thought that divine inspiration was a continual process within the life of the church. There were many things which were divinely inspired. Augustine suggested that Jerome wrote under the dictation of the Holy Spirit. Indeed, the same word used in 2 Timothy 3.16 – 'All Scripture is inspired by God' – was used by Gregory of Nyssa to describe a commentary on Genesis, and by the Council of Ephesus to describe their decision to condemn Nestorius.[11]

The Early Church, then, did not decide on the basis of divine inspiration, but on historical connections and theological truth. The Scriptures were inspired and authoritative *because* they were the genuine, authentic work of the apostles.

In the end, a consensus did emerge. A synod at Rome in 382 agreed with Athanasius' list. Synods were held at the wonderfully-named Hippo Regius in 393 and at Carthage in 397 and 419 under the leadership of Augustine, which further endorsed the list. At last some kind of agreement was reached.

Nearly four hundred years after the death and resurrection of its founder, the church finally issued an official list of the contents of the New Testament.

Priscillian of Avila

Back a bit. You might think with all this acceptance that the Bible had been tamed, that the dangerous book had been brought under control. But Christianity's rush to the heart of the empire did not remove the danger associated with owning and studying the Bible, it simply changed the source of that danger. Because in 385 AD, for the first time, the church killed one of its own.

Priscillian, the Bishop of Avila, was a devoted Bible scholar who had written a commentary on Paul's letters. Inspired by Paul's instruction to make the body 'a temple of the Holy Spirit within you' (1 Cor. 6.19) he argued that Christians should reject wealth and earthly honour and instead embrace a life of humility, discipline, and chastity. Such ideas may not be heretical in themselves, but the church was now part of the empire, and well on the way to adopting an entirely different set of values.

One of the key charges against Priscillian – and this is going to be a theme from now on – was that he allowed mixed groups of men and women to meet, pray and study the Scriptures. His views brought him into conflict with other bishops, who complained to

Pope Damasus I. At a Synod held at Saragossa in 380, Priscillian's teachings were condemned.

Despite this ruling, Priscillian's supporters succeeded in having him made Bishop of Avila. But in 383 the Emperor, Gratianus, was murdered in Lyons and a general called Magnus Maximus took control of Britain, Gaul, Spain and Africa. Maximus was a chancer and a thug, keen to curry favour with the church, so he reopened the trial of Priscillian. The Bishop was faced with trumped-up charges of sorcery and holding licentious orgies – ridiculous, given his insistence on celibacy. Nevertheless, he was condemned and, at Trier in 385, he and six others were executed. They were the first heretics ever executed by Christian authorities.*

At the time, there was concern: Bishop Ambrose of Milan, Martin of Tours and even Pope Siricius protested against the execution, arguing that an ecclesiastical case should not be decided by the civil powers. But a precedent was set. And in future centuries, the ecclesiastical authorities would only too happily create trumped up charges and then co-opt the civil powers to do the dirty work.

This then is the close of one chapter and the start of something new. By 419 AD the list of the Scriptures was pretty much settled and, although there would still be variants in the order and composition in years to come, the shape of the New Testament was established.

From now on the arguments about the Bible become less about the composition and more about how it is used and by whom. Debates about the status of different books will still crop up; but far more important are debates about access, about who should be allowed to read, to interpret and to translate God's dangerous book.

---

* At the Council of Toledo in 400, Priscillian's case was reviewed, and the most serious charge that they could find was that he'd mistranslated one word. Priscillian became a bit of a local hero in Spain. Indeed, it has been claimed that the remains at Santiago de Compostela are not those of Saint James, but Priscillian.

The Lindisfarne Gospels. Seventh century.

PART TWO: THE BIBLE IN THE WORLD

THE TRANSLATED BIBLE

One Sunday morning in November 403 AD, in a church in the North African city of Oea – modern Tripoli – there was a riot. The problem was not the preaching, not some strange gnostic doctrine expounded by a local heresiarch. The problem was the ivy.

The word 'ivy' that is. Because the bishop was reading from a new translation of the book of Jonah. It was all going fine, until he came to the bit where the plant sheltered Jonah, and then, instead of the word 'gourd' this new translation had 'ivy' and suddenly the whole thing went pear-shaped. Or gourd-shaped. The bishop was forced to climb down 'as he desired not to be left without a congregation—a calamity which he narrowly escaped'.[1]

The story of the riot comes from a letter by Augustine, Bishop of Hippo. He wrote to the translator, warning him of the danger of altering something so familiar, so cherished, something which 'had been chanted for so many generations in the church'

> I would much rather that you would furnish us with a translation of the Greek version of the canonical Scriptures known as the work of the Seventy translators. For if your translation begins to be more generally read in many churches, it will be a grievous thing that, in the reading of Scripture, differences must arise between the Latin Churches and the Greek Churches...

His correspondent replied that the Hebrew word in question was '*ciceion*' which in contemporary Syriac was '*ciceia*'

> It is a kind of shrub having large leaves like a vine... If, therefore, in translating word for word, I had put the word 'ciceia,' no one would know what it meant; if I had used the word 'gourd,' I would have said what is not found in the Hebrew.

There is a weariness to the way he closes his letter

> I beseech you to have some consideration for a soldier who is now
> old and has long retired from active service... I am contented to
> make but little noise in an obscure corner of a monastery, with one
> to hear me or read to me.

His name was Jerome and, at the time of this event, his 'obscure
corner of a monastery' was in Bethlehem. And far from making a little
noise, his translation was going to detonate an almighty blast which
would dominate the western church for the next thousand years.

Jerome and the Old Latin

Jerome – or to give him his proper name, Sophronius Eusebius
Hieronymus – was born in Stridon, on the borders of Dalmatia
and Pannonia, around 347 AD. He was a clever child and, when
he was twelve, he was sent to Rome to study rhetoric, philosophy
and classical literature. He was not an especially religious student,
although after bouts of drunkenness he would appease his
conscience by visiting the catacombs, to contemplate the tombs of
the martyrs and the apostles. Not, perhaps, the sort of behaviour
you associate with students.*

On a visit home to Stridon, however, he encountered old friends
who were living as monks at nearby Aquileia and who made a great
impression on him. Then, in 373, he nearly died during a journey
to the east. Drenched with fever, severely ill, he saw a vision calling
him to put aside his study of secular, pagan literature and devote
himself to God – and to the Bible.

He recovered and responded. He became a hermit in the Syrian
desert.† There he started to learn Hebrew from a converted Jew. Jerome
became a three language man, as Augustine called him, famous for
his knowledge of Greek, Latin and Hebrew. No other contemporary
scholar could rival him in this achievement.‡ He returned to Antioch
in 378 or 379, where he was ordained, and eventually made his way

---

* Except art students.

† Although, apparently, he 'was often present at dances with girls'. My kind of
monastery, really.

‡ Augustine himself knew only a few fragments of Greek and hardly any Hebrew.

to Rome where Pope Damasus made him his secretary. Damasus had secured the papacy by somewhat unorthodox means: in the run up to the election, he hired a gang of thugs to stone the church where his rival, Ursinus, had his headquarters. Some 137 people died in the resulting fight. Damasus was concerned for unity – not to say uniformity – and as part of this programme, he suggested that Jerome should revise the Latin Bible.

By now, the Roman empire in the west was in serious decline. As it crumbled, it lost touch with the Greek-speaking east. In southern Gaul (France) and north Africa, Latin was more common, and translators had already made Latin versions of the Bible. These pre-Jerome versions – known as the 'Old Latin' versions – were vibrantly colloquial and probably dated back a long way. Around 180 AD, a Christian called Speratus was arrested in the town of Scillium in North Africa. He was carrying a box which contained 'Books and letters of a just man, one Paul.' Since it was unlikely that the people of the region spoke Greek, this indicates that Paul's letters – and probably therefore the gospels – had already been translated into Latin before the end of the second century. Cyprian of Carthage (c.200–258) was the first to quote a Latin text. Other, independent versions were also translated in southern Gaul around the same time.

The multiplicity of texts brought problems. According to Jerome, each copy had its own variations. They were riddled with grammatical and textual mistakes. Partly this was due to careless copying and partly to translating errors. Quite often the copyist had inserted passages from one Gospel into another, just because he thought that a bit had been missed out.

So there was a need for an accurate revision. Jerome set to work: his revision of the gospels were published in 383, followed by his correction of the Old Latin book of Psalms. There was immediate controversy. Jerome's revisions were seen as meddling with a much loved text. Then, late in 384, Damasus died and Jerome was forced to leave the city. He took a boat to Syria, accompanied by his brother, a priest, and some other monks. At Antioch he was joined by other female followers from Rome who had decided to found their own community of nuns. Eventually this group settled in Bethlehem.

Jerome and the Septuagint

Bethlehem gave Jerome access to a number of important resources. He could visit the sacred sites with learned Jewish guides. He could keep in touch with Rome and other church centres via the large numbers of pilgrims making their way to and from the Holy Land. Most of all, he had what all scholars need – a library – the famous library at Caesarea, founded by Eusebius and Pamphilus, where Origen's famous *Hexapla* was still to be found.

At Caesarea, Jerome spotted a major problem. The Old Latin texts had been based on the Septuagint, but with the *Hexapla* in front of him, Jerome could see the imperfections in the Greek text. So Jerome took a momentous step: he decided that you couldn't just revise the Old Latin text – at least not where the Old Testament was concerned – you had to go for a new translation from the Hebrew.

It was a radical, controversial move. The Septuagint was, after all, a divinely inspired translation: hadn't the seventy elders emerged from their seventy separate cells with seventy identical texts? The outrage was the same as people felt in Victorian England about tampering with the Authorised Version. There was not a little anti-Semitism in the feeling as well: was not Jerome simply edging towards Judaism? Jerome – who knew that the Septuagint origin story was a myth – was determined to persevere.[*]

It was hard work. His desert-learned Hebrew struggled with the task of deciphering the vowel-less *Hexapla* version. He had no dictionary, no grammars, none of the standard tools of today's exegetes. 'How often I despaired,' he wrote 'and how often I gave up and in my eagerness to learn started again.'[2] He used local Jews to help him, although they weren't keen to make the connection public: one local Jewish instructor, secured at considerable expense, insisted on being smuggled in each night.

It was not just cherished words and phrases which Jerome jettisoned. It was entire books. He decided that whatever was not

---

[*] 'I do not know whose false imagination led him to invent the story of the seventy cells at Alexandria, in which, though separated from each other, the translators were said to have written the same words. Aristeas, the champion of that same Ptolemy, and Josephus, long after, relate nothing of the kind; their account is that the Seventy assembled in one basilica consulted together, and did not prophesy.' Jerome, *Apology for Himself Against the Books of Rufinus*, II.62–63

in the Hebrew Scriptures should be classed as secondary. That meant the extra books in the Septuagint – works which he classed 'apocrypha'. He translated Esdras and the Greek parts of Daniel, Tobit and Judith, but others he left alone.

The Horns on Moses Head

Jerome's insistence on the Hebrew text had an unfortunate consequence: it turned Moses horny.

In Exodus 34.29-35, when Moses came down after meeting God on Mount Sinai, his face was described as 'shining' – *qaran* in Hebrew. The Hebrew text, however, had no vowels in it, so Jerome was faced with *qrn*. He thought it was *qeren*, which in Hebrew means 'horned'. So that's how he translated it. This is why many drawings and paintings of Moses from that time and beyond show him with a peculiar horned hair-do. The most famous of these is Michelangelo's statue of Moses.

Jerome's translation was finished around 406 AD. It was not immediately successful, but from about the ninth century onwards it became the *de facto* Latin version used by the Catholic church. Not that they went along with all his conclusions. The Apocrypha went back in. Those books which he never translated – Wisdom, Ecclesiasticus, Baruch and Maccabees – were still included: compilers just used the Old Latin versions. And despite the fact that he'd completed a fresh translation of the Psalms from the Hebrew, most versions used the revised Latin version he'd done in Rome, way back when he started work for Pope Damasus.

The final version therefore was a kind of compilation. It was nicknamed the Vulgate, from the Latin word for common. And it became the standard Latin translation of the Bible. Even so, it was not until the Council of Trent in 1546 that the Catholic church declared Jerome's version to be the authorised Bible of the Catholic church. One thousand, one hundred and forty years since he put down his pen in his hermit's cave in Bethlehem, Jerome became official.

In his preface to Damasus, written to accompany the revision of the gospels, he wrote

> You urge me to revise the old Latin versions and, as it were, to sit in
> judgment on the copies of the Scriptures which are now scattered

Jerome's cell and memorial. Beneath the Church of the Nativity, Bethlehem

throughout the whole world... The labour is one of love but at the same time both perilous and presumptuous; for in judging others I must be content to be judged by all; and how can I dare to change the language of the world in its hoary old age, and carry it back to the early days of its infancy?

How indeed? The challenge and task of the translator has never been better expressed: to take the hoary old language back to its infancy. What Jerome did was to establish the need for translators to go back to the sources; even though it might cause uproar in the church. And what he faced was what Bible translators have always faced: people really don't like change.

The Rise of the Barbarians

The empire in the west was in trouble. When Augustine died in Hippo in 430, the Vandals were besieging the city; the Franks were rampaging in Gaul, the Lombards in North Italy, the Angles and the Jutes in Britain. It was not, frankly, looking hopeful. When, in 410 AD, Rome had fallen to the Goths, Augustine took comfort in the fact that at least they weren't atheists. The Goths may have been brutal invaders, but at least they were *Christian* brutal invaders. Because, in 350, the Bible had been translated into Gothic.

Ezra writes the Law. The frontispiece to the Codex Amiatinus.

Codex Amiatinus

There are over ten thousand extant Vulgate manuscripts, dating from the fifth century onwards. The oldest complete Vulgate, *Codex Amiatinus*, dates from the early eight century and was made in Jarrow, Northumbria. It's a massive book: 1040 vellum pages, weighing in at 75 pounds. Three copies were originally commissioned by Ceolfrid in 692. The order was so big that the monastery had to buy more land in order to raise the 2000 cattle required to provide the parchment. A later, ninth century copy of *Codex Amiatinus* is the personal Bible of the Pope. He probably needs some help lifting it.

The Gothic Bible is virtually the only literary remains of a once mighty race. The Goths, it seems, just didn't *do* literature. What they did do was violence – at which they excelled, first fighting the Romans, then establishing an empire which stretched from the River Don to the River Dnieper.* Christianity reached the Gothic Empire in about the third century, largely because the Goth raiding parties kept bringing back Christian priests to work as slaves.

The Gothic Bible was created by a descendant of one of these captured slaves, one Wulfila or Ulfilas (Gothic for Little Wolf). Wulfila was born around 311 AD. He was a Christian, who travelled with a Gothic delegation to Constantine's court to work as an interpreter. In Constantinople he took holy orders and was appointed Bishop of the Danubian Goths. In 350, he decided to translate the Bible

---

* In the east were the Ostrogoths and, in the west, were the Visigoths.

into Gothic, using the Septuagint as his source material for the Old Testament and translating the New Testament from the Greek.

There were three immediate problems. First, the Gothic language had no alphabet. Wulfila had to invent an entirely new alphabet, which he based on the Greek alphabet, mixed with some runic signs.

Second, Gothic lacked words for some of the concepts in the Bible. The Goths were the first race from outside the Græco-Roman world to have the Bible; so some concepts in the New Testament were simply unknown to them. They didn't use crosses so Wulfila used the word 'pole' instead. Other unknown concepts he solved using compound words (e.g., the word 'altar' was made up of the Gothic words for 'place of sacrifice') or simply introducing the untranslated 'Christian' word (e.g., 'gospel').

The third problem was the Gothic culture. For a warrior race, prone to hitting people with various weaponry, some concepts needed careful translation. For example, he used the word *fráuja* for 'Lord' instead of the alternative *draútins*. Both meant Lord or master, but *fráuja* denoted the lord in the peaceful context of his household, whereas *draútins* was used to describe him a warrior-lord, or leader of a war-band.

These problems – and solutions – are exactly the same problems which have faced Bible translators ever since. Alphabets have to be invented, concepts taken from the local culture and altered, and certain key Christian terms imported into the culture. What Wulfila started by the Danube goes on around the world today.

Other ancient translations

The Gothic Bible was the first of several ancient translations from the fourth century onwards. As missionary priests travelled to different lands (or as they were captured and taken as slaves) they took with them their scriptures – scriptures which needed to be translated into the languages and the cultures of the people around them.

Armenian

Armenia became a Christian state around 301, when its king Tiridates III was converted by Gregory the Illuminator.* According to the fantastically

---

* You could say Tiridates finally saw the light. Boom, and indeed, boom.

named historian Lazar of Pharb (c.500) there was a soldier called Mesrop Mashtotz* who became a Christian missionary. He created a new alphabet and then translated the Greek text into Armenian with the help of someone called Catholicus Sahak.† Certainly the Armenian translation is one of the earliest translations of the Bible.‡

Georgian

Go north of Armenia and you get to Georgia. According to tradition, Christianity was introduced to Georgia by a captured female slave called Nino, during the reign of Constantine. As with Armenia, an alphabet had to be invented for the Georgians to have the Scriptures in their own language. This happened by the mid-fifth century – around 450 AD.

Ethiopic

Some Christian stories link the Ethiopian eunuch of Acts 8.27 with the spread of Christianity there. It's more likely that it went there during the reign of Constantine the Great. Certainly inscriptions show that Christianity was established in Ethiopia by the fourth century. Parts of the Bible were translated into Ge'ez, as the language was called, by the fifth or sixth centuries. The Old Testament comes from the Greek text, the New Testament from a variety of different text traditions. The Ethiopic New Testament also includes two apocryphal books – 1 Enoch and Jubilees.

Coptic

The gospel spread early into Egypt. Alexandria, of course, was a hotbed of Christian theology and teaching, but most of that was in Greek. Egypt's own language was Coptic – divided into two main dialects: Sahidic in Upper Egypt and Bohairic in Lower Egypt. The Bible was probably translated into Sahidic by Christian missionaries as early as the mid-third century; and the Bohairic version the century after that. In time the Bohairic dialect triumphed to become the standard version of the Coptic church in Egypt.

Slavonic

As hordes of Asiatic people began to descend on the empire from the East during the sixth century, Emperor Heraclius decided that he needed some people to... well, just to get in the way, really, and act as a buffer zone. So he

---

*   d.439. The names just get better and better

†   aka Isaac the Great, 390–439. What did I tell you about the names?

‡   Armenians have been associated with Israel and Jerusalem since they converted in the fourth century. Many went to Jerusalem as pilgrims and stayed on as monks. In the eleventh century they bought the church on Mount Sion and dedicated it to Saint James, or *Surp Hagop* as he's called in Armenian. It became the centre of the Armenian community and they've been there ever since.

sent missionaries into Croatia to turn that region Christian. It is not certain if it worked, but certainly three centuries later there was a Moravian empire which made a request to Constantinople – the seat of the Byzantine Empire – for priests to be sent to conduct the services and generally teach the people. Emperor Michael III (842-867) sent two brothers: Methodius and Cyril, Greeks from Thessalonica. They had learned the Slavonic language in Thessalonica, where masses of Slavs had settled.

According to tradition, it was Cyril who devised the alphabet – known as Glagolithic – so that he could write the Bible in the Slavonic language. He based the alphabet on quite a flamboyant style of Greek, not to mention some Latin songs, a bit of Hebrew (or possibly Samaritan) and quite a lot of symbols that he just invented. Cyril died during the translating, but his brother finished the job. Eventually the centre of Slavic culture moved north, to Russia.

This is one of the most influential Bible translations of all time. Christianity became the state religion in Russia following the conversion of Prince Vladimir in 988. The Russians developed an alphabet based on the earlier Glagolithic script, and they called it Cyrillic, after Cyril.*

Significantly, the development of a Slavonic script was actually opposed by German clergy, notably the Archbishop of Salzburg, who claimed ecclesiastical oversight of Moravia, and wanted to see the Latin liturgy exclusively. It would not be the last time that allowing a Bible translation will be seen as tantamount to losing control.

---

* Good thing they didn't name it after Methodius, otherwise it would have been called Methodic. Or even Methodist. Actually Cyrillic was largely developed by a disciple of Cyril called Clement of Ohrid.

Meanwhile in England

'Sing me a song, Caedmon,' said the figure in the man's dream.

'What shall I sing?' replied Caedmon.

'Sing me the beginning of created beings.'

When he woke, Caedmon went to the Abbess of the Abbey where he was staying, who encouraged him to become a monk and to turn the 'whole series of sacred history' into verse. He started with the 'creation of the world, the origin of man, and all the history of Genesis' then moved on to the rest of the Bible.[3]

Caedmon lived in Whitby and he spoke Anglo-Saxon, rather than English as we know it. Sadly his work, a poetic retelling of Bible stories written around 670 AD, does not survive; the only fragment of it we have is inscribed in runes on a cross at Ruthwell in Scotland.

But it was, perhaps, the first vernacular version of the Scriptures made in Britain.

The tale of Caedmon's dream is told by Bede – the Venerable Bede, as he's known – author of the *Ecclesiastical History* and the most famous writer from Anglo-Saxon times. He lived at Jarrow between 673 and 735 and he, too, was a Bible translator of sorts. One story tells how, as he lay dying, he finished dictating the last sentence of his Anglo-Saxon version of John's gospel. This may be a myth, however, as no trace of it has ever emerged.

Other writers followed Caedmon's example; in the Bodleian Library at Oxford, there's a tenth century manuscript which contains a verse paraphrase of stories from Genesis, Exodus and Daniel. Originally believed to be the work of Caedmon, it is now thought to be the work of a school of poets which flourished a little later. But the English monks, for all their delight in illumination, were not big on Bible translation. There is no complete Anglo-Saxon Bible. Parts of the Bible appear to have been translated into Old English by Alfred the Great, including the Ten Commandments and bits of Exodus, which he used as a preface to his legal code; he also, reputedly, worked on a translation of the Psalms. Aelfric of Eynsham worked on a paraphrase of the Torah.* His writings show that he had reservations about the project – particularly that the uneducated might think that the Jewish laws still applied to Christians.

There are odd bits of translation, written between the lines of other manuscripts. The *Vespasian Psalter* in the British Library was produced in the mid-eighth century and contains an interlinear Old English translation of the Psalms.† It was produced in southern England, perhaps in St. Augustine's Abbey or Christ Church, Canterbury or Minster-in-Thanet. The Lindisfarne Gospels also contain an Anglo-Saxon translation between the lines. There is also a version of Matthew's Gospel, by a Yorkshire priest named Farman, written between the lines of another Latin manuscript.

---

* He began it in Dorset, but became Abbot of Eynsham in 1005. Since Eynsham is my village, and he lived about half a mile away from where I'm typing, I'm going to claim the work for us.

† It gets its name from where it was first shelved: in the Vespasian shelf section in the part of the library indexed by the names from a set of busts of the Roman Emperors on top of the shelves.

There was a version of the four gospels in early English, known as the West-Saxon or Wessex Gospels. Seven copies of this have survived and since we know that so many Anglo-Saxon manuscripts were destroyed at the time of the dissolution of the monasteries, it's possible that it had a fairly wide currency.

Nevertheless, attempts to translate the Bible into Anglo-Saxon seem sporadic. And they came to a halt completely in 1066, when the Normans invaded. William brought a new, French-speaking aristocracy into England – and a French-speaking clergy with them. These groups had no interest in an English, vernacular Bible. Indeed, the Norman invasion effectively killed off the Anglo-Saxon language. It was not until three centuries later that a recognisable form of modern English began to emerge, and with it the first true English Bibles.

Meanwhile in the East

And so, by the end of the ninth century, the Bible had been translated into many of the languages of the Western empires – including the languages of those cultures which were in the process of succeeding Rome. For most of Europe, the Vulgate reigned supreme. Latin was still the language of the church, as it would be for the next five hundred years or so. Further afield, entire alphabets had been invented in order to give people the Bible in their own language.

The plurality of languages was symptomatic of the fractured times. The unity of the Mediterranean world was disappearing. From the end of the third century the empire had effectively been split in two: a western or Latin part and an eastern or Greek part. In the west the old Rome crumbled: in the east, the new Rome – Constantinople – survived. In the sixth century, the great Byzantine emperor Justinian managed to reconquer large parts of the old empire, but his successors could not hold on to his gains and the empire was never again to be one entity.

From the seventh century onwards, Islam became a major threat. By 711 the Arabs had conquered North Africa and crossed into Spain, and in 717, the first of a succession of Islamic armies besieged Constantinople. Islam, of course, was another religion of 'the Book'. The Koran rejected the divinity and resurrection of Jesus, but it recognised both Jesus and Moses as prophets, and traced the origin of the faith back to Abraham, and the origin of the Arab peoples back to Ishmael.

The Bible was translated into Arabic, although we don't know exactly when. The spread of Islam forced Jews and Christians in the conquered lands to speak Arabic, and translation of the Bible was outlawed, so it had to be translated in secret. The oldest known manuscript of the Arabic Bible is *Codex Vaticanus Arabicus 13* which dates from the eight or ninth century. *

The Arab domination of the Mediterranean Sea made communication even more difficult. By 450 AD hardly anyone in Rome could read Greek; while after about 600 it was pretty rare to find anyone in Constantinople who could speak Latin. And so in the west, the Latin Bibles – especially Jerome's Vulgate – became the norm, while in the east there was the Septuagint and the Greek New Testament. If Greeks or Latins wanted to read each other's works they had to do so in translations. Few bothered, and without a shared cultural and linguistic background, the two churches began to move irrevocably apart.

There were theological differences as well, arguments over creeds and over the relative status of the different churches. From the early days, there had been a church in Rome, but in the old days it was the first among equals, with Constantinople, Antioch and Alexandria. Before Constantine, there had been a plurality and diversity in the Christian faith: different parts of the Christian world had their own approaches and, as we've seen, their own set of scriptures. Now as each side became more foreign, more 'other', both sides of the church became entrenched in their dogma and their traditions.

What this meant was that the church in the west lost touch with its roots. Christianity was an eastern faith, born in Palestine and nurtured in the churches of Asia and Syria, North Africa and Greece. Its scriptures were in Greek and Hebrew and Aramaic. But as the memory of those languages faded, the western church moved far away from its home. It was a church where everything was a translation.

---

* The Torah probably existed in Arabic much earlier – a Jewish reference talks of the Torah being in four languages: Hebrew, Greek, Aramaic and Arabic.

Meanwhile in China

One day, in China, a man called Wang Chieh made a book which he gave away to people in memory of his parents.

When I say he 'made' a book, he didn't write it. He had it printed from a carved woodblock.

It was May 11, 868. And Wang Chieh had invented printing.

THE MEDIEVAL BIBLE

Latin became the sacred language of the western church. Jerome's Vulgate eventually gained prominence in the west, but its dominance was never complete. In Africa – as indicated by the furore over the ivy – the Old Latin texts hung around. Damasus' dream of one universal Latin version was never realised.

The problem was the human factor. All Bibles were copied by hand, in the *scriptoria* of often isolated monasteries. The monks, slaving away with their quills and their soot-black ink, were craftsmen rather than scholars; they had no experience of alternative lists or traditions. Books were expensive, elite items. If you had a copy of the Bible or the New Testament, you didn't question its accuracy or pay a fortune for another one so that you could compare the texts. You just copied it and passed it on.

Missionaries making their way into barbarian lands weren't concerned with textual accuracy – they just needed a set of simple ethical ideas to which your average Goth, Slav or Hairy Savage could sign up. If that meant using Old Latin, Jerome's version or a hybrid of the two, they weren't worried – anything was OK as long as it did the job.

Thus, different waves of missionary activity brought with them their own text traditions. In Ireland, for example, the monks produced texts which conflated Jerome with the Old Latin; Spanish texts use Jerome as a foundation, but added all manner of marginal glosses and even legendary additions. In Northumbria a text-type formerly associated with Southern Italy was introduced by Ceolfrid and Benedict Biscop; this mingled with Vulgate and certain Irish text traditions to produce entirely new variants. The history of the Latin Bible text in the Middle Ages is like a breeding programme; different texts joining together, replicating, reproducing, mutating.

The Epistle to the Laodiceans

Some text traditions included complete books. There are over one hundred copies of the Latin Vulgate which include the *Letter of Paul to the Laodiceans*. At the end the tenth century, Abbot Aelfric claimed that Paul wrote fifteen epistles and put the *Laodiceans* after Philemon. Indeed, *Laodiceans* proved to be difficult to eradicate. It's the cockroach of uncanonical books. Even the invention of printing couldn't kill it: in 1488, the first German printed Bible included it – as did all eighteen German Bibles published before Luther's translation. The first Czech Bible (also in 1488) included it. It hung around the canon like an uninvited guest, ever hopeful of admission, until, in the end, the bouncers threw it out.

Alcuin and the standard edition

On Christmas Day 800 AD, the Pope crowned Charles the Great – Charlemagne, King of the Franks – as Emperor. Although Charlemagne sought some kind of endorsement from the east, the move only widened the split between the Greeks and Latins: the Byzantines clung to the idea of one empire, one emperor.

Charlemagne was personally committed to Christianity and very interested in theology. One of his prime concerns was to reform the education of the clergy – who were, in effect, his local leadership. As part of these reforms, he made several attempts to sort out the biblical text. He decreed that the copying of the text should only be carried out by suitably qualified monks with a concern for accuracy. And he charged Alcuin, head of his palace school, with the task of creating an authoritative, grammatical Latin text out of the many different versions.

Alcuin was an Anglo-Saxon monk and he knew hardly any Greek and even less Hebrew.* So this was no Jerome-like attempt at translation. This was holy proof-reading. His concern was simply to purge the text of errors in copying, punctuation and grammar, and to impose a consistency of appearance on the volumes – each measuring broadly the same dimensions, and each page containing two columns of 50–52 lines each. For the comparison, he used various Bibles sent to him from Northumberland. The completed text was probably presented to Charlemagne at his coronation.

---

* Alcuin was born near York around 730 AD.

Watch your handwriting

In the early Middle Ages, the Latin script followed the classical tradition – it was written in capitals without any spaces or punctuation. In Charlemagne's palace school at Aix-la-Chapelle a different script was developed, smaller, easier to read, with the letters joined together. It has become known as Caroline Minuscule.

Alcuin's Latin version, written in Caroline Minuscule. 9th century.

Sadly, Alcuin was fighting a battle which was almost impossible to win. The history of Bible production in the Middle Ages is largely one of glorious technical skills combined with really bad editorial. The illuminated manuscripts looked magnificent, but the texts were frequently full of errors and there were so many variants that finding one 'uniform' Bible was impossible. The task of copying a Bible by hand was too vulnerable to accident, boredom and ignorance.

The work of translation had continued, but in some very specific forms. In 830 a monk named Hrabanus Maurus, head of the monastery school at Fulda, translated the gospels into High German but, amazingly, the version he used was the *Diatesseron* of Tatian, written way back some 650 years earlier. Maurus' pupil Otfried von Weissenburg made a free translation of the gospels and not only in High German, but in verse. At St Gallen, a monk called Notker translated the Psalms.[*]

The main task of Bible production in this time was not in translation but illumination, which is, I suppose, a different kind of translation: words made into pictures.

Illuminated Bibles

We interrupt this programme for an Anglo-Saxon riddle

A life-thief stole my world-strength,

Ripped off flesh and left me skin,

---

[*] He had, apparently, a very large lower lip, giving him the nickname of *Labeo*, i.e. 'Lippy'.

Dipped me in water and drew me out,
Stretched me bare in the tight sun;
The hard blade, clean steel, cut,
Scraped-fingers folded, shaped me.
Now the bird's once wind-stiff joy
Darts often to the horn's dark rim,
Sucks wood-stain, steps back again
With a quick scratch of power, tracks
Black on my body, points trails.

The answer? It's describing the production and illumination of a Bible.[1]

The illuminated Bibles of the Middle Ages are some of the most remarkable works of art in the history of mankind. Astonishing resources were poured into these richly-decorated, highly crafted Bibles. At least two hundred lambs were killed and skinned – their world-strength stolen by some local life-thief – to provide the parchment for one copy. Expensive pigments were required: tissue-thin gold and silver leaf; deep lapis lazuli blue; vermilion from cinnabar (mercury ore – the best came from Spain, mined by prisoners, doomed to die, their lungs congested by the heavy metal fumes); madder, kermes, red and white lead, verdigris, yellow ochre, orpiment, oak gall, indigo and woad.[2]

Written on the smoothest parchment, they were often elaborately bound, in gold or silver, set with precious jewels and gemstones. Sometimes the covers were made of rare woods or ivory. This is the Bible as commodity, as a statement of wealth and power. The Bible had always been treasured: now it *was* treasure.

Handwritten, illuminated manuscripts were fabulously expensive. In 1309 the nuns of Wasserler in the diocese of Halberstadt sold a complete Bible they had for sixteen pieces of silver. Three years later the same nuns spent some of the money: five pieces of silver, which brought them 180 acres of land, two farmhouses, and a farm with two acres of woodland and another wood. In 1388 the Abbey of Johannisberg purchased a complete Bible for seventy florentines and arranged permission to pay the amount over four years. Seventy florentines would have bought them 35 plump oxen.

Lindisfarne Gospels

One of the most famous of all these illuminated works is the Lindisfarne Gospels, produced by a monk called Eadrith (later the Bishop of Lindisfarne) around 698 AD and bound by Bilfrid, who added precious gems and metalwork to the binding.

The book's survival is a miracle. In January 793, the gospels were hastily packed up and taken from the monastery to avoid invading Vikings. During their escape the boat carrying them was shipwrecked. Fortunately, the gospels washed ashore and were taken to Durham.

Despite their precious nature, the Lindisfarne Gospels were later written on by a priest, Aldred, who, sometime in the late tenth century, inserted a word-for-word Anglo-Saxon translation in the spaces between the lines of Latin text.

Treasure houses of knowledge

The cost of books meant that even the best stocked libraries were small by our standards. In 1170, Christ Church, Canterbury, had a library of over six hundred books. The Vatican library – then the largest library in the world – had about 1100 books in it. Books in these libraries were chained to the wall or shelf to make sure that no one stole them. The chains kept the books secure, kept the learning moored to the bookshelf. Thomas Farnilaw, Chancellor of York left his Bibles and prayer books to the churches of York on condition that they were 'chained up so that all men may use them'.

Chained library in Hereford Cathedral

The monasteries produced many thousands of Bibles. Over twelve thousand whole or partial manuscripts survive from this time – a small fraction of what was actually produced. *Scriptoria* became well-organised production lines. One monk dictated the text to ten or twenty others, who wrote it down. (Of course, this also led to more errors creeping in. One monk making a mistake in one manuscript is one thing, a mistake multiplied in twenty manuscripts is another problem entirely.)

Not that every monk approached their work with complete enthusiasm or professionalism. Indifferent copyists made clumsy mistakes. In a manuscript from Ireland there are some rather plaintive comments in the margins: 'God be praised, it's growing dark', 'St Patrick of Armagh, preserve me from this everlasting writing,' and 'Oh if I only had a nice glass of old wine in front of me!'*

Alcohol seems to have been something of a lure. Richard of Bury complained that the monks cared 'more about drinking beer than writing books.'† One codex, from the Monastery of St Gallen, has a drawing on the last page of an outsized tankard of beer, with a poem which runs

> 'If, Grimoal, you drink from this or a similar flagon,
>
> May the good liquor it holds, like vinegar choke and burn you,
>
> So that, coughing and gasping, you stay everlastingly thirsty.'

Who Grimoal was is not recorded. But he clearly liked a pint.[3]

Millennium fever

The books may have been secure, but the ideas inside them had a way of slipping their chains and causing all kinds of confusion. Revelation talked of the thousand year reign of Christ and, as the year 1000 approached, this led to a welter of millennial expectation. Was the world going to end? Would Christ descend on schedule, to rule in person on earth?

The millennium was a hornets' nest. Literally, in France, where a peasant called Leutard fell asleep in a field and dreamt of a swarm

---

* I know the feeling.

† See above.

of bees invading his body, entering through his groin, rising, stinging their way up and emerging from his mouth, 'bidding him to do things impossible to men'.[4] He was stung into action: when he woke, he went to the parish church where he smashed the cross and destroyed an image of Jesus. Soon his preaching attracted many followers, but when the local bishop condemned him as a heretic, he lost all his followers and threw himself down a well.

His is just one of many mad stories around the millennium: the time when the words of Revelation went viral. Even though the end had proved not to be quite as nigh as all that, the Bible was dangerous – to sanity, sometimes – and sometimes in more physical ways. In 1010, news reached Europe of the destruction of the Church of the Holy Sepulchre in Jerusalem by the Moslem messiah, al-Hakim. It was still an outrage that Jerusalem – the holy city of the Bible – was in the hands of Muslims. Something must be done.

Martin of Tours, in the fourth century, had seen clearly that Christianity was an anti-militaristic faith. 'I am Christ's soldier,' he said. 'I am not allowed to fight.'[5] But from Constantine's time onwards, many armies have been convinced that God was on their side. *Nobiscum deus* cried the Byzantine soldier on leaving camp – 'God with us' – the first cry in an arc which led to *Gott mit uns* on the belt buckles of Nazi soldiers.[6] God with us. Immanuel. The Wehrmacht wearing a name of Jesus.

Pope Urban II was certain of God's support. At Clermont in 1095 he launched the crusades with the phrase 'God wills it!' He backed up his medieval regime change with some agile biblical gymnastics, redefining the idea of 'taking up the cross' (Matt. 10.38). It wasn't just the New Testament which was wrenched into service, either: the imagery of Old Testament Jerusalem inspired the military order of the Knights Templar – the Knights of the Temple of Solomon – 'Christian' warriors, sustained by daily readings from the more militaristic parts of Joshua, Judges and the apocryphal book of Maccabees.

The Bible and the People
Although in the 1190s Pope Innocent III had stated that the desire for understanding the Holy Scriptures was a good thing, he also warned that

the secret mysteries of the faith ought not to be explained to all men in all places. For such is the depth of divine Scripture that not only the simple and illiterate but even the prudent and learned are not fully sufficient to try to understand it.[7]

The people had to be protected from the potency of the Scriptures. Access to the mysteries of the faith was closely guarded. Latin was one form of fencing the Bible off from the common herd. It made sure that only the learned could study it. 'Holy Scripture is God's dining room, where guests are made soberly drunk,' said one medieval writer.[8] The church was ever alert either for priests who quaffed too deeply, or for the unlicensed who had somehow broken into the drinks cabinet.

And there were clear signs of drunkenness. The power of the church and the fever around the millennium led to many people discussing Scripture. This was an age of spiritual longing; shut out from the mysteries of the church, the people began to turn away from a corrupt and venal orthodoxy. They compared what they knew of Jesus' teaching with the behaviour they could see in the church, and the church did not come out well.

The problems were particularly acute in France: 'Everywhere in our cities and villages, not only in our schools but at the street corners, learned and ignorant, great and small, are discussing the gravest mysteries' wrote the bishops of France to the Pope in 1140.[9] Some of this muttering resulted in strange heresies, like the 'Brethren of the Free Spirit' who preached a kind of apocalyptic pantheism. Or the Cathars of south west France, with their brand of medieval gnosticism – they believed that matter was evil, the world a creation of dark forces. Salvation lay in renouncing all that was worldly including, of course, the powers and authorities of the world.* In one of the darker and more disreputable episodes of church history, the Cathars were savagely crushed when the ironically-named Pope Innocent III launched a 'crusade' against them. The conclusive act was the capture of the Cathar fortress of Montségur, which the church authorities, borrowing a phrase from Revelation, termed

---

* The name came from the Greek word *katharoi* meaning pure or perfect. They were the 'perfect' people.

a 'synagogue of Satan'.[10] Montségur was captured and over two hundred of the Cathars were burned alive. One might wonder where the real Satanic powers were residing.

The Waldensians

Peter Valdes was a successful businessman in Lyons, who underwent a spectacular conversion. Around 1170, he did a dangerous thing: he took Christ literally. He sold all his possessions, left enough money to care for his wife and family, and gave the rest to the poor. Then he went into the streets, preaching and serving others.

An early biographer, Stephen of Bourbon[*], described Valdes as someone who was 'not well-educated, but on hearing the gospels was anxious to learn more precisely what was in them.' Others shared his desire. Valdes commissioned Bible translations in French and when they were read out in public, large crowds of people flocked to hear the gospels in their own language.

Valdes soon attracted the attention of the authorities and was ordered not to preach. He took his case to the Pope, who approved of his voluntary poverty but banned him and his followers from speaking anywhere but in church – not that any clergy were likely to invite him in. When Valdes and his followers carried on their unofficial preaching, they were excommunicated and driven out of Lyons. They became known as the Waldensians and, far from being destroyed by their persecution, their movement actually spread, establishing centres in Germany and central Europe.

The Waldensians were a biblical movement: they believed that every Christian had a vocation to preach and that the personal study of Scriptures was paramount. They emphasised the vernacular Scriptures: preachers were encouraged to memorise chunks of the Scriptures in the vernacular to use in their preaching. They were eventually driven underground, but small communities continued to exist in Italy, Bohemia and elsewhere, surviving centuries of persistent, low-level persecution. Eventually they emerged, blinking in the light of the Protestant Reformation, many of the ideas of which they had already come up with three centuries before. In the end they were to travel further afield, establishing the *Chiesa*

---

[*] That's his place of origin, not his preferred drink.

Evangelica in Piedmont and even travelling to America where, in the late nineteenth century, some Italian Waldensians established the town of Valdese, North Carolina. Reading the Bible takes people on strange journeys.

Paris Bibles

By the eleventh century schools of education had grown up around certain cathedrals. Their aim was to explore the problems and propositions of Christianity, to study the Scriptures: to do, in fact, theology. These were clerical institutions – for the professionals. Inside the fence. But soon the bigger of the Italian cities began to finance their own schools, drawing not on Christian models but on Muslim schools of higher education, such as the school of Al-Azhar in Cairo, with its lectures, professors and degrees. These, along with some of the northern cathedral schools, developed into universities. Chief among these was the University of Paris, which became the leading theological school in Europe. Indeed, it was a Paris scholar who popularised the term theology – the twelfth century monk Peter Abelard, who entitled one of his books *Theologia Christiana*.[11]

Scholars soon rediscovered the need for the basic tools of biblical scholarship. In 1312, the Council of Vienne issued a directive that chairs of Greek, Hebrew, Aramaic and Arabic should be set up at the major universities: Paris, Bologna, Salamanca and Oxford. (Typically, it took Oxford around two hundred years to implement this directive. There is a record of a converted Jew called John of Bristol teaching Hebrew and Greek there in 1320, but apparently he only lasted a year.)[12]

In Paris, the establishment of the School of Theology also led to demands for a standard 'academic' text. The ambition was encouraged by the Paris stationers who sensed the first market for an academic textbook. If all students were required to have one version, they stood to make some cash.

The result was the Paris Bibles. The basic text was Alcuin's Latin version but, to help students, it included a 'gloss' – an abbreviated commentary written in the margins and between the lines. These notes gave interpretations laid down by the Church Fathers and earlier authorities, explained unfamiliar or difficult Latin words, expounded on the doctrine and meaning of a particular passage, or corrected false or heretical teaching. Sometimes even the glosses had glosses, leading to Bibles where the text grew ever smaller, crushed beneath successive layers of marginal notes. Sadly, the attempt to impose a standard edition didn't work. The booksellers' rush to tap into the student market led to shoddy and irresponsible copying – with the result that neither the Bible nor the gloss were properly harmonised.

But that wasn't their real achievement anyway. The real achievement of the Paris Bibles was in their format. They set new standards in content and layout. Running heads at the top of the page identified which book the reader was in. For the first time, the order of the books in the Bible became uniform.

And they had chapters. Chapter division was not new in Bibles – it had been used since the days of the great Alexandrian codices– but there was no uniform system. The students at Paris came from a wide range of geographical backgrounds, and they brought with them their Bibles, often with different arrangement of chapters and a different order of books. A man named Stephen Langton, who was teaching in Paris at the time, devised a number system for the chapters which became popular in Paris and it is his chapter numbers which we use today.* The chapters were numbered and marked and tied to glossaries and notes at the end of the book. Bibles contained, for the first time, useful appendices, such as concordances and lists of Hebrew names.

The other big format change was that the Paris Bibles were portable. This was to not just to fulfil the needs of students: it was driven by radical preachers, out in the streets. The preaching orders – monks like the Dominicans and the Franciscans – spent a lot of time wandering from town to town in search of souls to save. And one of their biggest problems was how to take the Bible with them; most Bibles were so big you'd need a horse and cart. But the Paris printers and booksellers developed smaller, more portable Bibles, written on a special type of vellum, scraped as thin as tissue. The technique and workmanship of these Bibles was astonishing. Even today it is not easy to produce a legible, small, portable Bible; but

---

* The earliest known copy of the Bible with this numbering system actually dates from 1231 and was written not in Paris, but in Canterbury.

these were all hand-written. They wrote in small, slender letters, reducing the enormous lectern Bibles to a small, portable format.

The Paris Bibles changed the way in which people viewed the Bible. The Bible could be held, it could be handled. It could, both literally and figuratively, be grasped.

Biblia pauperum

In the twelfth century, two significant inventions reached Europe from the far east. The first was paper, which promised to free the book from the expense of vellum; the second was the wood block. For the first time, whole pages of books could be printed at one go. This was not moveable type – we are still some one hundred years away from Gutenberg's press – but whole pages carved out of one block of wood. Long blocks of dense text were too complicated to be carved in that way, so the process was better suited for illustrations. And, when it came to the Bible, illustrations were useful in telling the Bible stories to people who couldn't read.

Among the earliest woodcut books were the so-called *Biblia Pauperum* – Bibles for the poor. The Bibles themselves were still expensive, but they were bought by priests and used as a teaching aid. Each page was filled with illustrations. The central illustration would be an illustration of an event from the New Testament, then around it there would be other pictures – events from the Old Testament which were linked to the main theme, portraits of biblical characters or symbolic drawings. It allowed people to link well-known stories together. What made them different to other illustrated Bibles is that there was hardly any text. They were a kind of medieval Christian comic. Later, these would be printed using moveable type, starting with German versions in Bamberg in about 1462.

Story Bibles

Around 1170, the same time that Peter Valdes was preaching in the streets of Lyons, another Peter – Petrus Comestor, a priest in Paris, and sometime Chancellor of the University – produced the *Historia Scholastica*, a kind of story Bible. 'Comestor' means 'devourer' and refers to the fact that he was a voracious reader: he was Peter the Eater, 'devourer of books'.

Biblia pauperum showing various 'ascensions', starting with Enoch, then Jesus. Finally Elijah is taken to heaven in what looks like a go-cart.

Originally written in Latin as an academic help for students, the *Historia Scholastica* was a paraphrase, retelling tales from the Bible along with popular fables, nuggets of history from Josephus and other classical authors, and helps for the reader, such as geographical or etymological appendices. It broke out of the confines of the university and became popular with literate lay people in the later Middle Ages. For two hundred years this was the widest read book in Northern France. Indeed, it was translated into the vernacular all over Europe; there are versions in German, Dutch, Portuguese, Czech and even Norse.

It became a kind of Bible, in fact. Chaucer and Gower read it: it was used in preaching, in popular drama and as a basis for biblical versifications. It also formed the core of another retelling of the biblical stories – *Cursor Mundi*, a huge early English poem written about 1300, which tells the Old and New Testament stories, not to mention covering a bit of world history as well. Such paraphrases were not uncommon. There were rhyming Bibles written in the twelfth and thirteenth centuries, with the aim of helping people to memorise the text. They were feeding an increasing desire: the hunger of ordinary people for the Bible.

Beguines

One of the most interesting exmples of the hunger for the spiritual was the Beguines – a group of religious women who renounced property, embraced chastity and lived with their parents or in small communities.* Originating in Belgium, they were a kind of nunnery of lay people. With no common rule and no mother superior, they were autonomous 'cells' devoted to lives of austerity and service. Their community dwellings – known as a Beguinage or Begjinhof – were not remote, like monasteries, but right in the heart of their towns. They had the temerity to wear religious habits. and wandered around with no discipline and did not even obey their parish priests.

Their activities and their mystical writings alarmed the authorities. At the Second Council of Lyons (1274) a Franciscan called Gilbert of Tournai gives us a crucial accusation: the Beguines had unauthorised vernacular translations of the Bible which they read openly in the public squares. These Scriptures, he said, contained heresies – although he did not specify what those heresies were. It didn't matter, anyway. What mattered was that unlicensed, uncontrolled laity – *women* – were reading the Scriptures in their own tongue.[13]

Their most influential teacher was Marguerite Porete, author of a hugely popular book called *The Mirror of Simple Souls*. Her books were incinerated and she was imprisoned, but she refused to appear to defend herself before her accusers. 'This Soul responds to no one if she does not wish to,' she said. '...whoever calls this Soul does not find her, and so her enemies have no reply from her.'[14] On 1 June 1310 she was burned at the stake.

---

* The male counterparts were called Beghards.

A street in the Begjinhof in Lier, Belgium

The church has never recognised Marguerite Porete. It canonised St John of the Cross who, two hundred years later, wrote in virtually identical terms of the soul's union with God; it canonised Dominic, heretic hunter and father of the Inquisition; it beatified Pope Urban II, who launched the crusades. But not Marguerite.

'Beguine' was originally a derisive nickname. It originated from a revivalist preacher called Lambert le Bégue – Lambert 'the Stammerer'. These women were 'stammerers'; ignorant people who couldn't even speak properly. This habit of giving unorthodox religious groups derisive nicknames goes back centuries – back, in fact, to the Roman nickname, 'Christians'. It was a technique which the authorities tried to use on another group which arose at this time: the followers of John Wycliffe, known as the Lollards.

The Lollards

John Wycliffe was a Doctor of Divinity at Oxford University. From the mid-1370s he began a series of attacks on the corruption of the church and the claims of the papacy to rule. Such attacks were not unique at the time, but it was the extent of his criticisms which was unusual. Wycliffe was going right to the foundations of the church.

The cornerstone of his case against the church was the Bible. Wycliffe placed the Bible above the church and its traditions, above the dogma of the Church Fathers and the rulings of the Pope. He believed – with revolutionary fervour – that the Bible was the property of everyone, that it was through reading and understanding the Bible that people could reach divine truth.

Ordinarily Wycliffe would have been dealt with fairly swiftly. But political divisions in the country meant that he was allowed to continue his attacks. In the end, however, his refusal to keep quiet led to his condemnation at a synod in 1382. He was sacked by the university and, by default, the band of followers he had gathered around him were turned into heretics. Although Wycliffe retired to the small town of Lutterworth in Leicestershire, it was something of an active retirement, for he continued to issue his denunciations of the church, right up until his death in 1384.

Wycliffe's emphasis on the Bible inspired his followers to make the first real English translation. Although Wycliffe is often credited with the translation, it's highly unlikely that he played any real part in it. It was probably the work of two men: Nicholas of Hereford, who did a rather wooden version of the Old Testament and John Purvey, who revised the Old Testament and translated the New.* The translations follow the Latin Vulgate closely, sometimes word for word and even in the same word order, making them almost unreadable. Later versions show a greater fluidity and freedom.

Alarmed, the authorities did what they always do when faced with radical ideas: they passed laws. In 1407, Thomas Arundel, Archbishop of Canterbury, banned the making and reading of Wycliffite Bibles, without the approval of the church. Which, obviously, would never be given. The ban was therefore a *de facto* ban on the translation of the Scriptures into English. Arundel wrote of that 'miserable, pestilential John Wycliffe of damnable memory, so of the old serpent, forerunner and disciple of Antichrist.' Strong words from an Archbishop of Canterbury – especially in a letter to the Pope.

---

* This of course raises an issue for the international organisation the Wycliffe Bible Translators. Strictly speaking, they should be called the Purvey Bible Translators. Or perhaps not.

The 1407 ban served as a useful tool to allow the authorities to search and seize any heretical books. It was the Stop and Search law of its time. But the authorities also turned to ridicule. They called the Wycliffites 'Lollards', a word supposed to imitate the muttering, mumbling sound of a group of lay people, stumbling their way through the Bible.

No other part of Europe went to such lengths to stop people getting hold of the Bible in their own language. Although elsewhere vernacular versions were discouraged, they were never declared illegal. And it was to be another 150 years before England raised the ban. Why? Part of the reason was that Wycliffe's teachings had clear political overtones. This wasn't just about personal piety: this was about who was in charge.

Lollardry linked with active revolt. In 1414, the prominent Lollard Sir John Oldcastle marched on London with an ill-formed plan to establish some kind of commonwealth. His 'army' was easily dispersed, and Oldcastle himself captured and executed. He was found guilty of insurrection and heresy, and the linking of those two crimes burned deep into the psyche of the English authorities: the one, it was felt, leads to the other. Heresy leads to insurrection.

The Lollards, though, were persistent. Determined. They met in secret. They defied the authority of the church, appointing their own leaders. They allowed lay people to preach and to officiate at Communion. They used the Bible – their Bible – to define their terms and procedures. Lollardry was never exterminated: it was driven underground; the secret belief of traders and merchants and the professional classes. There were strong, local pockets of Lollardry in prosperous farming areas such as East Anglia, the Chilterns and the Cotswolds. It was a belief system which was associated with those by whom the ruling classes felt most threatened: the up and coming middle classes. People with real cash.

And despite the ban, the Bibles circulated widely. Over 250 manuscripts of Lollard bibles have survived to this day – mostly copies of all or part of the New Testament. Wycliffite Bibles are the single largest type of medieval literature still extant. When we consider that these are just the survivors, the fragments which

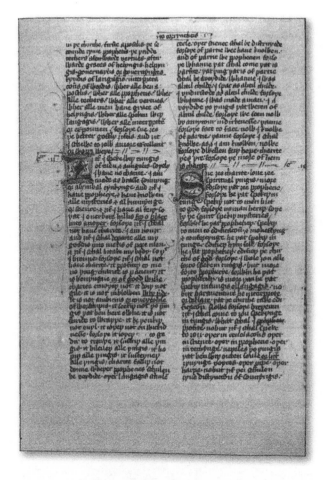

A page from
a Lollard New
Testament

escaped burning or decay, we can begin to grasp just how extensive was this underground literature.[15]

Wycliffe's opponents were never going to let a little thing like his death stand in their way. In 1419, an international council of the church at the Swiss city of Constance formally declared him a heretic. In 1428 – nearly forty years after his death – the English authorities duly dug up his corpse and burned it, a final, stupid, futile gesture against the man and his ideas.

They were decades too late. Wycliffe's ideas had already escaped the confines of the university, the confines of England, indeed. They were gone from the church and the universities to the artisans and tradesmen and urban classes of England; to Prague, where Jan Hus preached a message of independence from Rome. Hus was burnt at the stake in 1415, but the movement he inspired lived on elsewhere.

It's a funny thing, but authorities always think that burning things is the way to destroy them. Burn books, burn people, dig up corpses and burn them as well. But burning never works. You can't burn ideas; you can only melt them, turn them into gas, invisible, free of boundaries, like ashes, sprinkled on the river, flowing downstream, floating out to sea.

The Wycliffe memorial at Lutterworth, and, in the distance, the church where he spent his final years.

THE REFORMATION BIBLE

In 1454, the world changed. In Mainz, Johannes Gensfliesch – or Gutenberg to give him his more familiar name – invented the modern printed book.* And he launched his invention with – what else? An edition of the Bible.

Developing the technology took him years, working in conditions of great secrecy. Even when his first backers pulled out and took Gutenberg to court, he refused to tell people what he was doing with that big winepress and all that lead. Finally, in 1444, he revealed what he had been up to. The first printed works from his press were some calendars and a short Latin grammar. But these were squibs, novelties, doing little to lessen the weight of debt that was crushing him. He needed to think big, make a splash. So when a new business partner, Johannes Fust, supplied him with eight hundred guilders of new capital, Gutenberg decided to do something to make everyone sit up: he would print a Bible.

The Bible, after all, was the book which, above all others, was associated with the scribes and the *scriptoria*. But Gutenberg's edition would be better – more precise, more exact – than any calligrapher could ever achieve. He decided on two editions, one on paper and the other on parchment. He created everything – from designing the typeface to inventing the special ink. He cast 46,000 pieces of type, each of which had to be finished by hand.

Printing finally began in 1452. Even with six assistants, setting the type for one page took a day and you could only print at ten copies an hour. It took two years to print the first edition – just 150 copies, in two volumes of 648 and 634 pages. In 1457 he decided to print another, even bigger Bible: this one came in three volumes, totalling 1768 pages, with only thirty-six lines to the page.

---

* Johannes Gensfliesch means John Gooseflesh. He took the name Gutenberg – a wise move under the circumstances – from his father's estate near Mainz.

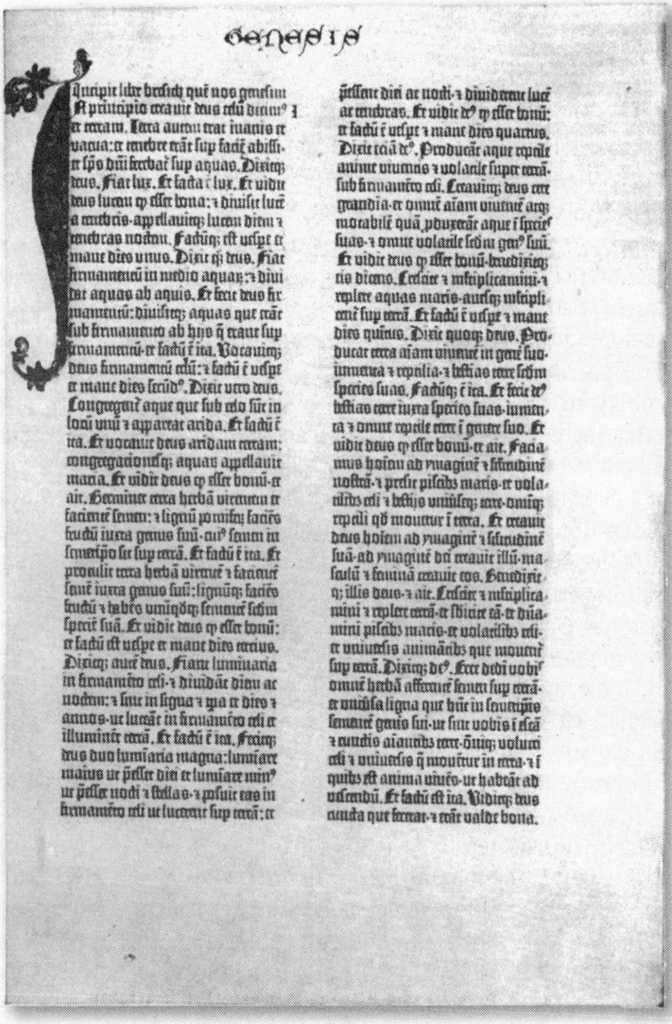

The first printed Bible: Mainz, 1454

The two Bibles were the only full-sized books that Gutenberg ever printed.

Like so many inventers, Gutenberg never grasped the true potential of his invention. He had produced huge, expensive luxury items, but what printing was to do was transform the book, so that it could be cheaper, smaller and mass-produced. Nevertheless, he was the first, the forerunner. He printed the first mass-produced books in Europe. And he changed the world.

The spread of printing

The production method of Gutenberg's Bible was new, but everything else was solidly traditional. Its two-column design was exactly the same as a hand-written manuscript; the typeface was based on contemporary handwriting. He even left a space so that the first letter of each chapter and the headings could be hand-drawn by an illuminator.

Others were quick, though, to spot the potential of this invention, and printing developed rapidly in Italy, France and Germany.* The cost of books, though never cheap, was made more affordable by printing smaller copies, and by using paper – another Chinese invention.†

The books from these presses were truly international. Latin was still the language of the educated elite, so a Latin book printed in Venice could be read by an educated reader in Edinburgh. It meant that ideas could spread much faster and much further than they ever had before. And the most printed book – the book which *everyone* wanted to read – was the Bible.

Not all the Bibles were in Latin, though. In Bamberg, Albrecht Pfister produced 'Poor Bibles', one in Latin and one in German. In 1466, Mentelin in Strasbourg printed a German translation of the Bible which was smaller and cheaper than Gutenberg's Bibles: 61 lines on the page, contained within one volume and retailing for

---

* It took twenty years for printing to reach England. In 1476, William Caxton set up a printing press in the precincts of Westminster Abbey.

† The earliest paper ever discovered was unearthed by archaeologists in a Tibetan desert town and dates from the late third century. It did not make it across to Europe until a thousand years later; the first paper-mill in Europe was founded in Germany in the thirteenth century.

only twelve guilders. Still expensive, but a bargain, compared to twenty guilders for Gutenberg's volumes.

Bibles began to flood from the presses. Eggstein produced another German Bible at Strasbourg. Joducus Pflanzman produced an illustrated Bible. Within a short time, printers were issuing Bibles in all shapes and sizes. In the years leading up to the Reformation over seventy thousand Bibles were printed in central Europe, and more than one hundred thousand New Testaments. There was the Latin Vulgate, of course, but also translations galore: Bibles in High German, Low German, Dutch, Catalan, Portuguese, Polish, Czech, French, Italian, Russian and even Ethiopian.

But not English.

Back to the Greek

In 1453, while Gutenberg was drying the inky sheets of his Bible, Ottoman forces finally conquered Constantinople. Constantine XI, last emperor of Byzantium, was lost among the brutal fighting in the streets. His body was never found.

In the west the news was received with genuine grief and dismay, even though the relationship between the two 'halves' of Christendom had been fractured for centuries. The split had become official in 1054, when Pope Leo IX sent three legates to Constantinople to try to sort out the disputes between the two churches. Things did not go well and the papal legate issued a Bull of Excommunication – clerical divorce papers slapped down on the altar of the Church of Hagia Sophia. The Patriarch of Constantinople responded in kind.* Yet in following centuries, even after the savage betrayal of the Fourth Crusade, there were sporadic attempts at reconciliation. Only twenty years before Byzantium fell, on 8 February 1438, Emperor John VIII of Byzantium and Joseph II, Patriarch of the Byzantine church, had met with the Pope in Florence, accompanied by twenty bishops and some seven hundred priests, monks and lay officials. It was the biggest show of ecumenical unity for a thousand years.†

---

* The bulls were eventually rescinded. In 1965. Nine hundred and eleven years later. Well, you don't want to rush these things.

† The meeting is recorded in what is the nearest the Renaissance came to an official summit photograph: the painter Benozzo Gozzoli recorded the delegates as characters in 'The Procession of the Magi' on the walls of the Medici chapel in Florence.

Their visit had a significant impact on the development of biblical studies in the west. During the Council, a scholar called George Gemistos Plethon gave lectures on Plato and Aristotle which, according to one listener, brought the spirit of Plato from the Byzantine empire to Italy. To scholars and clerics in the west it was a whiff of the ancient east, a tantalising, spice-like scent of previously unknown literary and theological treasures.

The Council of Florence actually came to an agreement on unity, but it was to no avail. Back east, the Greek citizens furiously rejected the terms. The result was that several prominent Byzantine bishops washed their hands of the east and returned west, to live in exile in Rome. Their number included Bessarion, Metropolitan of Nicaea, who had led the pro-union clergy at the Council. In 1450 even the Patriarch of Constantinople, Gregory Melissenos, fled to Rome.

They were just the high-profile refugees. Surrounding these galleons were a flotilla of Byzantine scholars, intellectuals, tradesmen and craftsmen who had made their way into the west during the fourteenth and fifteenth centuries. Many of these emigrés arrived as penniless refugees but they had something that, in western eyes, was invaluable: they could read and write classical Greek. The Byzantines had a form of further education, where anyone over the age of fourteen could study the works of the ancient Greek poets, historians, dramatists and philosophers. Any educated Greek in the Imperial service, therefore, would have undergone this education. Many Greeks found work as tutors, translators, scribes, editors.

One centre of Greek learning was at Venice – by the late 1470s there were some four thousand Greeks in the city. They were even given a wing of the church of San Biagio in which to worship in their own language. Venice was a major centre of printing and book publishing, so it was only natural that it was there, in 1476, that the first book ever to be entirely printed in Greek was produced. It was a Greek grammar, and it enabled thousands of scholars in the West to learn the language.

Expertise wasn't the only thing the refugees carried in their luggage. They brought texts with them as well – the writings of the classical authors – poetry, drama, scientific treatises, and many theological works and codices of biblical writing; the literary remains of the

Eastern empire, to fill the libraries of the West. In 1469, the Greek scholar Bessarion presented his library of eight hundred volumes to the church of St. Mark in Venice. In the 1490s the famous printer Aldus Manutius established a Greek press in Venice and based many of his editions on this collection.

Greek was fashionable – at least among the intellectuals. The world was full of Greek geeks. This revival in the teaching of Greek was to have a profound effect on the printing of the Bible. Because the publishers printing the Bibles needed expertise. Preparing the text for printing had revealed, once again, how varied and different all those hand-written manuscripts were. A printer-editor preparing a Latin Vulgate might have to choose between different readings in two or more different manuscripts. Only one could be correct, but which one? How was he to know?

Back to the Hebrew

The study of Hebrew was also on the rise, although in the virulently anti-Semitic medieval world, reading Hebrew was suspect: as a monk in Freiburg said 'Those who speak this tongue are made Jews.' In 1506, Johan Reuchlin produced the first Hebrew grammar, *De Rudimentis Hebraicis*.* He said of the Hebrew dictionary it contained that 'before me among the Latins no one appears to have done this.'[1]

The great centre of Hebrew printing was in north Italy. The small town of Soncino near Mantua was home to a press which in 1488 printed the first complete Tanakh.† Perhaps the most influential edition was printed in 1524, when Daniel Bomberg – a Dutch printer based in Venice – employed the Jewish scholar Jacob ben Chayim to revise the Hebrew text in accordance with the best manuscripts. Chayim was a refugee from Tunisia and his introduction gives a flavour of how, at its best, this quest for knowledge could bring different faiths together. 'God sent a highly distinguished and pious

---

* Reuchlin's great, great nephew was Philip Melancthon, the reformer who taught Greek literature and the Greek New Testament at the University of Wittenberg.

† Some of the vowel points and accents were inaccurate. Revised editions were issued from 1491–1494. Probably by then the Soncino Press had moved to Naples. Martin Luther owned a 1494 Soncino Tanakh.

Christian Daniel Bomberg to meet me,' he wrote. Bomberg asked
him to 'revise the books which I print, correct the mistakes, purify
the style and examine the works till they are as refined silver and
purified gold.'[2] The resulting text was, indeed, the gold standard for
the Masoretic text. Not only was Bomberg's 1524 edition widely used
by Jews, it was used by the Reformers in preparing later translations.
Luther's copy, with his notes, is still extant.

Erasmus and the Greek New Testament

The scholars of the sixteenth century were explorers. There were
new worlds out there, new continents to be discovered. Their studies
were the prows of ships, plunging into uncharted waters. And at the
head of these expeditions, their Columbus, their Magellan, was a
scholar called Erasmus.

Erasmus was a man of his age: scholar, intellectual, satirist,
celebrity. And Greek geek *par excellence*; he even Hellenised his
name: Herasmus Gerritzoon,
the son of a lowly priest,
became Desiderius Erasmus,
international scholar. It was
a subtle piece of rebranding.

In 1506 he began a new
Latin translation of the New
Testament, working from a
fifteenth century Greek text
used by eastern churches.
Controversially, he translated
several words differently,
such as the word *ekklesia*.
Although the Latin word was
the same – *ekklesia* – it had
come to mean, specifically,
the 'church'. Erasmus,
however, used the word
congregatio – 'congregation'.[*]

Erasmus. Wearing, apparently, a turnip
on his head.

---

[*] Our word 'church' derives from a later Greek word from the third century,
kyriakon, which means the house of the Lord, the building.

In 1509, Erasmus showed examples of his work to friends in England. Some were enthusiastic, but others warned him off. So he abandoned the project.

Then he discovered that Cardinal Ximénes, a Spanish cleric, had embarked on an ambitious project to publish both the Old and New Testaments in their original languages. What's more, the work had received some kind of official approval. Erasmus decided to act. He would produce an edited edition of the Greek text with a Latin translation, and he would use, not the fifteenth century manuscript, but several earlier manuscripts which he had since found in libraries in Basle and England.

Meanwhile, in Spain, Cardinal Ximénes and his team already had their Greek New Testament ready. All it required was a Greek glossary and a bull of approval from the new Pope, Leo X, to be printed as a foreword to the book. Erasmus, however, was a friend of Leo's and he used this friendship to queue-jump the Cardinal. He not only obtained papal approval for his project, he got an agreement from Leo that he would have sole rights to publish a Greek New Testament for three years. Ximénes had been outmanoeuvred.

And so, in February 1516, the publisher Froben in Basle published the *Novum Instrumentum omne*, Erasmus' Greek New Testament with accompanying Latin translation. It was a critical edition – that means it was drawn from a variety of manuscripts. Most of these were late manuscripts, from between the twelfth and fifteenth centuries. Erasmus had toned down the accompanying Latin translation to be less controversial. He also had to do a bit of guesswork: his only manuscript of Revelation was missing the last six verses. Rather than delay the publication while he hunted down a complete Greek manuscript, Erasmus simply translated the missing verses from the Latin Vulgate back into Greek.

He revised this rather rushed first edition three years later – using more Greek manuscripts which he'd discovered in the Netherlands and Hungary. Finally, in 1527, he published a new edition, with parallel columns of Greek, Latin Vulgate and his own revised Latin text.

The book unleashed a storm of controversy. Erasmus had omitted some passages from the Vulgate which were absent from the original

Greek text; familiar passages, which for centuries had been included, were suddenly no longer the word of God. And he retranslated certain key terms, not just *congregatio*, but other passages. Especially inflammatory was his translation of Matthew 3.2, where the Vulgate text has John the Baptist crying out *poenitentiam agile* – 'make penance'. The Catholic church had built a huge edifice on the idea of 'doing penance', but Erasmus translated it as *resipiscite* – repent, 'come to your senses'.

Erasmus' Greek text gave scholars a powerful tool for creating new translations of the New Testament. The Reformers that came after him were, above all, people of the book; scholars like Erasmus, exegetes, translators, for whom reading, interpreting and

Dürer, St. Jerome in His Study, *1492. This engraving, used as a frontispiece for* The Letters of St. Jerome *published by Nikolaus Kessler in 1492, shows Jerome as the Renaissance textual critic, with the Hebrew, Greek and Latin texts open in front of him. The lion refers to a legend where Jerome removed a thorn from a lion's paw.*

translating the Scriptures was *the* primary task. This can be seen in the representations of Jerome. Medieval paintings show him as a desert monk, a haggard penitent praying in the wilderness; the Reformers show him as a scholar, a proto-textual critic, sitting in his study, surrounded by books, diligently correcting the text.

Erasmus was no Protestant. He remained a member of the Catholic church: ironically detached, maybe, but publicly supportive of traditional doctrine, committed to peaceful, reasonable compromise. But by the time he died in 1536 his teachings had been overtaken by more passionate, more furious and far less reasonable arguments.

Complutensian Polyglot

Meanwhile, in Spain, Cardinal Ximénes' Greek translation had been gathering dust. The sheets of the New Testament were printed in 1514, but first Ximénes delayed until he could finish the Old Testament, then Erasmus jumped in to claim sole rights. Ximénes might have challenged this, had he not died in July 1517.

The printed sheets, ready to be bound, just sat there for seven years, until the book was eventually published sometime between 1520 and 1522. It is known as the *Complutensian Polyglot* and it is an astonishing piece of work.* It was published in five volumes, with an extra volume containing Hebrew, Aramaic and Greek dictionaries and study aids. Each page of the Old Testament has three parallel columns of text with the Greek Septuagint, Latin Vulgate and Hebrew Tanakh. At the bottom of each page of the Torah, the printers added the Aramaic *Targum Onkelos* with its Latin translation. And above each word of the Greek text was its Latin equivalent, while each word of the Hebrew text (which, of course, ran right to left) had a small letter at its start which keyed it to the Latin text. It was the *Hexapla* of its day, and it demonstrates how far the printing industry had come in the seventy years since Gutenberg.

The *Complutensian Polyglot* was published just before the texts became weapons in the theological war between Catholic and Protestant but, even so, it betrays a vulnerability, a nervousness.

---

* *Complutensian* because the scholars created it in the Spanish city of Alcalá de Henares, which, in Latin, was called Complutum; *Polyglot* because the Bible was in four languages.

The design of the book puts Jerome's Vulgate slap bang in central position, with the Greek and Hebrew versions either side. Thus, according to the preface, are 'the synagogue and the Eastern church set like the thieves on this side and on that, with Jesus (that is, the Roman Church) in the midst.' The *Complutensian Polyglot*, then, was all about sustaining the traditional status of the Catholic church and the Vulgate. That position was going to become increasingly uncomfortable over subsequent decades.

The Canon revisited

The pioneering work of Renaissance scholarship had significant consequences. Now anyone versed in the original languages could go back to the source material for themselves – and if they were not versed in the original languages, the booksellers would happily sell them the resources they needed to learn.

The publication of the ancient texts also reignited the thousand-year old debate over the authenticity of certain books. Jacob Thomas de Vio (aka Gaetano) denied that Paul wrote Hebrews and questioned the apostolic authorship of James, Jude and 2 and 3 John. Erasmus not only agreed, he also chucked 2 Peter and Revelation into the mix. Andreas Bodenstein – a friend of Luther (at least until they argued over theology – a common fate for Luther's friends) – wrote a treatise on the canon in which he questioned the authorship of James, decided that the apostle had not written 2 and 3 John, declared that Hebrews was not written by Paul, and argued that there was little reason for including Revelation in the New Testament at all.

Erasmus' work also raised that old chestnut of the approved text. Erasmus, as we've seen, worked from several Greek manuscripts. But which were the reliable ones? In 1550, a French scholar-printer called Robert Estienne (aka Stephanus) issued an edition of the Greek New Testament which was notable for a number of important features. Estienne included variant readings from some fifteen different manuscripts – many more than had been available to Erasmus. Each manuscript was identified by a different Greek symbol. His text was so widely used that it came to be known as the *Textus Receptus*, the 'received text'. It formed the basis for many subsequent editions of the New Testament.

Estienne printed four editions of his Greek New Testament – in 1546, 1549, 1550 and 1551, but it was the final edition which, in a way, has had more influence than any of his other Bibles. Because this one featured verse references. Others had done this before, but it was Estienne's verse division which stuck; it is his verse divisions which we follow today.*

Nowadays verse numbers are ubiquitous. But we should remember that these little numbers are not in any original. Some Christians weave intricate historically worthless theories around these numbers; of the link, for example, between John 3.16 and 1 John 3.16, or of finding the 'middle verse' of the entire Bible. Jesus didn't speak in verses; Paul didn't write tiny little numbers in his letters as he went along. It was Estienne who introduced the verses, 1400 years after the originals were written.

The first three editions of Estienne's Greek New Testament were printed in Paris. But the 1551 edition, verse numbers and all, was printed in Geneva. Estienne had moved, fled France, crossed the border and settled in Geneva. Geneva was safe. Geneva was a place where a Bible printer could pursue his trade.

Geneva was Protestant.

Martin Luther and Junker Jörg

In 1521, a German monk tore the religious and political fabric of Europe apart.

His name was Martin Luther, and he'd concluded that man could only be saved by faith. Confession, penitence, absolution, prayers to the saints – none of these made any difference. Where had he found this? In the heart of the Bible of course, in Paul's letter to the Romans, a lump of dynamite, hidden in plain view. So when the cash-strapped Archbishop of Mainz tried to raise money by selling indulgences – basically documents allowing the sinner to spend less time in purgatory after death – Luther was stung into action. Where was purgatory in the Bible? How could the Pope sell time off? He drew up his famous 95 theses and posted them in protest to the Archbishop.

---

* In 1448 Rabbi Nathan divided the Tanakh into verses; the first printed edition of this was printed in Venice in 1524. In 1527 the Dominican scholar Santes Paganini printed a Latin Bible with verse references, in Lyons.

Luther is a complex character. By no means the plaster saint of Protestant hagiography, he was a foul-mouthed, dogmatic, argumentative man; but he did more than anyone else to change the face of Europe. What made Luther so potent a force is that he understood the power of the new medium of print. He knew that print could not effectively be silenced. The books of the Lollards and the Beguines had been burnt, but the mass-produced books of the age of printing could not be so

Dürer's portrait of Luther. There's that turnip again.

easily suppressed; shut a printing press in one place and another would spring up somewhere else. Luther understood that the only thing that would see a book silenced was if there was no one to buy it. So he made his books and pamphlets urgent, readable, compelling, a must-purchase. He was incredibly popular. Not including the Bible translations, over 3,700 separate editions of his books or pamphlets were published in his lifetime.

Luther also understood the non-reading public. In his books he used drawings – sharp, satirical cartoons often. Art as theological propaganda. He commissioned his friend Cranach to draw sharply polemical prints, contrasting scenes from the Bible with scenes from modern life. In one scene, Christ is shown fleeing from the Jews because they are trying to make him king, while the Pope is shown wielding a sword to protect his earthly domain. You didn't need to read to get that message.

In 1520, Luther published three incendiary books. *To the Christian Nobility of the German Nation* called on the aristocracy to reform the church; *The Babylonish Captivity of the Church* attacked the traditional teaching about the sacraments; and *Of the Liberty of a Christian Man* restated his fundamental belief in justification by faith. Their publication saw Luther summoned to a council at Worms. He refused to recant. 'The Holy Scriptures and my conscience are my Emperor', he said. 'I cannot, and will not, withdraw what I have said. God help me. Amen.'

Luther's protector was Frederick, Elector of Saxony, who was playing a dangerous game himself, using Luther to break the power of the Emperor. On the way back from the hearing Luther disappeared. Kidnapped. Missing in action.

Around the same time, a bearded gentleman moved into a simple room in Wartburg Castle. The man, who called himself Junker Jörg – Knight George – spent hours in the room, scratching away, writing. And when he wasn't there, he was down in the marketplace, listening to conversations.

Clearly Junker Jörg was up to something.

Luther's Bible

It wasn't that there weren't German Bibles already. Eight editions of the Bible in German had already been printed before Luther was born. The first vernacular Bible ever printed in Europe was Johann Mentelin's Bible, printed at Strasbourg in 1466.* But Germany was a collection of mini-states with regional dialects; there was no standard German language at the time. Luther – who had been 'kidnapped' for his own safety – virtually invented a 'mean German', a common language intelligible from Saxony in the east to the Rhineland in the west.[3] *Koiné Deutsch*, if you like. And, disguised as Junker Jörg, in his small, sparsely furnished room, he set to work.

He had three key resources. First, the 1519 edition of Erasmus' Greek New Testament. Second, a Latin version (and a couple of earlier German translations – neither of which he consulted much). Third, and perhaps most importantly, he had the marketplace. Because the really important thing about Luther's translation – the thing which set it apart from the others – was that it used the language of the people. Luther was, emphatically, a man of the streets: that was what

---

* The Bible was also printed in Italian (1471), Dutch (1477), Catalan (1478) and Czech (1488).

gave his arguments their strength, their vitality, their vulgarity. But he was good at listening as well. According to the stories, he would go out in his Junker Jörg disguise, into the markets and the streets, listening to the way in which ordinary German people spoke. He later described this process in his *Letter of Translating*

> We do not have to ask the literal Latin how we are to speak German... Rather we must ask the mother in the home, the children on the street, the common man in the marketplace. We must be guided by their language, by the way they speak, and do our translating accordingly. Then they will understand it and recognise that we are speaking German to them.[4]

Luther worked at a white-hot speed. By the end of February 1522, a mere eleven weeks, he had completed the New Testament. It was printed in conditions of the utmost secrecy. Luther's name is missing from the title page. Just the words *Das Newe Testament Deutzsch* and the place – Wittenberg.

The room in the Wartburg where Luther translated the New Testament

The first edition was published in September, probably in an edition of three thousand copies – a huge amount at the time. It flew off the shelves. Its success so alarmed Luther's enemies that Duke George the Bearded – a man who Luther, with characteristic politeness, called 'the Dresden Hog' – made purchasing the New Testament a criminal offence and offered to buy back the copies of anyone who had already purchased it. Only four people surrendered their copies. A second edition followed in December, with some corrections: over the course of his life, Luther oversaw a further fifteen corrected editions. Johannes Cochlaeus, who had the job of stopping this phenomenon, lamented that

> Even tailors and cobblers, even women and other simple folk who had only learnt to read a little German in their lives, were reading it with great enthusiasm as though it were the fount of all truth, while others carried it around, pressed to their bosom, and learned it by heart.'[5]

Heavens. People learning the Bible. Whatever next.

Luther's command of the vernacular was one reason for its success. Another was the price. The price of a bound copy was between ½ and 1½ gulden, depending on the binding. 1 gulden was the cost of a pig ready for slaughter, so these were much more affordable books. Not cheap, perhaps, but as cheap as possible.[6] And one per cent of what a Gutenberg Bible had cost.

Then there was the design. It was the first Bible printed in single columns, making it much more readable (not to mention allowing Luther room to add many marginal notes). It had illustrations by Lucas Cranach which are as satirically polemic as you'd expect: in the picture of the fall of Babylon, the buildings shown collapsing are taken almost directly from the woodcut of Rome in the Nuremberg Chronicle. The portrait of the whore of Babylon shows her wearing the three-tiered papal crown.*

His enemies complained that he had added words to Scripture, specifically, that he added the word 'alone' to Romans 3.28, as in 'we are justified by faith *alone*'. Luther responded with an explosion

---

* Even some of Luther's supporters felt this was taking things a bit too far. In later editions, the crown was reduced to a single tier.

*A page from Luther's 1522
New Testament*

of abuse. His critics were 'brazen idiots… like Dr. Schmidt and Dr. Snot-Nose', but the truth was that he *had* added it. He justified this addition to the text on the grounds of it being a typically German way of expressing things, but it's not a convincing argument – in the end he resorts to just telling them 'Luther will have it so, and he says that he is a doctor above all the doctors of the Pope.' So there.

He went onto complain that 'everyone's a critic'

It was also like this for St. Jerome when he translated the Bible. Everybody was his master. He alone was totally incompetent, and people who were not worthy to clean his boots judged the good man's work. It takes a great deal of patience to do good things in public. The world believes itself to be the expert in everything, while putting the bit under the horse's tail. Criticizing everything and accomplishing nothing, that is the world's nature. It can do nothing else.

Or, 'Come and have a go, if you think you're scholarly enough.'

Luther and the canon

Luther may have declared *sola scriptura*, but he thought some *scriptura* more *scriptura* than others. He grouped the New Testament books into three categories:

1. Books which taught all you need to know about salvation, 'even if you were never to see or hear any other book or doctrine': John, 1 John, Romans, Galatians, Ephesians and 1 Peter.

2. The Synoptic gospels, the other Pauline epistles, Acts, 2 Peter and 2 and 3 John.

3. Doubtful books – Hebrews, James, Jude and Revelation.

He placed the last group of books at the end of his translation, an order which was followed by Tyndale, and by other English translations up to the Great Bible – the first really authorised edition – which returned the books to their pre-Lutheran order.[7] His doubts about these books is reflected in the table of contents: the first 23 books are numbered, then a blank space, then we have Hebrews, James, Jude and Revelation, all without numbers.

His reasons for these concerns were theological more than textual. He disliked Hebrews because it taught that there could be no repentance after baptism; he called James 'a right strawy epistle compared with the others' because of its emphasis on works; he thought Jude too reliant on 2 Peter and disliked Revelation intensely.* 'Whatever does not teach Christ is not apostolic, even though St. Peter or St. Paul does the teaching' he wrote.[8] And, of course, it was Luther who decided what did or didn't teach Christ.

In subsequent decades, disciples of Luther printed editions which reflected Luther's 'canon', most notably Jacob Lucius, who published

---

* He was later to revise his opinion of Revelation when he realised that the whole thing was really about the Catholic church. Once he'd identified the Pope as the Antichrist, he was a big fan.

a Bible at Hamburg in which the four disputed books were grouped under the title 'Apocrypha... That is, books that are not held equal to the other Holy Scripture.' For nearly a century after Luther, various Reformed Bibles continued to use his labels and follow his opinions.[9] (Not so the Genevan Reformers, who followed the traditional order of the New Testament.)

Luther secretly returned to Wittenberg on 6 March 1522. Once there, he began on the rest of the Bible. Using a 1494 edition of the Vulgate and a Hebrew Bible published in 1488, he published the books in sections: the Law in 1523, Samuel, Kings and Chronicles in 1524, the Prophets after a gap of ten years.

Compared with his sprint through the New Testament, the work on the Old Testament was sheer hard slog. At the time Luther had not descended into the rampant anti-Semitism that was to blight his later years, and he was helped in his work by the Jewish scholar, Matthäus Aurogallus. Yet even with such help and advice, it was hard going. 'Dear God it is such hard work and so difficult to make the Hebrew writers speak German!' he complained.[10] Later he was to grumble that his efforts were unappreciated. 'Ploughing is easy once the obstacles have been removed. But nobody wants to remove the trees and the stumps and prepare the ground. There is no gratitude in the world...' [11]

But his work on the Old Testament also made him realise – as Jerome had – that the Apocryphal Books were not part of the Hebrew Scriptures. There were arguments among various Protestant groups as to whether the Apocrypha should be included or not. Luther kept them in his Bible but he was by no means convinced about them.

Münster

The authorities had always feared what the Bible would do if ordinary people could read it. And they were right to be fearful. For the Reformation not only brought about theological and religious conflict, it led to political violence, fanaticism and rebellion. Luther had defied ecclesiastical authority; now others indulged in different forms of defiance.

There had been sporadic outbreaks of unrest throughout the fourteenth and fifteenth centuries, but the Peasants' War of 1524 onwards was specifically informed by their reading of the Bible. The *Twelve Articles of the Peasants,* written in March 1525 by Sebastian Lotzer, a tanner, and Christoph Schappeler, a Protestant pastor, not only called for the reform of rents, taxes and servitude, but also for the reform of the church, including the removal of pictures and images, the preaching of the 'pure' gospel, and the right to elect the parish priest.[12] It begins with the gospel

> First, the gospel is not a cause of rebellions or insurrections because it speaks of Christ the promised Messiah, whose words and life teach nothing but love, peace, patience and unity, so that all who believe in Christ become loving, peaceful, patient and united.

It's peppered with Bible references and phrases

> Third, until now it has been the custom for us to be regarded as a lord's personal property, which is deplorable, since Christ redeemed all of us with the shedding of his precious blood, the shepherd as well as the most highly placed, without exception. Thus, Scripture establishes that we are and will be free.[13]

The peasants looked to Luther for support but, although he sympathised with some of their concerns, he condemned their rebellion, arguing that the Bible clearly supported slavery – after all, didn't the patriarchs of the Old Testament have slaves? Didn't Paul tell slaves to be obedient? Then, when the violence started to rise, when things started to get bloody, Luther abandoned them to their fate. In a typically polemical tract, *Against the Robbing and Murdering Hordes of Peasants,* he declared that anyone who killed a rebellious peasant was doing God's will.

Over one hundred thousand peasants were slaughtered in 1525.

Luther was out of his depth. He wanted reformation, not revolt. Like so many church leaders, he thought that people should read the Bible in order to agree with him. But those who affirm the priesthood of all believers can't complain when the believers start to act like priests. Those who claim that Christ sets us free should not be surprised when people want that freedom to mean something.

As he got old and sick, Luther lashed out in pain. His later tracts, particularly the notorious *On the Jews and Their Lies* which advocated banning all rabbinic teaching, burning Jewish homes and synagogues and expelling from Germany all Jews who would not convert, were to reap a bitter harvest.

And then there was Münster.

From Revelation to revolution

The extreme radicals were radical because of the Bible. As they studied it for themselves, they realised that a lot of what they'd been told was in the Bible wasn't there at all. Nowhere, for example, was the Trinity explicitly stated. Jesus was utterly opposed to violence and war. And the Bible said nothing about church rites such as infant baptism.

So radical sects grew up who tried to follow exactly what Jesus said. They were pacifists. They started re-baptising people, for which they were given, as so often happens, a mocking nickname: the rebaptisers, or in mock-Greek, the Anabaptists. The Anabaptists were bitterly persecuted – by Protestants as well as Catholics. In 1526, the Protestant city leaders of Zurich had four Anabaptists drowned in the River Limmat. Harried, chased, exiled, they became a kind of Protestant underground. In Moravia, Joseph Hutter founded what would eventually become the Bruderhof; the Dutch Anabaptist Menno Simons started a community which became the Mennonites. These were people who based their lives on what they read in the Gospels and Acts. Most Anabaptists tried to live quiet, inoffensive lives, building small communities and practising a Christian communism.

Some of the more radical sects headed straight to the end of the Bible, to that ultimate book of the outsider: Revelation. It was clear, to them, that the end times were coming. In the German city of Münster, a former Lutheran pastor called Berni Rothman preached the imminent second coming of Christ, and that Münster would be the new Jerusalem. The city soon became a nexus for all sorts of disenfranchised, extreme Anabaptist groups. Jan Matthys replaced Rothman as leader and urged a violent revolution. His fellow leader, the dangerously unbalanced Jan Beuckelszoon (aka Jan of Leyden)

took things even further. He banned all books
except the Bible. You want *sola scriptura*, you got
it. The situation descended into chaos. The forces
of the Bishop of Münster and his troops blockaded
the city. The food ran out. Anarchy. Jan of Leyden
declared himself the new Messiah, the successor to
King David, playing out the life of an Old Testament
king, practising polygamy and living in luxury,
while all around him the people starved and their
fevered dreams died.

There could only be one outcome. In 1536
the city was captured; the new Jerusalem was
brutally and sadistically crushed; its leaders
tortured and executed and their bodies hung
in cages from the tower of the city church.

You can still see the cages
there today.

The Church responds...

When he retired in 1572, the
Wittenberg printer Hans Lufft
had printed some one hundred
thousand copies of Luther's
translation of the Bible.[14] There
were also reprints in Basle and
Augsburg and elsewhere. The
influence of Luther's Bible
was immense. Just a year after
the publication of his New
Testament, a Dutch translation
was in print. The following year
there was a Danish version, and
in 1526 a Swedish one. There
were Hungarian, Lithuanian,
Polish, Romanian, Bohemian,
Slovenian, even Icelandic
translations.

The punishment of the Münster rebels.

In 1523 an anonymous French version of the New Testament was published. It was actually the work of Jacque Le Fèvre d'Étaples, a Catholic and friend of Erasmus. He followed it with the complete French Bible in 1530, the title page of which was concerned to reassure people that his work which was translated 'in accordance with the pure and complete tradition of Saint Jerome'.[15] The version became the basis for the Louvain Bible of 1550, which was to become the standard vernacular edition for Catholic France.

But before that, in 1535, a Protestant version was published in Geneva, the work of Pierre Robert Olivetan, a relative of Calvin. This claimed to be based on the Greek and the Hebrew, but it was actually based largely on Le Fèvre's Catholic version. And then, Olivetan's version was used as the basis for the revisions which created the Louvain Bible. So there is a criss-crossing of influences, Catholic and Protestant, each relying on the other, and each claiming to be better than the other. Olivetan's version was revised by Calvin, Beza and others at Geneva and the edition of 1588 became the standard French Protestant Bible.

The Louvain Bible shows that the issue for the Catholic church was not about the language, but about tradition and authority. Defending the Vulgate – the traditional version – was paramount. And authority: in Italy, for example, an official Italian version was done in 1471 by a Venetian monk called Niccolo Malermi. His translation, which received official approval from the Inquisition, remained in print until 1567. An unauthorised 1530 Italian version by Antonio Brucioli, based on Greek and Hebrew, was placed on the Papal Index of banned books in 1559.

The Vulgate must be defended at all costs. At the Council of Trent in 1546 – 1150 years after he'd written it – Jerome's version finally gained the stamp of approval and it was finally established that the Vulgate was the official, approved, authorised Latin edition. However, even the Catholic authorities admitted that the Vulgate was in a bit of a mess. So, the Council ordered a complete revision – one more attempt to establish an official, authorised text.

The revision proved an enormously difficult job: so difficult, that forty years after the proclamation, it still hadn't been completed. Then, in a decision which he must have deeply regretted, Pope Sixtus

V decided that if you want a job doing, you'd better do it yourself. He set to work. His version was released in 1589. Sadly it was such an error-strewn, sloppy piece of work that it was withdrawn in embarrassment a few months later (after the Pope died.) It was the first Bible to be issued with a product recall.

It wasn't until 1592 that the corrections and amendments were made and the official version finally approved. And it is this version, the Sixto-Clementine as it is known (named after the unfortunate Sixtus V and his successor Clementine VIII) that became the standard edition of the Vulgate from then on.

Sweeter than honey

Meanwhile the Bible continued to make its way into the vernacular languages of Europe. How hard the church came down on those who dared to produce an unauthorised translation seems to vary geographically.

In Spain, for example, the Inquisition turned on Protestants with a vengeance. In 1543 Francisco de Enzinas, a young Spanish student living in Wittenberg, translated the New Testament into Spanish. Enzinas dedicated it to the Spanish Emperor Charles V. Charles V, hearing that a Spanish edition was in preparation, ordered its suppression. Nothing daunted, a few days later Enzinas sought an audience with the emperor and handed him a copy. The emperor agreed to sanction the translation providing his spiritual advisors approved it. This was never going to happen. The copy was examined by de Solo, the emperor's confessor, who immediately had Enzinas arrested. Enzinas escaped a year later, eventually making his way to England, where he ended up professor of Greek at Cambridge.

In 1551, the first index of banned books issued by the Inquisition forbade any translation of the Bible into Castilian or any other Spanish vernacular. So when a revised edition of the Spanish New Testament was produced at Geneva by Juan Perez di Pinedo, they used a false imprint – the printer was 'Juan Philadelpho' and the location given was Venice. This and many other Protestant books were smuggled into Spain. In 1557, one Julian Hernandez filled two great barrels with copies of Perez' New Testament and a Spanish Psalter, and landed them at Seville. He was later executed for his activities.

It was an escapee from the Inquisition who first translated the complete Bible into Spanish. Cassiodoro de Reina was a monk who converted to Protestantism in the late 1550s. Initially he worked in London, but he was under constant harassment, and he was accused of heresy and homosexuality and anything else his critics could throw at him. The Inquisition burned him in effigy in 1562. Seven years later his Bible – the first Spanish Bible translated from the Hebrew and Greek – was published in Basle.[*] It had a picture of a bear tasting honey on the title page – the emblem of the Bavarian printer Mattias Apiarius, 'the bee-keeper'. The Bible became known as *Biblia del Oso* – the 'Bible of the Bear'.

'How sweet are your words to my taste,' says Psalm 119, 'sweeter than honey to my mouth!' By then all Europe was tasting the Bible, bear-like, snouts in the sweetness of Scripture.

Even England.

*The engraving from the title
page of the Biblia del Oso*

[*] Portugal had to wait a century longer for its first New Testament and the whole Bible was not available in Portuguese until 1719. But for sheer delays, nothing can beat the New Testament in Basque, which was written in 1571 but not published till 1900, 329 years later. That is one lengthy editing job.

The woman seduced.   Genesis.   2

23 Then the man said, *This now is bone of my bones, and flesh of my flesh. She shalbe called 'woman, because she was taken out of man.

24 *Therefore shal man leaue ? his father and his mother, and shal cleaue to his wife, and they shalbe one flesh.

25 And they were bothe naked, the man & his wife, and were not ? ashamed.

THE SITVACION OF THE GARDEN OF EDEN.

Because mencion is made in the tenth verse of this seconde chapter of the riuer that watered the garden, we muste note that Euphrates and Tygris called in Ebrewe, Perath and Hiddékel, were called but one riuer where they ioyned together, als they had foure heades: that is, two as their springs, & two where they fel into the Persian sea. In this countrey and moste plentiful land, Adam dwelt, and this was called ' Paradise: that is, a garden of pleasure, because of the frutefulnes and abundance thereof. And whereas it is said that Pishon compasseth the land of Hauilah, it is meant of Tygris, which in some place, as it passed by diuers places, was called by sundry names, as some time Diglito, in other places Pasitygris, & of some Phasin or Tison. Likewise Euphrates towarde the countrey of Cush or Ethiopia, or Arabia was called Gihon. So that Tygris and Euphrates (which were but two riuers, And some time when they ioyned together, were called after one name) were according to diuers places called by these foure names, so that they might seme to haue bene foure diuers riuers.

CHAP. III.

1 The woman seduced by the serpet, 6 Entiseth her housbãd to sinne. 14 They thre are punished. 15 Christ is promised. 19 Man is dust. 22 Man is cast out of paradise.

1 NOw *the serpent was more ᵃ subtil then anie beast of the field, which ý Lord God had made: and he ᵇ said to the woman, Yea, hathe God in dede said, Ye shal not eat of euerie tre of the garden?

2 And the woman said vnto the serpet, We eat of the frute of the trees of the garden,

3 But of the frute of the tre, which is in the middes of the garden, God hathe said, Ye shal not eat of it, nether shal ye touche it, ᶜ lest ye dye.

4 Then *the serpent said to the woman, Ye shal not ᵈ dye at all,

5 But God doeth knowe, that when ye shal eat thereof, your eyes shalbe opened, & ye shalbe as gods, ᵉ knowing good and euil.

6 So the woman (seing that the tre was good for meat, and that it was pleasant to the eyes, & a tre to be desired to get knowledge) toke of the frute thereof, and did ⁱ eat, and gaue also to her housband with her, and he ᶠ did eat.

7 Then the eyes of them bothe were opened, & they ᵍ knewe that they were naked, and they sewed figtre leaues together, and made them selues ʰ breeches.

8 ¶ Afterwarde they heard the voyce of

a.ii.

PART THREE: THE ENGLISH BIBLE

THE ENGLISH BIBLE

The sleepy Cotswold town of Burford is not a place that one associates with danger and protest. Yet, spend a few hours there and you can see much of the history of the English Bible – and the battles it engendered – written on the walls of the buildings. The town is a kind of book itself, a little tale, a diary, an observation of the progress of the Protestant ideas, official and unofficial.

Start inside the church. On a wall in a side chapel there is some old, black-letter writing. It is hard to decipher, but it consists of two quotes from the Bible – the work of two of the greatest of the English Bible translators. One is from Romans 13.12–14, in William Tyndale's translation

The writing on the wall in Burford church

The nyght is passed and the daye is come nye. Let us therfore cast awaye the dedes of darcknes and let vs put on the (Armoure) of lyght. Let vs walke honestly as it were in the daye lyght: not in eatynge and drinkynge: nether in chamburynge and wantannes: nether in stryfe and envyinge: but put ye on the Lorde Iesus Christ. And make not provision for the flesshe to fulfyll ye lustes of it.

The other is the work of Miles Coverdale. It is taken from a book in the Apocrypha – Ecclesiasticus 14.19

> All transytory thynges shall fayle at the last & the workere thereof shall go withall.

The writing is big, overt, triumphant; the texts favourites of the Reformers. Clearly Burford supported the Protestant cause. The lettering was done between 1550, when the old stone altars were being removed from the churches, and 1553 when Mary tried to take the country back to Catholicism.

By that time Tyndale was dead and Coverdale was in Europe, on the run. And both of these events were intrinsically tied to the English Bible.

The danger of reading

With the spread of print came a widespread suspicion of the act of private reading. The Catholic church engaged in what has been called a 'demonising of reading'. In Venice, in the late sixteenth century, a silk worker was denounced to the Inquisition because, it was said, 'he reads all the time.' A swordsmith who 'stays up all night reading' was arrested.[1] Reading was dangerous. Books were carriers; infected, contagious with ideas, plague-ridden with revolution. Keep them shut. Chain the books up again.

Women, particularly, were vulnerable. Some men believed that women should not learn to read at all in case they received love letters. Others wanted women's reading heavily restricted, lest they get too over-excited. This is one reason why pictures of the Virgin Mary reading – which were relatively common in the Middle Ages – largely disappear after 1520. Reading was not a respectable habit, even for the mother of Jesus.

And in England groups of people reading together could only be up to no good. Because wasn't that what the Lollards tried to do? The legislation of 1407, banning the making of English Bibles, was still in force. In principle that allowed for an authorised translation to be made but the last thing the authorities wanted was for the Bible to be opened up to the lower classes. Henry Knighton complained that the translations of the Lollards meant that 'the pearl of the gospel is scattered abroad and trodden underfoot of swine, and what is wont to be the treasure of both clerks and laymen is now become the jest of both.'[2] Thomas More argued that if you were to put the Bible into English it would be treated 'presumptuously and unreverently at meat and at meal.'[3]

But the real fear was not that the people in the taverns would mock the Bible; the real fear was that they would take it seriously. This was a prospect which horrified Henry VIII. Henry, who had come to the throne in 1509, was a staunch Catholic. He wrote a book attacking Luther's ideas, a book which inspired Pope Leo X to call him *Fidei defensor* – 'Defender of the Faith'.[*] When it came to Bible translation, Thomas More – one of Henry's Chancellors – argued speciously that there was no point in translating the Bible because not enough people could read. This was patently a lie. Publishers routinely published ballads and manuals aimed at a working class artisan audience and, more to the point, numerous heresy trials of the time show that ordinary people could read enough to get them into trouble.

The idea of an English version of the Bible was inherently bound up with Lollardry. Searches for Lollard books continued throughout the fifteenth century. In 1476 the University of Oxford told King Edward IV that they had discovered and burnt some texts during a search for Wycliffite material. In 1523, the year after Luther reignited the whole debate, Archbishop Tunstall was still muttering about 'Wycliffite heresies'.[4]

Lollardry had always been strong in the Thames Valley, out west in the rich sheep farming lands of the Cotswolds. In our 'sample' town of Burford, for example, charges of Lollardry were made against several citizens in 1521. John Longland, Bishop of Lincoln was on an inquisitorial tour; pest control, eradication of unhealthy belief. In Burford, fifteen men and women were accused of a variety of

---

[*] The book was *Assertio septem Sacramentorum adversus Martin Lutherum.* It is probable that Henry didn't write every word himself. Thomas More had the job of 'a sorter-out and placer of the principal matters contained therein.' Luther immediately struck back and, in typically restrained manner, called the king a pig, a dolt and a liar, who deserved to be covered in excrement. Theological debate was a bit more robust in those days.

offences, including reading forbidden books, reading and reciting the Scriptures in English, discussing biblical themes and ideas and speaking against pilgrimages and the adoration of saints. The ringleader was one John Edmunds, a tailor, in whose house the group met. He suggested that instead of going on pilgrimage, people should offer their money to the image of God: 'the poor people, blind and lame.' The group had even been visited by a dealer in contraband texts and ideas, one John Hakker from London.*

For these offences they were punished: they were branded on the cheek, and forced to march around the town carrying a faggot of wood – a reminder that they could have been burned at the stake had the bishop not been merciful. A hard mercy, though. Tough love. Because after this they were incarcerated, committed as prisoners to a monastery or abbey, there to serve life sentences of perpetual penance, effectively slaves of a religious institution, usually far from their homes. Such was the fate awaiting all those who dared to take the Bible into their own hands. Imprisonment among the monks. Burnt with red-hot irons. Reading the Scriptures in English could leave you scarred for life.

This fear of revolution runs deep in the English government's response to the Reformation. Henry never lost his paranoia about the printed word. In his final speech to Parliament, he moaned that the precious jewel of the Bible was 'disputed, rhymed, sung and jangled in every alehouse and tavern.'[5] In July 1546, just a few months before his death, Henry banned all unofficial versions of the New Testament and any works by certain authors, especially Wycliffe, and the Bible translators Tyndale and Coverdale.[6]

The soundtrack to Henry's statement should be the sound of stable doors and bolting horses. For by the time of his death, Tyndale and Coverdale's work was to be found on the lectern of every church in England.

---

* Hakker, or Hacker, alias Ebb, was 'a great reader and teacher' in Lollard circles. He was known as 'Old Father Hacker' and had links into the Lollard underground. He was arrested in 1527 and 'so hard set upon' that he revealed the network of forty-eight other Lollards with whom he was in contact. By then he was working mainly in Essex.

William Tyndale

William Tyndale is one of the greatest figures in English history. You won't find him taught much at school. You'll hardly, indeed, find him mentioned in church. You won't find his face on stamps or bank notes.* And yet he has had a greater impact on British Christianity than any mitred archbishop, or miracle-working saint; and a greater effect on the English language than any other writer – more even than Shakespeare.

He was born in Gloucestershire and, after studying at Oxford, went to work as a tutor and chaplain in the house of Sir John Walsh at the charmingly named Little Sodbury. It was around this time that, hearing of Luther's New Testament, he conceived the idea of translating the Bible into English. According to one story, his increasingly radical views led him into a dispute with a local cleric who believed that the tradition of the church was more important than the law of Scripture: 'We were better to be without God's laws than the Pope's.' Tyndale was outraged. 'If God spare him life,' he said, 'ere many years he would cause the boy that driveth the plough to know more of Scripture than he [the cleric] did.'

God did not spare Tyndale's life for long. But long enough. Long enough.

He went to London where, naively, he approached John Colet, the Bishop of London, for help. Colet refused to have anything to do with the idea and Tyndale was forced to work alone on his project. After some months working on his translation, his ambitions were discovered and he was forced to flee the country. He went first to Germany, to Wittenberg, home of Martin Luther. Within a year, using Erasmus' Greek version, he had succeeded in translating the New Testament. The Tyndale New Testament was fresh, vibrant, new. Whereas the Lollard Bibles used the Vulgate, Tyndale went back to the Greek. The title page ran: 'The new Testament diligently corrected and compared with the Greek by William Tyndale.' Not, then, a Lollard book. Far more dangerous than that.

Tyndale moved to Cologne, where he'd heard that there would be printers willing to print his book. The Cologne printers had connections as well; warehouses in St Paul's churchyard, the centre

---

* Perhaps it's just as well. He was not what you'd call 'conventionally attractive'.

of London's book trade. But one of the printers involved let slip a remark in a tavern: that they were printing a book which would make England Lutheran. The local magistrates raided the printing house and Tyndale was forced to make a hasty exit to Worms, carrying those sheets which had been printed with him.* When he arrived in Worms he started on new editions.

William Tyndale by an unknown artist

Tyndale was a truly great translator. It was not just that he had a good grasp of Latin, Greek and Hebrew – many men had that; it was that he had a genius for English. His writing ripples with vigour and energy. Many phrases still in use come from Tyndale's words: 'lead us not into temptation but deliver us from evil,' 'a law unto themselves,' 'knock and it shall be opened unto you,' 'the apple of his eye,' 'a land of milk and honey,' 'let there be light,' 'the powers that be,' 'the salt of the earth' and many more come direct from Tyndale's translation.

The book, unlike Luther's editions, was small – pocket-sized. You could carry this around easily. You could hide it. And you could smuggle it into England.

And that's what happened. Finally, in 1526, the work was ready for shipping. It made its way, hidden in barrels, behind timber, in bales of cloth, by way of Antwerp and Rotterdam, to the Hanseatic merchants; then it was stored in London. One of the main distribution hubs was in Honey Lane, a narrow road adjoining Cheapside near to the old Church of All Hallows. Copies were available on the black market for nine pence each. Another hub was the house of a man with the appropriately biblical name of Simon Fish, 'dwelling by the

---

* Only 31 pages of that original edition survive. They are in the British Library.

Whitefriars in London' who was a wholesaler of heresy. He provided multiple copies of Tyndale's work to interested parties. At one point he was linked with the purchase of two hundred copies, brought in by a 'Duche man'.[7]

Despite the best efforts of the authorities, it was an underground success. Copies even made their way up the Thames to Oxfordshire, swimming like salmon towards Gloucestershire, where Tyndale had been born. In Burford in 1530, one Simon Wisdom was charged with possessing some of the Scriptures in English – either in whole or part. Wisdom was no peasant radical, he was a wealthy merchant. Several buildings in the town bear his mark and he was rich enough to found a school and endow some almshouses. Burford, once again, was a barometer of dissent.

The 'best efforts' of the authorities were quite remarkably stupid at times. On the orders of Bishop Tunstall, a merchant in Antwerp called Augustine Packington bought up one entire edition of the 1526 New Testament in order to burn it. Tyndale was delighted. Not only were all his debts paid off, but he had enough money to print a second, corrected edition. And the people were not happy with the idea of the Bible being burned. The first burning took place in October 1526, at Saint Paul's Cross, London. Those witnessing the biblioclasm muttered that the book 'was not only faultless, but also very well translated'. They thought that it was burned to stop people discovering the shocking truth: that there was nothing wrong in it.[8] Burning manuscripts; this was medieval thinking. One gets the feeling that neither Packington nor the Bishop of London had quite grasped the principles of either PR or the book trade.

Even so, Tyndale was condemned as a heretic and went into hiding. While on the run, he learned Hebrew so that he could start on the Old Testament. He published a copy of the English Torah in Antwerp in 1530, probably with the help of his assistant Miles Coverdale. He started work on the rest of the Bible, and also wrote some polemical tracts. In 1530 he wrote *The Practyse of Prelates*, which opposed Henry VIII's divorce on the grounds that it was unscriptural. If Tyndale could have supported the King's action, he might have been able to return to England when Henry broke with the Catholic church. But he could not betray his principles, and Henry became an enemy for life.

 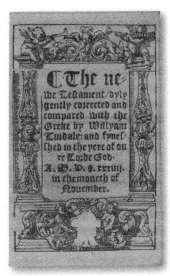

Left: a page from the Cologne New Testament, printed in 1525.
Right: the title page from Tyndale's 1534 revised New Testament

He was not the only one. The most vehement opponent of Tyndale was Thomas More. More is a saint, canonised by the pope in 1935 and also celebrated in the Anglican calendar of saints and heroes of the Christian church. Which is curious, because More spent much of his time trying to suppress every copy of the English Bible and to burn anyone who had a hand in it.

More pursued heretics with a murderous zeal. When he was appointed Chancellor there had been no burnings at the stake in England for eight years.[9] The policy changed. The first victim was Thomas Hitton, a priest who had spent some time with Tyndale in the Low Countries and who had come to England to arrange distribution for Tyndale's work. He was seized near Gravesend, and found to be in possession of incriminating letters. He was burnt at the stake at Maidstone on 23 February, 1530. In 1531, Richard Bayfield, a graduate of the University of Cambridge and former Benedictine monk, was burned at Smithfield for distributing copies of Tyndale's English translation of the New Testament. In 1532 John Bainham was condemned for distributing books by Luther and Tyndale. Broken under torture, he initially recanted, but a few months later he wrote a public letter to the Bishop of London, renouncing his retractions. He then walked into church clutching two banned works by Tyndale. For this flagrant act of disobedience, he was arrested and burned at Smithfield in April 1532.

More's argument was not with the *idea* of an English translation – although he believed that if there were such a thing, only bishops should be allowed to buy it, and they could only lend it to trustworthy clerics. In More's eyes, he was not burning the word of God, but a faulty translation filled with heretical opinions. More's biggest complaint was a familiar one – that Tyndale had translated *ekklesia* as 'congregation'. When Tyndale pointed out that Erasmus – More's great friend – had done the same, More replied that the difference was one of intent: Erasmus was interested in scholarship, Tyndale was clearly bound on sedition.

Tyndale was brimming with seditious ideas. He believed that God commanded us to love the Turks and we should try to convert them – which might make soldiers unwilling to go to war against the Turks. He disagreed with the death penalty for theft. He disagreed with putting heretics to death.* Above all, Tyndale argued that God's law was superior to the authority of kings: if the king ordered something contrary to God's law, then the king should be disobeyed. In an argument that was going to come back and bite him, More argued that those who refused to obey the king because of their private consciences were, by their very nature, seditious.†

More was never to get his man. In a strange mirror-image, Thomas More – the man who argued that Tyndale was seditious because he put his conscience above the king – did exactly the same thing. In 1533 Henry VIII had married Anne Boleyn and split from Rome. When required to swear an oath to uphold the break with Rome, More refused. On the morning of 6 July 1535 More was executed.

---

* More pointed out that where Lutherans were in power, they were putting those they consdiered to be heretics to death.

† The scale of More's hatred of Tyndale can be seen in the size of the book containing these arguments: his *Confutation of Tyndale's Answer* was nearly half a million words long, five times as long as *Tyndale's Answer unto Sir Thomas More*, the book which had given rise to it.

In words that could have come straight from Tyndale, he told the assembled crowd that he was the king's servant, but God's first.*

Not that this helped Tyndale. In 1535, Tyndale's enemies caught up with him. A fanatical Englishman called Henry Phillips betrayed Tyndale to the Antwerp authorities. The Low Countries were ruled at the time by the Spanish, who had no truck with Protestants. Tyndale was imprisoned in the castle of Vilvoorde near Brussels. From his cell he wrote of his loneliness

> I ask to have a lamp in the evening; it is indeed wearisome sitting alone in the dark. Most of all I beg and beseech Your Clemency to urge the Commissary that he will kindly permit me to have the Hebrew Bible, Hebrew grammar and Hebrew dictionary, that I may pass the time in that study.

The work had not been completed. The Old Testament needed translating. Although Thomas Cromwell made moves to get him released, Tyndale was condemned for heresy and, in 1536, he was burned at the stake. As an act of mercy and in light of his fame, he was allowed to be strangled at the stake before the flames were lit. His last words, according to *Foxe's Book of Martyrs,* were a prayer for Henry VIII, that his eyes would be opened.

But Henry's eyes were already open. One year after Tyndale's death, two printing shops in London issued copies of the English Bible. In 1539, the first officially sanctioned English Bible was published, with a picture of the king in the frontispiece.

And much of the text in that Bible – and all of the New Testament – was the work of William Tyndale.

Miles Coverdale

When Henry VIII broke from Rome it was expected that there would be an English version of the Bible. But Henry remained silent on the matter. The most significant influence was Anne Boleyn, the king's passion. Anne was an intelligent, learned and highly committed

---

* Thomas More lied to Parliament, lied to the public and was involved in acts of torture, and sent people to their deaths. He's also the patron saint of politicians and statesmen. Really, you couldn't make it up.

Above: The death of Tyndale, from Foxe's Book of Martyrs. *Right: the Tyndale Monument, in Vilvoorde, near Brussels.*

Protestant and she supported the idea of the English Bible. More support came from Henry's henchmen Cranmer and Cromwell – although they were more concerned with promoting a translation without Tyndale's Lutheran bias. Finally, in 1534, the Bishops petitioned the king for an English Bible, and Henry agreed.

The opportunity was grabbed by Miles Coverdale who had been Tyndale's assistant in Antwerp but who had escaped arrest. In 1535, while Tyndale languished in a Vilvoorde dungeon, Coverdale published the first complete Bible in English. The text was constructed from Tyndale's work, with the rest newly translated from various Latin versions and Luther's Old Testament. It was printed in Cologne and, astutely, Coverdale removed Tyndale's 'seditious' marginal notes and opened the book with a flattering dedication to Henry VIII, suggesting that reading the Bible would make people better subjects both to God and king.[10] This version is known as the Coverdale Bible.

Coverdale was a kind of one-man Bible industry in Reformation times. He not only worked on the eponymous Coverdale Bible, he also edited the Great Bible and then helped prepare the Geneva Bible, while on the run in Europe. He also issued editions of the Psalms and Latin/English versions. Indeed, his translation of the Psalms is still the one in use in Anglican liturgy today.

Matthew's Bible

The tide, apparently, had turned. In 1537 another new Bible appeared. It is known as the Matthew's Bible, after its supposed translator, one 'Thomas Matthew'. But Thomas Matthew didn't exist; he was a cypher, a pseudonym. Instead, the Bible was probably the work of a man called John Rogers. He compiled it using Tyndale's Torah and New Testament and some new material of Tyndale's (Joshua – 2 Chronicles). What was missing, he filled in from Coverdale's version. Anne Boleyn had a copy of this Bible.

But still a pseudonym, still nervousness, anxiety about the English vernacular versions. Henry had given them his tacit approval, but the king was not known for his consistency. John Rogers knew that the activity could get him into trouble. (As, indeed, it eventually did.) Better keep low. Hide away. Wear the clothes of Thomas Matthew.

'Set forth with the kinges most gracyous lyce[n]ce. But even so, John Rogers used a pseudonym.

The Great Bible

These versions were all very well, but they were still freelance, unauthorised. What England needed, it was decided, was an official version. A royal Bible. So, in 1538, Thomas Cromwell and Archbishop Cranmer – mouthpieces of the King – ordered the production of 'one book of the whole bible of the largest volume in English'. Copy deadline: Christmas 1538.

Coverdale, that great survivor, was appointed editor, and he used Matthew's rather than his own version, as a basis.

Known as the 'Great Bible' because of its size, the Bible was published in 1539 and was the first to appear with a royal stamp of approval. Since, by law, every church had to buy a copy, this Bible made a lot of money. Specifically it made Cromwell a lot of money, since a royal proclamation of 14 November 1539 gave him the exclusive printing rights to this Bible for the next five years. He didn't live to profit from it – he was executed in 1540 and his coat of arms removed from subsequent editions.[*] Bible printing was to remain a Crown-controlled monopoly for centuries. Elizabeth I renewed the privilege

---

[*] His death forced Coverdale into exile, since Cromwell had been his protector. Coverdale returned to England in 1548, only to flee again on the accession of Mary in 1553. He never had an easy life.

and conferred it on the Royal printers and the Universities of Oxford and Cambridge.*

One look at the title page tells you all you need to know about the Great Bible. Where Coverdale's title page had the name of God at the top, the Great Bible has a large image of Henry with a tiny, bodiless Jesus hovering over him like a bird. On the left, Thomas Cranmer, Archbishop of Canterbury, passes the Bible to the bishops; on the right, Thomas Cromwell gives it to the nobility. Below the bishops, a preacher expounds the Scriptures to the common people, who celebrate by shouting 'Vivat Rex' – long live the king. Henry is in charge, and don't you forget it.

Curiously, there is a prison on the title page, in the lower right hand corner. Is this a symbol of the Bible escaping from the shackles? Or a warning to those who use a different Bible? The people on this page have speech bubbles emerging from their mouths but all but two speak in Latin. This is not a Bible for lay people. It's a Bible for the Latin-literate priests. In his preface, Cranmer writes that people need Scripture, but they cannot be allowed just to get on with it. 'Go to thy curate and preacher' he advises.[11]

It's hard not to look at this title page without feeling slightly ill. This is ecclesiastical spin for Henry and his government: the old monster, magnanimously handing out the Scriptures which for so long he'd tried to withold. He never did change his mind about who should be allowed to read the Bible. In an act of 1543, he attempted to restrict Bible reading to certain groups, on the grounds that it only created disorder among the uneducated. The groups of people allowed to study the Scripture are illuminating: noblemen could read it to their families; noble- and gentle-women, and merchants could read it to themselves. Lower-class women and men – merchants, apprentices, artisans, yeomen, farmers, manual labourers were all banned from reading the Scriptures.[12]

Mary and the martyrs

After the Great Bible, no new versions of the English Bible were published in England for the next sixty years. During the reign of

---

* That monopoly is still in force. Only Cambridge University Press, Oxford University Press, HarperCollins and the Queen's Printers have the right to produce the Authorised Version.

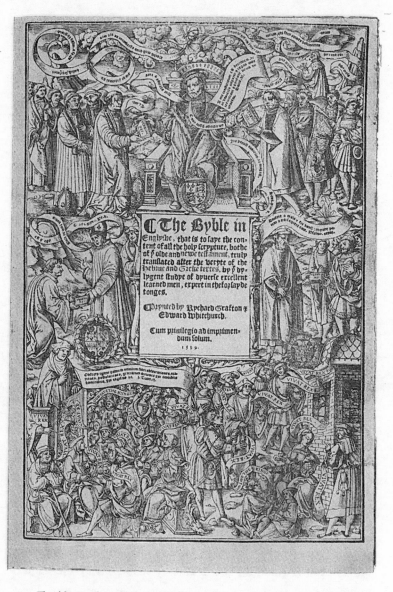

The title page from the Great Bible. Henry VIII generously shares the scriptures with his subjects. Certain subjects, anyway.

Edward VI, new editions of the Great Bible and the earlier versions were printed. And then along came Mary.

The daughter of Henry VIII and his first wife, Catherine of Aragon, Mary was a devout Catholic who sought to rescue England from the curse of Protestantism. By whatever means necessary. She wasn't entirely alone in her wish; the pace of change in the reign of Edward VI had unsettled many people. There was even a rising in the south-west of England, where the leaders called not only for the restoration of the Latin Mass but also a ban on the English Bible.[13]

Mary ascended to the throne on 19 July 1553 and a month later issued a decree banning the public reading of the Bible. Two years later she banned the import of works by Tyndale, Coverdale and Cranmer. She set up the Company of Stationers to control the publication of books; from now on all books would have to be authorised by this company. It was the official board of censorship. Not a single Bible was printed in England during Mary's reign. The English Bible was not used in church services and Bibles placed in church were taken out and burned.

Not just the books. The people as well. Indeed, the first of the Marian martyrs was John Rogers, alias Thomas Matthews, creator of the Matthews Bible. He was burned to death at Smithfield on February 4, 1555. He was followed by five bishops, including Cranmer. The bulk of those martyred under Mary, however, were not famous or wealthy or influential: they were ordinary tradesmen and labourers and women.[*]

The violence and persecution of Mary's reign – commemorated in one of the all-time best sellers, John Foxe's *Book of Martyrs* – led to many Protestants fleeing the country. They ended up in Geneva, a city which, under the leadership of Farel and then Calvin, had become the homeland of European Protestantism. And it was there that group of emigrés set to work on one of the most influential, ground-breaking Bibles of all time.

---

[*] Mary's reign led to so many Protestant printers fleeing that they had to import liturgical and Catholic books from abroad.

The Bible from Geneva

In Shakespeare's *Hamlet*, written around 1600, there is a scene where preparations are being made for the duel between Hamlet and Laertes. A courtier called Osric reels out a load of technical jargon about duelling and Horatio quips 'I knew you must be edified by the margent ere you had done.'* The line refers to one of the most popular books of the Elizabethan era – the Geneva Bible where, in the preface, editors tell the readers that for 'good purpose and edification' they 'have in the margent noted' certain things. They certainly did. The Geneva Bible, produced in 1560, is stuffed full of notes, comment, maps, pictures, diagrams, indexes and all manner of helps for the user. It is one of the most remarkable books of the seventeenth century.

The man behind it was William Whittingham, the chaplain of the English colony in Geneva. Driven out of England by Mary's persecution, for three years he and a small group of scholars pored over Tyndale and Coverdale's text, labouring to make it more accurate and readable. The Bible they produced is sometimes known as the Breeches Bible – from Genesis 3.7

> Then the eyes of them both were opened, and they knewe that they were naked, and they sewed figge tree leaues together, and made them selues breeches.

This mocking nickname was probably given to it by jealous Elizabethan bishops, whose ponderous Bishops' Bible of 1568 was such a commercial flop. It's not a fair nickname, since other versions also used the word (most notably Wycliffe).[14]

Instead it is usually named after the city in which it was produced: the Geneva Bible.† A version of the New Testament and Psalms was published in 1557. The next year Mary died – to be succeeded by Elizabeth – and many of the exiles went home. But three or four

---

* You had to be there, really.

† This name has also been used of other versions, simply because so many were printed at Geneva. During the bitter religious wars which tore France apart there is an account of Huguenot women in the town of Orange left lying in the gutter, their bodies pasted over with leaves torn from 'their Genevan Bibles'. These were French Bibles printed at Geneva.

stayed on to complete their work and, in April 1560, the full Geneva Bible was printed.

Hold a Geneva Bible in your hand and you soon realise just how revolutionary a document the book is. The title page promises not only the Bible, 'translated according to the Ebrew and Greeke, and conferred with the best translations in diuers languages' but also 'most profitable annotations upon all the hard places, and other things of great importance.'

In later editions, printed in London, turn the page and there is a prayer – written in the form of a poem. On the opposite page is a diagram drawn up by one 'T. Grashop' demonstrating 'Howe to take profite in reading of the holy Scriptures.' According to this diagram, the Scriptures contain matters concerning not only 'Religion and the right worshipping of God', but also 'Common wealthes and gouernments of people.' The reader is advised to mark and consider the 'coherence of the text, how it hangeth together' and to take the opportunity to 'Reade interpreters if he is able' as well as listen to sermons and 'conferre with such as can open the Scriptures. Acts 8.v.30,31&c.'

Turn the page again and you come to 'THE FIRST BOOKE OF MOSES, CALLED *GENESIS.' The asterisk signifies a note, of which there is a positive cataract, flooding down the inner and outer margins, and across the foot of the page, distinguished from the text by two thin red lines.

Each book of the Bible has its own introduction; in fact, each chapter has its own mini introduction or summary as well. Turn the page again and you come to a wonderful map, showing the 'Situation of the Garden of Eden.' There are running heads on each page showing not only the chapter numbers, but what's happening: 'The creation of man... The creation of woman... The woman seduced...'

There are pictures, maps and diagrams scattered throughout the book. The map of the Exodus (Numbers chapter 33) contains not only all the points along the way, but also tiny pictures of the towns and the events. There are drawings of the Temple, the Tabernacle and Ark of the Covenant, Solomon's palaces, the High Priest, the Holy Land at the time of Jesus... There is even a diagram showing who, under the Levitical law, was allowed to marry whom.

*Above: the opening of Matthew's Gospel
from the Geneva Bible
of 1560.
Right: an example of the illustrations
accompanying
the text.*

At the end of the Bible there are two lists, one a glossary of proper names and their meanings, and the other a concordance of 'the principall thinges that are conteined in the Bible' with their chapter and verse references.

This Bible is an amazing piece of information design, one which is totally focused on the reader. Everything in this book has been designed to encourage the reader to study Scripture for themselves. It was printed in Roman type, rather than the eye-wateringly difficult Gothic black letter type. It was the first English Bible to use verse numbers within chapters – taken from Estienne's 1551 Bible. It was priced affordably. Like Tyndale's New Testament, it was portable. The 1587 edition, for example, is just over 6 inches by 8.5 inches, which made it both affordable and portable. The Great Bible was designed to be forbidding to the average user – that was the point. But the Geneva Bible was the perfect travel Bible. It was the Geneva Bible which the Puritans took with them to the New World. You couldn't have taken the Great Bible.*

As others had found with Tyndale's New Testament, the size made it easy to smuggle. Because for large portions of its life, the Geneva Bible was officially *scriptura non grata* in England. Even so, huge quantities were smuggled in from the printshops on the continent.

The 1587 edition is a compact version. Maps, which previously covered two pages, have been reduced in size. The information is given in a more compact way. Even the translation itself has been improved. Later editions of the Geneva Bible include a revision of Tyndale's New Testament by Laurence Tomson which has been 'translated out of Greeke by Theod. Beza'. Beza was a learned scholar and Calvin's assistant at Geneva. He had studied Greek manuscripts which were earlier and more reliable than those used by Erasmus and he published these in 1565. In other words, the Geneva Bible was not a Bible which stood still. It availed itself of the latest scholarship.†

---

* Unless you hollowed it out and used it as a boat.

† It wasn't just the latest text, either. The diagram in front of the Geneva Bible of 1578 and onwards is by one T. Grashop. We know little about him, but he was also known as Thomas Gresshop or Greshop. Or Gressop. A former army chaplain, he was in London at the time when the Geneva Bible was originally printed. His advice on 'How to take profite in reading of the Holy Scriptures' appeared for the first time in 1578. It shows that the Geneva Bible did not stand still, but developed. New aids were added.

The Geneva Bible enabled ordinary people to interact with the Bible in a way that they had never done before. The Jesuit William Weston travelled round England in the 1590s. He records the activities of groups reading their Bibles

> Each of them had his own Bible and assiduously turned pages and looked up the text cited by the preachers, discussing the passages among themselves to see whether they had quoted them to the point and accurately.'[15]

In particular the Bible was often used for 'prophesyings' – small meetings where, after studying the Bible, 'a man shall speak or enquire of God as shall move his heart.' These were basically Bible study groups: people would gather together, their Bibles in their laps, reading the Scriptures and responding to what they read. They were attended, according to their critics, by 'men, women, boys and girls, labourers, workmen and simpletons'.[16] Ordinary people sharing ideas, labourers reading the Bible, people holding the clergy to account: it was Henry VIII's nightmare. And his daughter's as well: Elizabeth I ordered Archbishop Grindal to suppress the meetings – an order which he refused to carry out, much to her rage.

The Geneva Bible had a long history, remaining in print for over eighty years and running to at least 140 editions. It became the classic family Bible and, in 1579, was the first Bible to be printed in Scotland – paid for by a public subscription from every parish. George Fox quoted from it in tracts written during the reign of Charles II. When he writes from prison in 1674, it is the Geneva Bible that he quotes. It is still being read, still being used, and still the Bible of dissent and religious disobedience.

And, frankly, when you're quoted in a Shakespeare play, you know you've made the mainstream.

It was the Geneva Bible which, more than any other English Bible, gave the Scriptures to the people. It succeeded so well, that, fifty years later, King James decided to take them back.

Douai Bible

Like the Protestant emigrés, many Catholics fled England once Elizabeth ascended to the throne. The Pope had declared more or less open war on Elizabeth, the Spanish were preparing to fight; this was no time to be a Catholic in England.

Towards the end of Elizabeth's reign, these Catholic emigrés did exactly the same as their Protestant counterparts in Geneva – they produced an English language Bible. The New Testament was translated at Rheims in 1582, the Old Testament at Douai, and the final version published in 1609.

This Bible, known as the Douai-Rheims Bible, was not a good translation. In many places it actually made the text more opaque than before. Some of the words it invented were so obscure that the reader might as well have been reading Greek or Hebrew. The book needed to include a glossary at the back to help the reader. Some of these words were taken up and have since passed into English usage – victim, co-operate, adulterate, neophyte – but others remain baffling: 'prefinition', 'azymes', 'scenopegia', not to mention the 'parasceve of the pasch'.*

And, like the illegal Protestant Bibles, the Douai-Rheims came with a set of notes – this time promoting Catholic doctrine – and was also widely smuggled into England for the use of oppressed English Catholics. With several revisions, it remained the basis for the Catholic English translation well into the twentieth century.

Welsh Bible

While the Catholic emigrés were torturing the English language in Rheims, a Welsh Bishop was translating the Bible into Welsh. The Welsh translation of 1588 was known as Bishop Morgan's Bible, after its translator – William Morgan – who became Bishop of Llandaff and then St. Asaph.

It had an enormous impact on the language and culture of Wales. Indeed, it was instrumental in preserving the language. Welsh had been outlawed as an administrative language in the mid-sixteenth century and the Reformation decrees of the 1530s and 1540s had

---

* As in John 19.14 'And it was the parasceve of the pasch, about the sixth hour, and he saith to the Jews: Behold your king.'

imposed the English Bible and the book of Common Prayer in the churches. To worshippers in Wales – many of whom knew no English – they might as well have stayed with the Vulgate.

In 1567 a Welsh New Testament was published – the work of William Salesbury, a remarkable scholar and a man who had laboured for years on the task. The book was scholarly and accurate but only achieved a lukewarm reaction. Morgan's translation was a thorough revision of Salesbury's work, as well as the first Welsh version of the Old Testament and Apocrypha. The success of Morgan's translation lay in exactly the same areas as those of Tyndale and Luther: he understood the Welsh language and he understood the people. He knew how they spoke. He loved the language itself. His work gave the Welsh language status. And, strangely enough, it was to be the Welsh translation which, centuries later, was to propel the Bible out into the world in a way it had never known before.

The Bishops Bible

Elizabeth disliked the Geneva Bible – she mocked the metrical psalms which were often included with it as 'Geneva jigs' – but, concerned as she was with rebuilding the country after the trauma of Mary's reign, she did not want it to become a big issue.

But the Geneva Bible was deemed too puritan to be the official version, so Elizabeth instructed her bishops to produce yet another version. This Bible was to be based on the Great Bible but, above all things, it had to be uncontroversial. The bishops were instructed to 'make no bitter notes upon any text or yet to set down any determination in places of controversy.' Unedifying passages were to be marked out so that 'the reader may eschew them in his public reading.' It was dignified, it was safe, it was incredibly dull.

This Bishops' Bible as it was known, was published in 1568, complete with a frontispiece showing Elizabeth, the Earl of Leicester and Burghley. It was not widely admired, but it served as the basis for the next major translation: the most famous book in the English language.

THE AUTHORISED BIBLE

In 1870, some scholars revised the King James Bible. In the preface, they wrote in hushed, nervous tones of the presumptuousness with which they approached a Bible which 'for more than two centuries and a half had held the position of an English classic.'

Perhaps they would have had a more relaxed time, if they'd realised that this assumption was almost entirely wrong. The King James, or Authorised Version, was not recognised as a classic on its first publication. In fact, it was widely ignored, and for one very good reason: hardly anyone wanted it in the first place.

Queen Elizabeth I died in 1603, to be succeeded by James VI, King of Scotland. James had been raised in about the most disruptive, turbulent atmosphere possible. His mother, Mary I – Mary Queen of Scots – married the Dauphin of France, but only ruled as Queen of France for a few months, before he died. Back in Scotland, she married Lord Darnley – James' father – then he was found dead in his garden in suspicious circumstances. When Mary then married the man who many believed to be Darnley's murderer, there was an uprising. Mary was forcibly dethroned, in favour of her one-year-old son, James. She fled to England, where she was arrested. After nearly two decades spent in prison, she was executed for treason following her apparent involvement in three plots to assassinate Queen Elizabeth.

In the meantime, James had grown up under the influence and control of the Scottish Puritans, a group so strict and dour they made their English cousins look like frivolous, woolly liberals. Their attitude to James can be seen in the statement of Andrew Melville, Rector of St Andrews University, who told the King

> Sirrah, ye are God's silly vassal; there are two kings and two kingdoms in Scotland: there is king James, the head of the commonwealth; and there is Christ Jesus, the king of the Church, whose subject James

the Sixth is, and of whose kingdom he is not a king, not a lord, not a head, but a member.

When a Puritan theologian calls you 'God's silly vassal' you remember it. James was never a Puritan. Yes, he was Scottish – which for Calvinists is always a bit of a head start – but he was also scandalously bisexual and profligate with money.* Most of all, he was king. He was – or believed himself to be – a divinely appointed monarch. He wrote two books – *The Trew Law of Free Monarchies* and *Basilikon Doron* (Royal Gift) – which outlined an absolutist ideology of monarchy. Kings, in James' view, were higher beings than other men.

All this lies behind James' behaviour when he became King James I of England. When a deputation of English Puritans asked for church services to be modified, he agreed to moderate a conference to be convened at Hampton Court in 1603. But it was to be a conference on his terms. No More Mr Nice Guy. Or Mr Puritan Guy, at least.

At the conference the Puritans made their case: John Reynolds, President of Corpus Christi College Cambridge, urged a new translation of the Bible, arguing that those Bibles 'which were allowed in the raignes of Henry the eight, and Edward the sixt, were corrupt and not aunswerable to the truth of the Originall.' The Bibles he was talking about were the official versions: the Great Bible and Bishops' Bible. Reynolds was probably pushing for the official recognition of the Geneva Bible. The Bishops were not in favour: 'If every man's humour should be followed,' said Archbishop Bancroft, 'there would be no end of translating.'[†] James seemed to agree with Reynolds. 'I could never yet see a Bible well translated in English,' he replied, at which point the English Puritans must have got their hopes up. But then he performed a switch: 'But I think that of all,' he continued, 'that of Geneva is the worst.'

---

* In Scotland James was suspected of being lured into 'carnal lust' by the Earl of Lennox – the first of a succession of male favourites. His Puritan masters imprisoned James for a time and forced Lennox to flee. When James ascended to the English throne, his extravagance was notorious. In 1614, relations with Parliament collapsed, because Parliament was no longer willing to fund the extravagant court, with its sexual scandal, intrigue and licentiousness.

† Judging by the amount of different translations today, he may have had a point.

Having torpedoed the Puritan hopes, James suggested that a new translation should be done by 'the best learned of both Universities.' And then he revealed his *real* aim: he commanded that his new version should remove all the marginal notes, 'for in the Geneva translation,' he said 'some notes are partial, untrue, seditious and savouring of traitorous conceits, as when from Exodus 1,17 disobedience to kings is allowed.'

James believed utterly in the divine right of kings. The translators of the Geneva Bible also believed in divine right, except, in their case, they believed in the divine right of an actual divinity. Kings, they believed, were subject to the same laws as every other man. The note singled out by James suggested that the Hebrew midwives who disobeyed the Pharaoh's command to kill all baby boys had acted lawfully. 'Their disobedience herein was lawful,' ran the note, 'but their dissembling evil.' To James, disobedience to a royal command – *any* royal command – was sedition. His new Bible would fix that, once and for all.

In fact, what James proposed was incredibly conservative. This was no radical new version, but a revision of previous versions. The text of the Bishops Bible was to be 'as little altered as the truth of the original will permit'. He instructed that 'the old ecclesiastical words to be kept, viz. the word Church not to be translated Congregation.' And, of course, 'no marginal notes at all to be affixed, but only for the explanation of the Hebrew or Greek...'

So, later that year 47 scholars were appointed to work in six 'companies': two on the New Testament, three on the Old and one on the Apocrypha. The work took three years, but in 1611 it was complete. The result was the King James Bible, one of the monuments of English culture, and a book wrapped in more myths than any Bible since the Septuagint.

Appointed to be read

The first thing that hits you is the size of the thing. And, actually, if it did hit you you'd be in A&E, because compared to the Geneva Bible the first edition of the Authorised Version (AV) is *enormous*; 42cm by 28 cm (16.5 inches by 11 inches) wide. This is not so much coffee table book as a coffee table. It is, literally, a weighty tome, designed to crush the other editions.

And once you've mustered the strength to open it, you immediately notice the difference in content. Whereas the Geneva almost overwhelms the reader with helps and instructions, the AV opens with a lengthy preface followed by the lectionary – 'The Table and Kalender expressing the order of Psalmes and Lessons to be laid at Morning and Euening prayer.' The Geneva Bible tells you how to read the Bible for yourself; the AV tells you what bits will be read to you, and when.[*]

It has running heads, as in the Geneva Bible, and chapter summaries, but no introductions to the books. It has no illustrations. (It does have 34 pages of genealogies and a huge and rather wonderful map of the holy land and Jerusalem, with a gazetteer of places.) The only marginal notes are cross-references, or explanations of alternative readings of certain words.

And it is printed in dense 𝕲𝖔𝖙𝖍𝖎𝖈 𝖇𝖑𝖆𝖈𝖐 𝖑𝖊𝖙𝖙𝖊𝖗 𝖙𝖞𝖕𝖊.

Looking at this huge tome and comparing it to the Geneva Bible, it is clear that the powers behind the AV didn't want the people to read the Bible: they wanted it read *to* them. A book designed to be read out to congregations or families or domestic staff does not require illustrations or notes or maps. A book appointed to sit on a lectern and to be read in churches, under carefully controlled conditions, by people who were licensed to deal with this dangerous object, does not need to be portable.

This was about control and authority. The church didn't want people learning about their Bibles. The Puritan William Prynne believed that the authorities hated the Geneva notes because they might 'overmuch instruct the people in the knowledge of the Scriptures'. A Bible-reading layman might end up knowing as much or more about the subject than the officially appointed priest. Can't have that, can we?[†]

---

[*] It's never, in fact, been officially authorised; it was 'appointed to be read in churches', but that's not really the same thing. However, from very early on it does seem to have been accepted as the 'official' version. Archbishop Ussher called it 'the authorised Bible' in 1620.

[†] The notes were so valued that later on, when the Geneva text was no longer used, Puritans actually imported the Geneva Bible notes into editions of the AV.

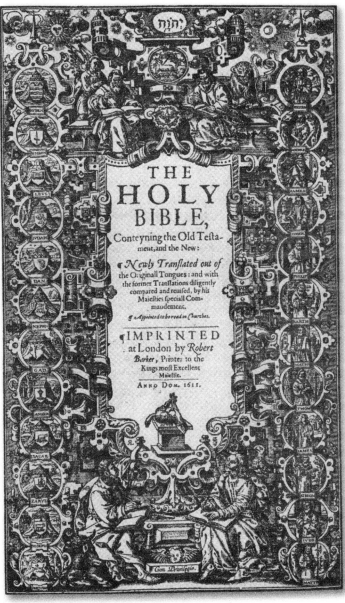

Title page of the 1611 Authorised Version.

With the tongues of men and angels

But what, I hear you ask, about the language? What about that undeniably beautiful, sonorous, lingering prose? If ever a Bible made the words of God sound like honey, this is the one. A passage such as 1 Corinthians 13 has such tone, such cadence

> Though I speak with the tongues of men and of angels, and have not charity, I am become as sounding brass, or a tinkling cymbal. And though I have the gift of prophecy, and understand all mysteries, and all knowledge; and though I have all faith, so that I could remove mountains, and have not charity, I am nothing. And though I bestow all my goods to feed the poor, and though I give my body to be burned, and have not charity, it profiteth me nothing

It's a beautiful piece of writing. But the beauty is deceptive. (And we'll come back to the word 'charity' later.) For one thing, it's so much more beautiful than the original. The rough and ready style of the Greek Scriptures was always embarrassing to scholars versed in classical Latin and Greek. It pained even such a biblical die-hard as Calvin. Writing on Romans, he bemoaned the 'faults in his [Paul's] language' although he consoled himself with the opinion that the weakness was actually a strength

> the singular providence of God has passed on to us these profound mysteries in the garb of a poor style, so that our faith might not depend on the power of human eloquence, but on the efficacy of the Spirit alone.[1]

For Calvin, the important thing was that the Bible was *not* the construct of literary men, but divinely inspired words transmitted through people who were, frankly, a bit rubbish at writing

> For it was also not without God's extraordinary providence that the sublime mysteries of the kingdom of heaven came to be expressed largely in mean and lowly words, lest, if they had been adorned with more shining eloquence, the impious would scoffingly have claimed that its power is in the realm of eloquence alone.[2]

These complaints about the style were obviously keenly felt by biblical scholars. In a curious work called *The glorious triumph of God's most blessed word*, Thomas Becon wrote in the character of the Bible, defending itself against common criticism: 'they object that I am rude, gross, barbarous, impolite, untrimmed, unpleasant, uneloquent, etc.'[3] Perhaps the most potent evidence for the disdain felt for the Bible's literary style comes, curiously, from the files of the Elizabethan secret police. In 1593, the poet Christopher Marlowe was accused of blasphemy. He was charged with saying that Adam could not have been the first man, that Moses was an Egyptian-trained juggler and that, if his father was the Holy Ghost, then that made Christ illegitimate. But the great poet is also accused of saying that 'all the New Testament is filthily written'.*

Crucial evidence. It shows what a classically trained scholar – Marlowe was a Cambridge man – thought of the style of the New Testament. He might have been exaggerating (he might have been drunk) but, in essence, he was saying nothing that Calvin hadn't said: New Testament Greek was not good. In a culture where the riches of language were everywhere evident, it was embarrassing to discover that God didn't write stylish Greek.

The translators of the AV dealt with the embarrassment of the Bible's literary style by upgrading it. They made a deliberate, conscious effort to improve the language of the Bible: they were not so much God's secretaries as his copy-editors. No one, after all, could ever accuse the AV of having the 'garb of a poor style'. Its critics, in fact, accused it of going too far in the opposite direction. The translators chose – created, really – a style of language which was not one spoken in Jacobean England: which, indeed, had never really been spoken by anyone, at any time. They were deliberately archaic. They used terms and phrases which were already out of date in 1611.[4] They were trying to create the 'Bible of Old England', to create a Bible which sounded like it had been written a century before.

It was the world's first mock-Tudor Bible.

The result was that people really didn't understand it at the time, let alone later. Writing in the middle of the seventeenth century,

---

* The testimony comes from a man called Richard Baines. Whether Marlowe said any of this is a matter of dispute.

John Selden observed that the language of the AV was 'well enough so long as scholars have to do with it, but when it comes among the common people, Lord, what gear do they make of it.' Anthony Johnson, writing less than ninety years later, stated that the absence of notes from the AV led to complaints from some readers that 'they could not see into the sense of the Scriptures.'*

The Bones of Tyndale

If the bodywork was flashier – all chrome words and polished phrases – the engine was pure Tyndale. Just as Coverdale repackaged Tyndale's work as Henry's 'Great Bible', the translators of the AV did the same. James hadn't commanded a new translation, he'd ordered that they make 'out of many good [versions], one principal good one.' So the AV is a tapestry, a collage of previous versions: including the Bishops Bible, Coverdale's, the Geneva Bible – even bits from the Catholic Douai translation. The translators or revisers did refer in places to the Greek and the Hebrew, but the texts they used were not even the best ones available at the time. As we've seen, forty years earlier, Theodore Beza had prepared an edition of the Greek New Testament which drew on all the latest manuscripts. But the translators didn't use this: they used Erasmus's text, published nearly a hundred years earlier in 1516.

Nevertheless, it is Tyndale who provides the bones and the muscles and the sinews. At least 83 per cent of the New Testament comes from Tyndale's translation and 76 per cent of the Old Testament.† The table on page 206 shows a comparison of Matthew 5.1–12 in the two versions. You can see how little the difference between the AV and Tyndale's version. The AV has added bigger words like 'multitude'; it has added unnecessary words 'they which do hunger and thirst after righteousness'. But it is Tyndale's version, undoubtedly.

The AV has majesty and stateliness. It is the prose equivalent of highly polished oak; Tyndale's is more rough-hewn timber. But Tyndale has a levity, a homeliness which is entirely absent from

---

* It was not just the English. The American Benjamin Franklin wanted to produce a version of the AV in modern English. He even submitted a sampling of his suggested translation of a few verses from the book of Job.

† Some scholars put it as high as ninety per cent of the New Testament. Whatever the case, it's a lot.

the AV. When the serpent tempts Eve in Tyndale's version he says 'tush ye shall not dye'. The AV has 'Ye shall not surely die' (Gen. 3.4).[5] According to Tyndale, 'The Lord was with Joseph and he was a lucky fellow'; according to the AV 'the Lord was with Joseph and he was a prosperous man' (Gen. 39.2).

See? Joseph's gone up in the world. Just like the Bible.

The old ecclesiastical words

Let's return, just for a moment, to 1 Corinthians 13. 'Though I speak with the tongues of men and of angels, and have not charity, I am become as sounding brass, or a tinkling cymbal,' it begins in the AV. 'Charity suffereth long, and is kind; charity envieth not; charity vaunteth not itself, is not puffed up... Charity never faileth... And now abideth faith, hope, charity, these three; but the greatest of these is charity' (1 Cor. 13.1, 4, 8, 13).

One of the things which James hated about the Geneva Bible was its terminology. It's the same problem which dogged Jerome and Erasmus. The Geneva Bible, following Tyndale, translated *ekklesia* as 'congregation' not 'church'. It used the word 'elder' instead of 'bishop'. These were loaded terms. If there were no bishops and no church in the Bible, how would the church justify its power?

Tyndale's version of the same passage runs: 'Though I speake with the tonges of men and angels and yet had no love I were ever as soundinge brasse: or as a tynklynge Cymball... Nowe abideth fayth, hope and love, even these three: but the chefe of these is love' (1 Cor. 13.1, 13).

Love. Not charity. *Love*. The Greek word is *agape*, which means not romantic, erotic love, but love or good will, love between Christians, love for your neighbour, the love of God for his children. When Jerome was at work it, he had a problem, because the Latin word *amor* was too gross, so he fell back on *caritas*. That got turned into 'charity' and that, for the church, got turned into an awful lot of money. By the sixteenth century 'charity' represented not just the giving of alms, but the whole edifice of church giving. The church's income was derived from 'charity' – albeit an official, enforced charity of the tithes. So, if the greatest of these is *not* charity, then there was the danger of people stopping their financial support to the church.

Matthew 5.1–12. A comparison of Tyndale and AV

When he saw the people he went up into a mountain and when he was set his disciples came to him and he opened his mouth and taught them saying: Blessed are the poor in spirit: for theirs is the kingdom of heaven. Blessed are they that mourn: for they shall be comforted. Blessed are the meek: for they shall inherit the earth. Blessed are they which hunger and thirst for righteousness: for they shall be filled. Blessed are the merciful: for they shall obtain mercy. Blessed are the pure in heart: for they shall see God. Blessed are the peacemakers: for they shall be called the children of God. Blessed are they which suffer persecution for righteousness sake: for theirs is the kingdom of heaven. Blessed are ye when men revile you and persecute you and shall falsely say all manner of evil sayings against you for my sake. Rejoice and be glad for great is your reward in heaven.

Matthew 5.1–12. Tyndale[*]

And seeing the multitudes, he went up into a mountain: and when he was set, his disciples came unto him: And he opened his mouth, and taught them, saying, Blessed are the poor in spirit: for theirs is the kingdom of heaven. Blessed are they that mourn: for they shall be comforted. Blessed are the meek: for they shall inherit the earth. Blessed are they which do hunger and thirst after righteousness: for they shall be filled. Blessed are the merciful: for they shall obtain mercy. Blessed are the pure in heart: for they shall see God. Blessed are the peacemakers: for they shall be called the children of God. Blessed are they which are persecuted for righteousness' sake: for theirs is the kingdom of heaven. Blessed are ye, when men shall revile you, and persecute you, and shall say all manner of evil against you falsely, for my sake. Rejoice, and be exceeding glad: for great is your reward in heaven:

Matthew 5.1–12. AV

---

[*] I have updated the spelling of the Tyndale.

All this lies behind James' third instruction to the translators – 'The old ecclesiastical words to be kept...' He didn't want congregations, he wanted churches – of which he was the head; he didn't want elders, he wanted bishops, whom he could appoint. And he didn't want love; he demanded charity. At times this gets ludicrous. Take Acts 1.20, where the Geneva Bible has

> For it is written in the booke of Psalmes, Let his habitation be void, and let no man dwel therein: also, Let another take his charge.

The AV has

> For it is written in the book of Psalms, Let his habitation be desolate, and let no man dwell therein: and his bishoprick let another take.

It is difficult to imagine the writer of Psalms ever had in mind someone taking over a bishopric. There were other, subtler, differences. The Geneva Bible uses the word 'tyrant' over four hundred times to describe wicked kings and emperors. But you won't find the word at all in the AV. It's the king's Bible – how can a divine monarch ever be a tyrant?

AV verses Geneva

The aim of the Authorised Version was to wrest back control of the Bible. The idea behind the project was never to give the people a new Bible to read; it was to stop them reading the one they already had. That was why it stripped out the notes. That was why it was printed in a massive format. That was why it uses an opaque, ornate language.

And that was why it was not exactly acclaimed on its arrival. The ordinary readers kept faith with their Geneva Bibles, with the notes and the maps and the pictures. They understood that. It spoke their language. The AV, on publication, was greeted with almost complete apathy.

It certainly wasn't a critical success. There is not a shred of evidence for any critical acclamation at the time. But there are lots of instances of condemnation. Puritan scholars lambasted it for its inaccuracies. Here's Hugh Broughton

> Tell His Majesty that I had rather be rent in pieces with wild horses, than any such translation by my consent should be urged upon poor churches... The new edition crosseth me. I desire it to be burnt. *

Even the translators themselves didn't use it. Lancelot Andrewes, chairman of the AV translators, used the Geneva Bible for his sermons, as did several other bishops. Archbishop Laud, the man later given the task of suppressing the Geneva Bible, based his sermons on the Geneva Bible until the mid-1620s.† Amazingly, even in the AV itself, in the preface, Bishop Smith makes a quote – and he quotes the Geneva Bible!

Shakespeare used the Geneva. Milton used it. Bunyan was still quoting the Geneva in 1672, long after it had ceased to be printed.[6] When the Puritans from the Mayflower set foot on America, it was the Geneva Bible they carried with them, not the King James. It seems odd to think that nowadays the heartland of the King James-only movement is the Bible-belt in America. And yet the first Christians who arrived in America wanted nothing to do with the King James version and didn't bother to pack it.

We don't know how many copies of the AV were sold on publication as there's no entry for it in the Stationers' Register. What we do know is that the Geneva Bible continued to sell and in huge numbers. Indeed, the Geneva proved so popular that in 1616 the King was forced to ban the printing of the Geneva Bible by any English press.

This didn't work: people simply imported copies. Printers in Amsterdam and Dort grabbed their opportunity and Bibles were imported from the continent. Even the King's official printer got in on the action. Robert Barker – the man appointed to print the AV – also did a very handy trade in smuggled Geneva Bibles. He bought a bulk lot of Geneva editions from Holland, stamped the date 1599 on them to make them appear as though they had been printed before the ban, and flogged them to the waiting public. At least eight editions were printed in Holland around 1630 and shipped into England with fake '1599' title pages.

---

* He was, admittedly, very bitter. His intemperate language and Protestant opinions meant that he was ignored when they were choosing the translation committees.

† Even later, along with the AV, he gives alternative readings from the Geneva Bible.

The Success of the AV

How, then did it succeed? How did the AV establish itself as a classic? How did this mock-Tudor, politically-motivated version come to be one of the best-loved books of the English world? Three main reasons: it had a monopoly; it was associated with royalty; and because age lends enchantment.

As we've seen, the rights to print Bibles were sold as monopolies, and had been since the time of Elizabeth. At the time of its publication, English printers were still producing Geneva Bibles. And when it became clear that these were outselling the AV, the authorities simply banned their production.

The Geneva certainly had better proof-reading. From the start, the printing of the AV was beset by confusion and disaster. The very first edition is known as the 'He-Bible' because of a spelling mistake in Ruth 3.15 where it reads 'he' instead of 'she'.* The owner of the monopoly, Robert Barker, 'Printer to the King's Most Excellent Maiestie', was catastrophically bad at collating and proof-reading. His business was so chaotic that he eventually ended in debtor's prison.

The Wicked Bible

The history of the various editions is littered with misprints, some of which have become legendary. The so-called Wicked Bible of 1631 missed out the word 'not' from Exodus 20.14, and thus had Moses declaring rather entertainingly 'Thou shalt commit adultery'. The mistake cost Barker a £3,000 fine and forced him into bankruptcy.

These printing errors so angered William Kilburne that he dedicated an entire book to them. In 1659 he published *Dangerous Errors in Several Late Printed Bibles to the Great Scandal and Corruption of Sound and True Religion*, in which he claimed to have identified twenty thousand errors in the various editions! One example was Numbers 25.17–18, where the Israelites were instructed to 'Vex the Midianites, and smite them: For they vex you with their wives.' The last word should have been 'wiles.'

And in 1682, the Oxford University Press issued a sumptuous edition featuring the parable of the vinegar, rather than the vineyard.

In the nineteenth century, a scholar by the wonderfully appropriate name of Dr. Scrivener attempted to collate all the editions of the AV

---

* The 1613 edition is therefore known as the 'She-Bible' because it corrected this. It made up for this by muddling the names of Jesus and Judas at Matthew 26.36.

then in circulation. He found there were more than 24,000 variations between them. The AV took us back to a time of the scribes and the copying errors. The fact is that it was not until 1762 that a standard edition of the AV was decided upon. Before then, no such thing as the one, true Authorised Version ever existed.

This suppression of the Geneva Bible and the monopoly for the King's Printers kept the price of the AV artificially high. It did not reduce in price until the 1680s as a consequence of competition. Eventually, however, the ban was effective. Gradually, the AV became the only Bible you could buy. In a straight shootout, the AV might never have survived.

A second reason is that it was the 'King James' Bible – it was associated with royalty. A little under thirty years after its publication, England was plunged into civil war. When Cromwell's soldiers marched to battle, they carried with them a Soldier's Bible, a little book of helpful verses from the Bible – and all in the Geneva version. The Geneva Bible was associated with rebels and revolutionaries; with joy-killing, fun-hating Puritans; with, indeed, regicide. It was the Geneva Bible lot who killed Charles I. After the collapse of the Commonwealth and the Restoration, few people wanted anything to do with the Puritans. When Charles II returned to the throne, it was the Bible associated with his grandfather which people wanted.

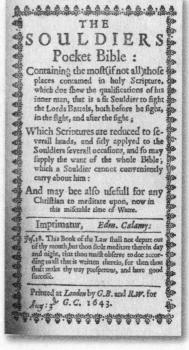

Finally, it had no major predators. No other versions of any significance were made, partly because tampering with the Bible was seen as symbolic of the religious fervour of the civil war years. And nobody wanted to go back to that again. So, without any serious competition, its sonorous, beautiful, fantastic prose wove itself into our culture.

Its translators were brilliant phrase-makers. As with Tyndale, the expressions of the AV have become part of the vocabulary of the English-speaking world: phrases like 'labour of love'; 'a thorn in the flesh'; 'the root of all evil'; 'the fat of the land'; 'the sweat of thy brow' all come from the AV. As a showcase of what English can do, it is magnificent. The historian Macaulay wrote of their version, 'If everything else in our language should perish, it alone would suffice to show the extent of its beauty and power.'

Its privileged position means that the AV has taken on a symbolic value. Just as everyone loves old English churches, but fewer and fewer go to worship, we cherish the AV, but hardly anyone reads it. A copy of the AV is what every household has, along with a dusty volume of the complete works of Shakespeare.*

This is why the AV is the non-Christian's version of choice. It allows them to enjoy the language without having to obey the thing.[7] Because, deep down, we want a God with a big white beard and a nice line in Jacobean poetry. We don't want a God who talks in the language of tradesman's Greek; a God who sounds like a shopkeeper or a housewife or even a carpenter; we want a God who sounds old and ancient and mysterious. The logical conclusion of this is the mind-bogglingly stupid statement of Charles Allen Dinsmore, who declared the AV to be 'a finer and nobler literature than the Scriptures in their original tongues.'[8] As the *Cambridge History of the Bible* puts it, the AV's text 'acquired a sanctity properly ascribable only to the unmediated voice of God.'[9]

Why do we love the King James Bible? Why did it come to dominate our culture?

Because it sounds better than the original.

---

* A survey taken in 1990 revealed that nearly 80% of people owned a copy of the Bible.

THE RADICAL BIBLE

On 1 April 1649, around twenty poor men took possession of a plot of common land in Saint George's Hill, Surrey. They plunged their spades into the ground and prepared to sow seed and cultivate the soil. Their activites earned them the mocking nickname of the Diggers, and the Surrey community was the first of some 34 communities which held property in common and sought to reclaim land which they believed had been taken from them. They were inspired by the Bible – specifically by the picture of communal living in Acts and the garden in Eden. Their leader Gerrard Winstanley wrote that the people of England

> are all children of the Land and the earth is the Lord's, not particular men's that claims a proper interest in it above others, which is the devil's power.[1]

Winstanley was writing in the aftermath of the civil war. Indeed, he was calling for land captured during the war to be redistributed, that the 'parks, forests, chases and the like may be set free to all that have lent assistance...' That, he claimed, would 'turn swords into ploughshares and settle such a peace in the earth, as nations shall learn war no more'.

Winstanley is typical of the era. The decades after the publication of the AV were years of huge political unrest in England, when multitudes of small, revolutionary dissenting groups flourished, mingling politics and religion (in the seventeenth century there was no real distinction between the two) and all demanding change. It was a time when print really began to have an impact. Cheap, disposable news-sheets meant that information was freed, democratised. There was a constant running battle between the emerging publishing industry, and the church and state. And at the heart of all this turmoil was the Bible.

The English – like no other European nation – became a people of the book. It has been estimated that over a million Bibles were published in England between the Reformation and the Revolution in 1640.[2] The sheer joy of people reading the Scriptures for the first time is captured in the words of a Welshman with the splendid name of Arise Evans

> I looked upon the Scripture as a history of things that passed in other countries, pertaining to other persons; but now I looked upon it as a mystery to be opened at this time, belonging also to us.[3]

The Bible was everywhere. Children learned to read from the Bible. In this pre-novel age, Bible stories were sources of popular entertainment. Biblical characters became metaphors for the events of the age. Adam became a symbol for everyman ('We may see Adam every day before our eyes walking up and down the street,' wrote Winstanley); Nimrod stood for all tyrants; Cain a symbol of exploitation.* The light of the Bible was turned on the events surrounding them. It was a guide, an interpreter to these tumultuous times. Arise Evans thought that Revelation 8 and 11 described the civil war. Many soldiers – shades of Münster – believed the war was the prelude to Christ's return and the thousand-year reign.[4]

Above all, it was from the Bible that the people drew their ideas of human individuality and dignity – ideas which were to become central to British culture. The Bible, that document of priestly authority, allowed people to question the authority of the priests. Arise Evans wrote that the Bible used to be 'in great men's hands, so that they might do as they pleased with the people that knew little or no Scripture'. Since the rise of printing, however, 'knowledge is increased among the people... so that they will not be ruled by the kings set up after the manner of the Gentiles any more.'[5] This led, inevitably, to people making their own interpretations. As the Duke of Newcastle commented ruefully, 'The Bible in English under every weaver's and chambermaid's arm hath done much harm... For

---

* The use of these handy codewords has been a feature of subversive writing and preaching throughout history, from Revelation's use of the name Babylon, to Communist Romania when the priest László Tokes was able to make comments on the rule of Ceauşescu, by preaching on Nebuchadnezzar and other evil monarchs from the Old Testament.

controversy is a civil war with the pen which pulls out the sword soon afterwards.'[6]

Previously, the government had tried to exert some form of control over these revolutionary ideas through censorship, but as the country descended into civil war, this proved impossible. In 1641 the Star Chamber – the main tool of censorship – was abolished. Now, anyone could get their ideas into print – at least if the printer thought there was money in it. Many people who wrote upon the Bible in this period were 'illiterate' in terms of a classical education. Academics sneered at John Bunyan for his lack of education: he reminded them that the only person in the Bible who spoke Hebrew, Greek and Latin was Pontius Pilate.

Bibles were more affordable than ever. With no state-controlled monopoly – or, at least, not one which was effectively enforced – in the early 1650s a Bible could be had for from twenty pence to 2s. 4d. The 1656 Bible was sold at no more than twelve shillings at the insistence of Cromwell.* After the Restoration the monopoly was restored and the prices shot up again.

'Freeborn John'

The writings of the various radical movements which sprang up before, during and after the Civil War are soaked in Scripture. In the sixteenth and seventeenth centuries, as one writer puts it, 'for leftist writers [the Bible] had to do in the absence of Marx'.[7] In the 1640s and 1650s a succession of radical Protestant groups found inspiration in the Bible's support for the poor and the humble. People such as John Lilburne, leader of the radical political movement the Levellers, were devout Christians. Lilburne had previous, when it came

---

* That's old money, of course. Twelve pence in a shilling, twenty shillings to the pound and all that pre-decimal stuff. Comparing prices across the centuries is notoriously tricky, not least because of industrialisation, but the daily wage of a tenant farmer in 1662 was around six pence.

to seditious writing. In 1638, at age 22, he'd been arrested for importing unlicensed religious publications from Holland. This began a series of trials during which he campaigned for his 'freeborn rights' – trials which earned him the nickname of 'Freeborn John'.

Frequently pilloried and whipped and kept in solitary confinement, Lilburne drew comfort from the Bible. Didn't Paul undergo exactly the same treatment? Didn't the psalms show God's followers being treated cruelly and unjustly? Didn't Revelation predict this exact kind of persecution? In a tract called *A Worke of the Beast*, he wrote a psalm-like defence

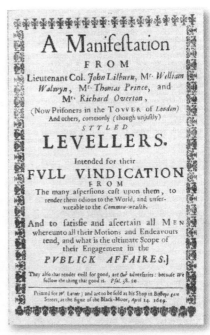

A Leveller manifesto, published in 1649, complete with Bible reference.

> For openly I to their face did there truly declare,
> That from the Pope our Prelates all, descended still they are,
> And that I might for what I said, make confirmation
> I nam'd Chapters the 9 and 13 of Revelation.[*]

Lilburne was said to have the Bible in one hand and the writings of Sir Edward Coke in the other.[†] The Levellers, like the Diggers, pointed to Eden. In the Garden of Eden, 'all men were Levellers'.[8] Women were the equal of men: 'we are assured of our creation in the image of God, and of an interest in Christ equal unto men, as also of a proportionable share in the freedoms of this commonwealth,' wrote Elizabeth Lilburne, John's wife. They called for the franchise

---

[*] Great political agitator; lousy poet.

[†] Coke (1552–1634) was a judge and MP who wrote extensively on common law and supported individual liberty against arbitrary government.

to be extended to all working men; for one year Parliaments, the abolition of the House of Lords, religious toleration.[*]

It ended, as these things tend to, in bloodshed. In Burford. In 1649, two Leveller regiments who were marching to present their grievances to Cromwell, were captured while they were asleep and locked up in Burford church. On the lead font, you can still see the engraved graffito of one of their number: 'Anthony Sedley. 1649. Prisner.' Three days later, on 17th May, four of their leaders were taken out to face the firing squad. The rest of the prisoners were lined up on the roof to watch. Cromwell had three of them shot; the fourth was reprieved, leading to widespread belief that he was a traitor. They are buried somewhere in the churchyard, in unmarked graves, and Cromwell marched on to establish his police state.

The Leveller's Memorial, Burford Churchyard

A few months later the Digger communities, too, were gone, broken up by landowner-orchestrated campaigns of violence, harassment and arson. But in their protests we see the birth of the socialist movements of the nineteenth and twentieth centuries. Indeed, in their protests we see claims for many of the essentials of parliamentary democracy that we now take for granted: one person one vote, religious toleration, free speech, human rights.

Illustrated Bibles

There was money to be made in Bibles: a ready market, eager customers. Thomas Guy, the founder of Guy's Hospital in London,

---

[*] They also called for MPs to have no outside interests. We're still waiting...

made most of his fortune in retailing Bibles. The hub of the business in London was St Paul's Cross Yard – ironically, the place where Tyndale's books had been burnt. There, a multitude of shops satisfied the craving for dangerous theology. With no house numbers in those days, the names of the shops were indicated by the sign hanging over the door. There were many variants of the Bible – The Bible, The Three Bibles, The Bible and Anchor, Bible and Crown, Bible and Peacock.* But also other Bible terms: the Angel, the Brazen Serpent, the Holy Lamb, the Trinity, and curiously Tobit's Dog.[9] The very geography of the area was religious: Paternoster Row, Ave Maria Lane, Amen Corner.†

Printer-publishers began to accumulate around the church as early as 1515, when Julian Notary was 'dwellynge in powles chyrche yarde besyde ye weste dore by my lordes palyes' in 1515, his shop sign being the Three Kings.' There were 'respectable' shops in the houses around the yards, but also a great number of bookstalls, ramshackle sheds, dealers to the theology addicts. Sometimes their drugs were not one hundred per cent pure

> Dr. Us[s]her, Bishop of Armath, having to preach at Paules Crosse, and passing hastily by one of the stationers, called for a Bible, and had a little one of the London edition given him out, but when he came to looke for his text, that very verse was omitted in the print.

When the Great Fire hit the capital in 1666, the trade was devastated. Evelyn tells us that soon after the fire had subsided the other trades went on as merrily as before, 'only the poor booksellers have been indeed ill-treated by Vulcan; so many noble impressions consumed by their trusting them to ye churches.'[10]

The selling of Bibles for profit caused some anxiety. To the public, it did not seem right that people should profit from selling the Scriptures. In 1725 a royal order was issued, requiring all printers to state the price for the unbound, printed sheets of the Bible clearly on the title page. The bookseller would make his profit by adding a variety of bindings to the book.

---

* The peacock was a symbol of the resurrection.
† Paternoster Row originally got its name from the shops selling paternosters, or prayer-beads.

Of course, the real money was to be made in printing. But that was a closed shop. A monopoly. Only the Kings Printers and the Universities were allowed to print the thing. Some enterprising booksellers sought to get round this by purchasing German and Dutch engravings of biblical scenes and then binding them into already printed Bibles. A Worcester bookbinder called Francis Ash purchased a large number of engravings and bound them into the famously austere Edinburgh Bible and made a fortune. When the Royalist armies besieged Worcester in 1642, Francis hid his fortune in the privy. A few weeks later he went to dig his money out, was overcome by the fumes and died.[11]

After the Restoration, booksellers and publishers began to take greater liberties. Only certain companies could print the Bible, but what exactly, asked the publishers, does 'the Bible' mean? If you added a commentary to the Bible, then technically you could argue that you were printing a commentary, with just extracts from the Bible. Long extracts. Long extracts which were actually the entire text. Still, it was worth a gamble. So, from around 1720, printers without the royal privilege started to print Bibles with commentaries and claimed that they were actually commentaries with Bibles. When no-one was prosecuted, they reduced the size and number of the notes. Finally they printed the notes right on the edge, so that the bookseller could simply trim the notes off and sell the book. It was now a Bible commentary, only without the commentary.

Another alternative was to brand these as 'Family' or 'Educational' Bibles, package them with illustrations and notes and explanatory diagrams and claim that the text was really just an accompaniment to the illustrations. Sort of like a very long caption.

Some of these illustrated Bibles were disassembled by their owners, who then inserted their own prints and drawings to accompany the text.[*] For real fans, this could bloat the Bible to enormous proportions. One set owned by Elizabeth Bull, whose father was a print collector, ran to 25 volumes; she'd inserted thousands of engravings and woodcuts into the text. The most extreme case was that of the printer Robert Bowyer. He added 6,293 prints to his Bible.

---

[*] The practice is called Grangerizing, after James Granger, who started the craze for adding to old historical texts in this way.

It ran to 45 volumes and was so huge it needed a special bookcase to keep it in. The first volume contains 126 prints and illustrations, and only gets as far as Genesis chapter 4 – just 81 verses. That's 1.5 prints per verse. He later claimed that the cost of the prints had forced him into bankruptcy.

Attempts at revision

The publication of the Authorised Version did not see the end of new translations. Between 1611 and 1880, some seventy English translations were made, but on the whole they were of marginal interest: unable to gain the traction needed to dislodge the impregnable fortress of the Authorised Version.

Strangely, when the Puritans took power under Cromwell, there was no concerted attempt to reintroduce the Geneva Bible. Part of the reason was financial – Cromwell had sold the rights to the AV to the printers Henry Hills and John Field, and they had little interest in a rival edition.

Others demanded a more substantial revision. In January 1657, Parliament's Grand Committee for Religion recommended that a sub-committee be asked to 'consider of the translations and impressions of the Bible, and to offer their opinions therein to the committee.'[12] (The word 'translations' shows that the Geneva Bible was still very much around.) A group of learned scholars gathered together making 'divers excellent and learned observations of some mistakes in the translations of the Bible in English...' but shortly afterwards Parliament was dissolved and observations were the only things ever made.[13]

Sometime during the 1650s, a Baptist cleric, Henry Jessey, spearheaded another effort. Jessey's knowledge of Hebrew and Greek was so extensive he was known as 'a living concordance'. He believed it was a duty 'to have the whole Bible rendered as exactly agreeing with the original as we can attain' and he recruited other scholars in a desire to 'have a more pure, proper translation of the originals than heretofore'. His translation was almost finished – it got as far as just needing a warrant for its publication – and then it disappears without trace. No-one knows what happened to it, or why it disappeared.[14]

Most probably the translation – like Jessey and the independent congregations – fell foul of the return of Charles II. Although Charles declared that no man would be called into question over differences in religion, once he was restored to the throne in 1660, he failed to live up to his word. He set about suppressing the congregations of those on the radical fringe of the church: Brownists, Baptists, Quakers, dissenting pastors, independents and those with similar leanings within the Anglican church. Jessey died in prison on September 4, 1663.

Bible translating was dangerous in the shiny newly-restored regime. In 1685, Richard Baxter published a *Paraphrase on the New Testament* which resulted in him being imprisoned.[15] Bible reading could still be subversive. One of the first people arrested under the new regime was Jessey's close friend and fellow pastor, John Bunyan. Significantly, Bunyan's great work *Pilgrims' Progress* begins with the dream of a ragged man reading a book; 'I looked, and saw him open the book and read therein.' An ordinary man, a sinner, and he's reading the Bible. (The Geneva, of course. Bunyan was still quoting his presumably battered old Geneva Bible in the 1670s.) Bunyan spent around one third of his adult life in prison; he was not viewed at the time as a writer of moral or improving literature, nor as the father of the English novel, but as a social revolutionary.[16]

The radical dissenters were marginalised and suppressed and, while they survived, their Bible did not. The final printing of the Geneva Bible was in 1644, after which this book, the greatest of the sixteenth and seventeenth century Bibles, fades from view.

The official text

In the reign of Charles II, the AV began to establish its status as the official text. Over the next century it travelled on the same arc as that taken by the Vulgate. The variant readings, printers' errors and archaic spellings were filtered out, and gradually a standard edition was established.

In 1745 William Whiston – well known as the translator of Josephus – published a kind of revised AV, called the *Primitive New Testament*, which corrected the AV in accordance with the latest archaeological discoveries. Then, in 1762, Dr. Thomas Paris issued an edition which corrected the many errors; modernised the spellings and – shock horror – introduced 360 marginal notes. It was this edition – 150 years after the first edition – which has subsequently become the standard text. Where Cambridge went, Oxford was bound to follow, and in 1769 the Oxford University Press issued their revised AV, edited by Dr. Benjamin Blayney. According to one expert, this contained over 75,000 differences from the version issued in 1611. This became known as the Oxford Standard Edition.

Still there was discontent. Because by the mid-eighteenth century, the AV was already becoming difficult for the ordinary reader to understand. In 1768, John Wesley issued a revised version, with over twelve thousand emendations, called *The New Testament With Notes for Plain Unlettered Men who know only their Mother Tongue.* Wesley was a man with his finger on the pulse of the working class – a preacher to Cornish miners, an open-air revivalist, the movement he started was given another mocking nickname: the Methodists. Wesley knew what others suspected, that the AV was difficult for the ordinary reader to understand.

In the same year, Edward Harwood published the snappily titled *Liberal Translation of the New Testament: Being an Attempt to translate the Sacred Writings with the same Freedom, Spirit and Elegance with which other English Translations of the Greek Classics have lately been executed.* The title doesn't exactly fill you with hope, but he too had recognised that the Bible needed revision, although he addressed the problem by the rather unusual means of making the AV even more tortuous than it was before. Here's his version of 'Our Father, who art in heaven':

> O thou great governour and parent of universal nature – who manifestest thy glory to the blessed inhabitants of heaven...

And it goes downhill from there. Harwood talked about 'the bald and barbarous language of the old vulgar version'. Those who had read the Bible all their lives became accustomed to its oddities and archaic language, but those who came to it afresh found themselves lost in a sea of obsolete terms: almug, chode, habergeon, hosen, kab, neesed, ring-saked, trode, occurrent, ouches, tatches... Or the

Jacobean fantasy-language of the original Jacob who 'sod pottage' (Gen. 25.29) and 'removed that day the he goats that were ringstraked' (Gen. 30.35)

Increasingly incomprehensible, the Bible was increasingly ignored. As one eighteenth century Bible historian wrote

> to our shame, be it spoken, whatever Reputation the Holy Bible has been had in, it is now treated with the utmost Slight and Neglect, and is scarce anywhere read but in our Churches.[17]

But as the eighteenth century gave way to the nineteenth, the problem was not to be that the Bible was ignored and unread.

On the contrary, some people were reading it more closely than ever before.

Let there be luminaries...

In a curious volume in the Bodleian Library there is a bound collection of pamphlets, including an account of the execution of Lords Kilmarnock and Balmerino ('After the first blow, his Lordship's head fell back upon his shoulders, but being afterwards severed at two more gentle blows was then received into a piece of red bayes...') and a rather racy account of the proceedings of the bill of divorce between the Duke of Norfolk and Lady Mary Mordaunt, (William Bayly, servant: 'She used to come there about four or five a Clock in the Afternoon, and might stay there about two or three hours... By all that's good, I never saw them in Bed together.') But tear yourself away from these and you get to the Reverend Alexander Geddes' *Proposals for Printing by Subscription A New Translation of the Holy Bible*. Written in 1788, Geddes argues that a new translation needs to be made because the Hebrew text had been found to be defective

> The true signification of many words, to which the rabbins [sic] had affixed a wrong or vague meaning was discovered or determined by having recourse to the Arabic and other kindred dialects, and by a more particular attention to the antient versions.[18]

He offers two samples of his new translation: Genesis 1 and some bits from Exodus 8, 14–16. They are not very good.* But what is interesting is that Geddes was responding to a new approach to the 'antient versions': the study of the language, the editions, the methods of transmission. He was responding to the rise of textual criticism – the study of the linguistic accuracy of various editions and translations. In 1707, John Mill published a Greek text based on some 98 versions of the text – collected from manuscripts, early versions and quotations in the works of the church fathers. He claimed that there were thirty thousand variant readings – mistakes, misprints, additions, omissions.† Mill's work was taken on by Johann Bengel, a student at the University of Tübingen. He collected as many Greek manuscripts as he could and realised that, although there were variants, there were nowhere near as many as claimed by Mill. He published his Greek text in 1734, but the challenge it posed to the *Textus Receptus* caused him to be ostracised. Then along came Tischendorf, who viewed his task as 'the struggle to regain the original form of the New Testament'. Tischendorf published more manuscripts and fragments during his lifetime than any other scholar.

There are variants in these texts, as we've seen. But there is also a great, unbroken testimony as well. What they really confirm is the extraordinary accuracy with which the biblical text has been transmitted since the first century AD. In terms of the canonical manuscripts, no significant variations have ever been found; there are odd verses, some different stories, copying errors and later emendations, but these are minor issues and can usually be solved through comparison of the different texts.

---

* God, for example says 'Let there be LUMINARIES in the expanse of the heavens... Let the earth produce ANIMATED CREATURES according to their kinds, 'CATTLE, REPTILES and other TERRESTRIAL ANIMALS according to their kinds.' Geddes published two volumes of his translation before he (and his readers, presumably) ran out of steam.

† Most of these were minor: the difference, for example, between 'wait for' and 'await'. Some of these are well-meaning attempts to make sense of potentially baffling verses. For example, some much later manuscripts have Jesus talking about putting a *kamilos* (ship's rope) through the eye of a needle instead of a *kamelos* (camel).

The Bible was under scrutiny. A new age of science and reason trained an enquiring, critiquing light onto the Scriptures. But in many ways, science and reason were to enhance the understanding of the Bible rather than undermine it. While the textual critics began to explore the ancient manuscripts with a new zeal, others were exploring in a more literal sense, as archaeologists and explorers set out to discover and excavate the biblical sites.

Edward Robinson mapped hundreds of ancient biblical sites, as well as discovering the remains of Hezekiah's tunnel in Jerusalem. In 1868 a German missionary discovered the Moabite Stone – a monument carved with the oldest Hebrew script known, commemorating the defeat of Israel by Mesha, king of Moab. In Mesopotamia, thousands of cuneiform tablets were discovered in the abandoned libraries of long-forgotten emperors. Tischendorf made his trips to Egypt in the 1850s. The *Codex Sinaiticus* was published in facsimile in 1862 and the *Codex Alexandrinus* in 1879–1883. In 1880, the American scholar Ezra Abbot was able to reconstruct Tatian's *Diatesseron* from quotations in an ancient Armenian commentary, leading, in turn, to the identification of a complete translation of the *Diatesseron* in an Arabic manuscript in the Vatican library.* The Cairo *genizah* was uncovered in the 1890s; *Codex Sinaiticus* was purchased by the British Library in 1933; the Nag Hammadi library was discovered 1945 and 1952; and the Dead Sea Scrolls in 1947.

One find in particular led to a completely new understanding of the nature of the New Testament. It took place at Oxyrhynchus: a nondescript site in Egypt. There are no temples at Oxyrhynchus, no pyramids, no statuary. But there are some old rubbish dumps. Some very old rubbish dumps. And in 1895 a couple of British archaeologists called Grenfell and Hunt started to explore those rubbish tips. And what they found there was amazing.

Letters from an Egyptian dump
Back to Elizabeth's secret police. Reopen the file for a moment. Remember Marlowe's assertion that the New Testament was

---

* This was published in 1888. Another Arabic manuscript of the *Diatesseron* was discovered in the library in 1896.

'filthily written'? He was right, in a way. Greek as a literary language had reached a high point during the classical period – from around 500 to 323 BC – the era of the great playwrights and poets and philosophers. The people of the Hellenised Roman world couldn't speak classical Greek – they spoke a far more everyday version. The *literati* of the ancient world continued to write in classical Greek, but the ordinary people spoke *koiné* or 'common' Greek. Naturally it was the best Greek, the literary Greek that ended up being preserved in the libraries, because that was the language used by the best writers. The New Testament had been preserved in spite of its style, rather than because of it.

As we saw, this was an embarrassment to the translators of the AV, schooled as they were in classical Greek. In fact it was an embarrassment much earlier than that: Origen wrote that 'In the apostles there was no power of speaking or of giving an ordered narrative by the standards of Greek dialectical or rhetorical arts...' By which he meant that the Greek wasn't of a very high standard.[19]

It was not just the rough, sometimes ungrammatical style. It was that the New Testament also contained some five hundred words – around ten per cent of the vocabulary of the Greek New Testament – which were not found anywhere else in secular Greek literature up to that point. These five hundred words, it was thought, were special words, coined by the direct inspiration of God, freshly minted for the New Testament church. It was, the German theologian Richard Rothe suggested, 'the language of the Holy Ghost'.

It wasn't actually. Not unless the Holy Ghost was an Egyptian housewife. For what Grenfell and Hunt found in Oxyrhynchus was a treasure trove of papyrus fragments – wills, receipts, letters, accounts, the kind of writing that never gets collected and put into libraries. And those fragments, those mundane, ordinary scraps, contained many of the five hundred unique, Greek words from the New Testament.

For example, Matthew and Luke, in their account of the Lord's prayer, include a word found nowhere else in secular Greek: *epiousion*, as in *ton arton ton epiousion* – our daily bread (Matt. 6.1; Luke 11.3). But what exactly did this word *epiousion* mean? Did it mean bread for the next day, or bread just for survival? Or did it mean the bread used in the Eucharist? (Jerome thought so, he translated it as *supersubstantialis* – literally 'the bread above the substance'.) This uncertainty led people to think that it didn't mean real bread at all. In the early third century Origen suggested that it was a metaphor: 'the bread for which we should ask is spiritual,' he said. And then scholars started reading the Oxyrhynchus finds, and they found the very word: *epiousion*. It was in a shopping list just after a request for chickpeas and straw.[20]

Jesus was referring to *real* bread. The kind you went down the shops to buy. Fresh bread. Daily bread. The finds at Oxyrhynchus revolutionised the translation of the Bible, because they showed that the New Testament was written in the language of ordinary Greek-speaking people of the first century. It was written for the housewife and the trader and the soldier and the artisan. In that sense, Tyndale's Gloucestershire prose was much more authentic than the Jacobean richness of the Oxford and Cambridge dons.

Revised Greek text

The emergence of these texts increased the dissatisfaction with the AV. Not only was the language hard to understand, but the Greek texts it had worked from were now shown to be faulty. As new texts emerged from the dust of old libraries and the sands of the desert, the *Textus Receptus* – which was developed exclusively from medieval Greek manuscripts – badly needed revising.

In 1881 two English scholars – Brooke Foss Westcott and F.J.A. Hort – published a landmark book: *The New Testament in the Original Greek*. They broke new ground in textual studies; it was Westcott and Hort who first classified the manuscripts into four groups: Syrian, Western, Alexandrian and neutral. *Codex Vaticanus* was the neutral text – the one they believed to be closest to the original Greek. Over time this was changed into the Alexandrian family, the Caesarean Family, the 'Western' Family and the 'Byzantine' Family. The Alexandrian family (e.g. *Sinaiticus, Vaticanus, Alexandrinus*) is considered the most accurate by the majority of scholars.

Seventeen years later saw the publication of Eberhard Nestle's Greek text, the *Novum Testamentum Graece* in 1898. Nestle simply compared Tischendorf's text with that of Westcott-Hort. Where they

Sources for the modern Greek texts

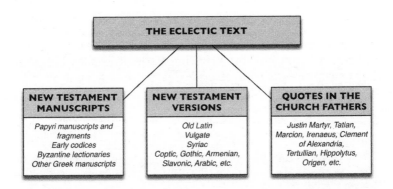

differed he went to another edition; where they agreed he took that as a standard reading. The result was a kind of compromise edition, and it was so successful that it lasted for seventy years. With revisions by Kurt Aland, the Nestle-Aland edition is still widely used today.[*]

These Greek New Testaments are what is known as eclectic texts – they are not taken from one single manuscript, but from a wide variety of sources. The eclectic text weighs each reading and decides which is the better one. This has become a crucial field of battle for those still wedded to the AV, which was translated from the combination of only six or seven manuscripts, all from the Byzantine tradition.

Scholars have three primary sources for New Testament texts: New Testament manuscripts; different translations of the New Testament and quotations taken from the works of the church fathers. Whereas Old Testament scholars have a paucity of ancient texts, the New Testament scholar is overwhelmed with choice. There are at least 5,400 known fragments or manuscripts of the New Testament, with more being discovered all the time.[†] Add in the thousands of copies of the various translations and you've got some serious work on

---

[*] This edition also formed the basis for the United Bible Societies' Greek Text – the only difference being the textual apparatus.

[†] For example, the recent discovery of lost pages of *Codex Sinaiticus*. See p.104.

Major sources of the Greek text

Chester Beatty Collection

In 1931 the Chester Beatty Library in Michigan acquired eleven papyrus fragments and manuscripts of the Bible. Dating from the third century AD, they are written in Greek and consist of seven fragments of Old Testament books, three from the New Testament, one from the Book of Enoch and one unidentified Christian sermon. They were bought from a dealer and probably originate from a Coptic graveyard in Egypt

Rylands Papyrus

Rylands Library Papyrus P52 is a fragment from a papyrus codex. The fragment only measures some 3.5 by 2.5 inches (8.9 by 6 cm) and it contains lines from John's gospel (18.31–33 on the front and 18. 37–38 on the back). Dated to between 117 and 138 AD, this is the earliest known manuscript of the New Testament.

Bodmer Collection

In 1956, Martin Bodmer purchased a number of biblical papyri for the eponymous Bodmer Library in Geneva. It includes a manuscript of John – or most of it at any rate – written about 200 AD. This manuscript also contains many alterations and corrections in the margin and above the text – presumably the work of a copyist. The collection also includes the earliest known copy of Jude and 1 and 2 Peter (200–300 AD) and the earliest known fragment from Luke (175–225 AD).

Codex Ephraemi

The fifth century palimpsest decoded by Tischendorf in 1841–1843. Scholars have used infra-red photography and chemical processes to retrieve the text – and found that Tischendorf had been very accurate.

Codex Bezae

A codex written in Greek on one side and Latin on the other. It dates from the late fifth/early sixth century. It was found in 1562 at Lyons, France by Theodore Beza – hence the name. It contains many variant, expanded readings.

Codex Washingtonianus

Aka the Washington Manuscript of the Gospels or The Freer Gospel, this codex containing the four gospels was discovered in 1906. It was written in Greek on vellum in the fourth or fifth century.

Lectionaries

Portions of the Greek New Testament are also preserved in Byzantine lectionaries. Around 2135 of these are known.

THE GLOBAL BIBLE

The first English Bible produced in English in the United States was the New Testament, printed in Philadelphia in 1777 by Robert Aitken. There had been a book of metrical psalms – the *Bay Psalm Book* – printed in 1640 but, before independence, it was illegal for American printers to publish a Bible in English. The British monopoly holders didn't want to miss out on the chance of a sale – even as far away as America.

During the War of Independence, Bibles were difficult to obtain. Initially Congress had explored the idea of a government sponsored version, inviting tenders from interested publishers. They eventually decided to import twenty thousand English Bibles from Holland, but Aitken – who had submitted a tender for the government version – decided to take the risk. His American entrepreneurship was rewarded: the New Testament was such a success that it ran into four reprints.[1]

Significantly, he used the AV. The first settlers, as we've seen, used the Geneva Bible. But the ban on printing English Bibles meant that this never established a foothold in America. Instead, Aitken chose the Authorised Version. Not that they called it that: in the newly independent America, a king had no right to authorise anything any more, so the version became known as the King James Bible, rather than the AV.

The other thing that firmly established the AV as America's favourite Bible (or favorite, perhaps) was the sheer scale of the printing. With typical American gung-ho, Bibles were stacked high and sold cheap. The Philadelphia printer Matthew Carey sold them as low as $3.50 a copy; by the 1840s, using new printing technology, the American Bible Society was selling whole Bibles at 45 cents each and New Testaments at 6 cents. By 1880 more than thirty-two million copies had been printed.[2]

As the first printed book in independent America, and the most widely distributed, the AV (or the KJV) embedded itself into American consciousness. More so than in Britain, the translation became sacred. What happened with the Septuagint in Egypt and the Vulgate in Europe happened with the KJV in America; the translation got confused with the original. Today the United States is the heart of the King James only movement. The KJV is fanatically – often viciously – defended by American pastors and churchgoers who believe it to be a truly inspired version, a version translated under the control of the Holy Spirit.

The King James Bible was the pet project of an extravagant, heavy-drinking, bisexual King, who agreed to it because he wanted to quash some republican marginal notes. Today it's the beloved version of the American right-wing, teetotal, anti-homosexual, ultra-Republican Bible belt. As many of its most vehement fans might say, 'Go figure.'

You Say 'Bible', I say 'Up-Biblum'

The AV may have been the first English Bible printed in America under independence, but it was not the first time the Scriptures had been printed. It was John Eliot who, in 1661, printed the first Bible printed in North America. Just not in English.

It was the 1661 Eliot Indian Bible or, to give it its proper name, the *Mamusse Wunneetupanatamwe Up-Biblum God*. It was a Bible in the language of the Algonquin natives, who were living in Massachusetts, and it was translated by John Eliot (hence the rather easier name). It was the first real missionary Bible since the Slavonic Bible of Cyril and Methodius. The work was supported by an organisation in England – the Corporation for the Promoting and Propagating the Gospel of Jesus Christ in New England.* The New Testament was printed in 1661 and the complete Bible in 1663. How much of a success it was is debatable. Eliot carried on his missionary work with it for twenty years, but after his death it was never printed again and the language itself has died.

Nevertheless, it led the way in the next great phase of the life of the Bible: the translation into many languages.

---

* I wonder if they called it CFTPAPTGOJCINE for short. Probably not. It was founded in 1649, by an Act of Parliament during the Commonwealth.

The president of the Corporation for the Promoting and Propagating, etc. etc. was Robert Boyle, the famous physicist. As well as being a noted scientist, he was an accomplished linguist who could read Greek, Hebrew, Syriac and Aramaic. Boyle was also a director of the East India Company and he gave money towards sponsoring missionaries to go East. Those missionaries required Bibles as well, so in 1677 the *Gospels and Acts in Malay* was produced. Boyle was a bit of a one man Bible Society: as well as the money he gave towards the Malay Bible, he also gave £70 towards printing the Bible in Turkish, and £700 towards printing the Bible in Gaelic.

The Corporation for the Promoting and Propagating, etc., etc. disappeared after Boyle's death, but two new organisations sprang up in its place: the Society For Propagating Christian Knowledge (1698) and the Society for the Propagation of the Gospel in Foreign Parts (1701).[*] Initially the aim of the SPG was to support the colonists in America, but then they expanded their vision to include the 'evangelisation of slaves and Native Americans'.

Societies sprang up all over Europe, sending missionaries out to all parts of the world. And these missionaries needed Bibles. One of the greatest missionaries – the founder of modern mission – William Carey founded a school of translation in Calcutta which translated the Bible into over forty languages.

The problems facing these translators were immense. Like Cyril and Methodius a thousand years before, they often had to start at the root. Missionaries had to create their own alphabets, and learnt to cast their own typeface. They had to try to get the multifaceted Bible into languages which sometimes contained only a few hundred words. They went into the places and had to find out all they could about the culture.[†] Many times it went wrong, as in the story of the missionary who purportedly translated 'Heavenly' as 'Sky Blue' leading to the prayer 'Our sky-blue Father...' Then there was the whole issue of culture. In countries which have never seen a sheep, what word do you use for the Lamb of God? (The translator working among the Inuit went for 'seal-pup'.)

---

[*] The former is now known as the Society for Promoting Christian Knowledge (SPCK) and the latter as the United Society for the Propagation of the Gospel.

[†] There is the story of one native whose name for the missionary was 'the white man with the book who torments us with questions.'

When Luther translated the Bible into German, only fifteen translations of the Bible had been made. By 1600, that figure had risen to forty; by 1700 it had risen to 52. By the start of the nineteenth century, the Bible had been translated into about seventy languages, mostly of middle Europe and the Mediterranean region.[3] In the nineteenth century the pace of translation and distribution was going to change dramatically.

The Bible and education

Before people could read the Bible they had to learn how to read. Few books have been responsible for more literacy than the Bible. And few men have done more to link the two than Robert Raikes: another of our candidates for the ten pound note, and another example of God's dangerous book bringing about real change. Raikes was a publisher, the proprietor of the *Gloucester Journal*.[4] A committed Christian, he saw how many people locked up under the Poor Law were there because they had no education. But where were they to get that education? There was no state education in the mid-eighteenth century.

So in 1780, Raikes started a school for boys in the slums. And since most of the boys worked from Monday to Saturday in the factories, he ran it on a Sunday. It was the world's first Sunday School. It was intended as a way of teaching the boys the basics of Christianity, but it started with teaching them to read: and their textbook was, of course, the Bible.

This was not, admittedly, modern education. Raike's curriculum was that 'The children were to come after ten in the morning, and stay till twelve; they were then to go home and return at one; and after reading a lesson, they were to be conducted to Church. After Church, they were to be employed in repeating the catechism till after five, and then dismissed, with an injunction to go home without making a noise.'*

Some were outraged. The schools were mocked as 'Raikes' Ragged Schools'. But the schools were enormously successful. By 1831, Sunday schools in Great Britain had a weekly attendance of 1,250,000

---

* Happy days.

children, an astonishing 25 per cent of the population. They were the forerunners of the state school system, a system which was not in place until the Elementary Education Act of 1870.

It was obvious to Raikes that people should start to read with the Bible. It was not indoctrination, because the evidence shows us that the Bible was, indeed, a book which ordinary working class people were desperate to read. Some, in fact, would walk miles...

Mary Jones and the Bible Society

In 1800 a young Welsh woman bought a Bible, and, in doing so, helped to inspire a new wave of Bible printing and distribution, on a scale never seen before.

Her name was Mary Jones. She came from a poor background – her parents were weavers – but Mary had taught herself to read and had saved up to get a Bible. It took her years to save up the money, and even then she was not sure where to get one. Bibles were scarce in Wales; in 1799 the SPCK had printed ten thousand Welsh Bibles and two thousand New Testaments, but by April 1800 the entire edition had been sold out and, due to lack of funds, the SPCK had been unable to publish any more.

Mary heard a rumour that a clergyman in Bala called Thomas Charles had some copies. It took her two days to walk the 25 miles from her home in Llanfihangel to Bala only to find, on arrival, that the Bible had been promised to someone else. Exhausted, she broke down in tears. Moved by her plight, Thomas Charles relented and sold her a copy he'd promised to someone else. Mary got her Bible, and in it, showing her halting command of English, she wrote 'Mary Jones His the True Onour of this Bible.'*

Charles, moved by the scarcity of Welsh Bibles, decided to do something. At a meeting of the Religious Tract Society in 1802, he raised the issue of the need for Welsh Bibles. The Secretary of the Society, the Reverend Joseph Hughes, suggested that 'a Society might be formed for the purpose.' Then he added, 'But if for Wales why not for the Kingdom? Why not for the world?' Two years later the British and Foreign Bible Society was formed.

---

* Mary's Bible is owned by the Bible Society. She dated it 1800 – she got hold of one of the last copies of the 1799 edition.

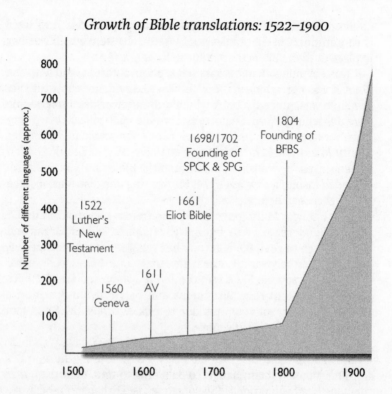

Growth of Bible translations: 1522–1900

That's the story, anyhow. And it's become a foundation myth of British Bible translation. In all probability, however, Mary Jones' story wasn't quite so crucial at the time. She did walk to Bala just to get a Bible – but she apparently bought two at the time, so maybe they hadn't quite run out. It took Charles another two years before he raised the issue, and, in the discussions and meetings which led to the foundation of the society, no hint of Mary Jones can be found. The earliest known reference to the story isn't until sixty years after the event – in *The Bible Society Reporter* for January 1867.[5]

But maybe that's the point. Mary's case was not unusual; that there were many people so desperate to lay their hands on a Bible that they would walk for miles and spend their life savings on it.

There were *thousands* of Marys – young, working class people who had learned to read and desperately wanted to read the Bible in their own language.

The demand for Welsh Bibles shows just how desperate they were. In July 1806 ten thousand Welsh New Testaments reached Wales, two years later a further thirty thousand New Testaments and twenty thousand Bibles were sent. For the next ten years, an average number of eleven thousand copies of the Scriptures in Welsh were distributed in Wales. Never mind the boys at the plough, the lads down the pit were also starting to read the Bible for themselves.

The British and Foreign Bible Society was only the first of many. Over the course of the next decade, there were Bible Societies founded in Germany, Switzerland, Holland, Sweden, Russian, Finland and Hungary. In 1816, the American Bible Society was founded. Their work coincided with the expansion of the European empires and the growth of the missionary movement.

By 1800 the Bible – or parts of it – were available in over five hundred languages, by the middle of the twentieth century that number had risen to over eleven hundred languages – eight hundred of these translations had been produced by the British and Foreign Bible Society. No organisation in history has done more to make the Bible available throughout the world.

The Bible Society worked to a number of principles. First, they decided that, in order to escape the problems caused in previous centuries, all their Bibles would be without marginal notes or interpretations. They were just going to deliver the plain, vanilla-flavoured texts. This approach ensured that the Bible Society was supported by Christians of many different denominations; it was a truly ecumenical programme.

Secondly, they decided that all Bibles should be sold, not given away. Bibles were objects with value; the buyer should pay something, even if it was not much. So the Society employed colporteurs – Bible salesmen – who spent their time on the road.* The colporteurs went to many remote places, where money was scarce, so they often received goods instead – bartering for the Bible. A Bible might be

---

* The word comes from a French word for an itinerant peddler of books and newspapers. When the Society used the word it was quite a modern term – the first recorded English use is in 1796.

exchanged for a new caught rabbit or new laid eggs or bunches of grapes. A Spanish blacksmith shod the colporteur's donkey in return for a New Testament. In Morocco, an Arabic gospel was exchanged for a pail of water for the colporteur's horse, while passing sailors at Port Said offered fans, chopsticks, cigars, sunshades and musical instruments in payment for Chinese and Japanese Scriptures.

These colporteurs made heroic efforts to take the Bible to people. At Chelyabinsk in Siberia, the Society's colporteur used a horse and sledge; in Algiers, an elderly Frenchman who had pioneered work in the Sahara made 'journeys of three month's duration by camel, far into the desert'.[6] They were not always welcomed. In some Muslim countries, they met with opposition and even violence. In Austria, it was considered a criminal act to sell a New Testament in the street. In Spain and Portugal, colporteurs were routinely arrested. In 1905 a Spanish colporteur was arrested for 'devoting himself to the sale of books which are contrary to morals and religion.' That'd be the Bible, then.[7]

In Konigsburg in 1911, one of the colporteurs reported that 'When I offered them the Scriptures they answered with blasphemy. It is impossible to describe their hatred of the Bible and they fight it with every weapon in their armoury.' 'The universal experience of our colporteurs,' reported the Bible Society's agent in Germany 'is that the Socialist surpasses all others in the virulence of his hatred of the Book, and in the depth of his contempt for its teachings'. There were 'dead walls of opposition among vast bodies of the working classes'.[8] This was different in England, where the socialism of Ruskin, Morris and the Fabians had a definite Christian feel to it. Socialism in Britain and America was rooted in, rather than opposed to, the Bible.*

The Revised Version
The Church of England eventually made concessions to the modern age. They agreed that, perhaps, the time had come for a revision of the Authorised Version. But from the start this revision was hobbled. Just as King James insisted that his translators should adhere to

---

* The American Christian Socialist and Baptist minister Francis Bellamy was the author of the original pledge of allegiance: 'I pledge allegiance to my Flag and the Republic for which it stands, one nation indivisible, with liberty and justice for all.'

the previous editions and to the 'traditional wordings', the powers behind the revision decided that it should stick as closely as possible to the AV. They even followed the AV's production method, with fifty-four scholars working in different 'companies' on different areas.

It was hoped that this would be a transatlantic version, with committees set up both in the UK and in the USA. However, the American committees did not like the strict guidelines issued from the UK. They wanted to make more radical changes (such as 'Holy Spirit' for 'Holy Ghost'). Thus, the process actually resulted in two new editions: in the UK there was the Revised Version (New Testament 1881, whole Bible 1885), while in the USA there was the American Standard Version (1901).

The Americans' instincts were right. The Revised Version failed because it ducked the issue. It tried to fix faulty foundations by redecorating. As one of the translators ruefully noted, 'It was a mistaken directive, in commissioning the Revised Version, to limit the language of the new text to the vocabulary of Tudor and Jacobean authors.'[9]

For some Christians, however, the appearance of the Revised Version was just another example of the erosion of the old certainties. The geologists and biologists had tampered with Genesis, now renegade Christians were trying to tamper with the AV. It was around this time that the idea of the AV as a God-given, inspired version began to grow. Their position was summed up in Edward Hill's words

> ...if we believe in God's providential preservation of the Scriptures, we will retain the King James Version, for in so doing we will be following the clear leading of the Almighty.[10]

Along with those who sanctified the AV for religious reasons, there were many who idolised it for literary reasons. As the British Empire began to unravel, the AV became an object of nostalgia, a holy relic from the days when Britain was great. The AV was praised by people such as Matthew Arnold as 'a great national monument'. Writers made outlandish claims for the quality of its language

...above them all [i.e. Shakespeare, Milton, etc.] is the prose of our Common Version. It is more sustained than any of them, more uniformly strong and melodious in its flow... And it has largely contributed to the fixation of the language at this its best estate, since the number of words in it the meaning of which has become obsolete in the course of nearly three subsequent centuries is so small that they may almost be counted on the fingers.[11]

Presumably the writer had a lot of fingers. The English scholar John Livingstone Lowes praised its 'utter simplicity, limpid clearness, the vividness of direct, authentic vision'. All arrant nonsense, of course. The AV has many qualities, but 'utter simplicity' would not be one of them. In Britain, it was to be another sixty years before a wholesale revision of the AV. But by that time people had become fed up waiting and, as we shall see, they had started to do the work themselves.

As the nineteenth century came to an end, there was still a thirst, a demand for the Bible, not only in Britain, but across the world. In 1905 the BFBS shipped 5,857,000 copies of the Bible; in 1909, 6,620,024 copies; and five years later, in 1914, they distributed over ten million copies.

And then the world turned dark. The Scriptures, it seemed, came to life on the fields of Flanders: at least those parts that talked of apocalypse and death and dark judgment. In his report for 1916, the Secretary of the Bible society turned to apocalyptic language

These last three years have shown us what unsuspected chasms are yawning under our feet. We feel like men who must grope their way on some strange planet, which is full of awful energies and incalculable perils. For us the fountains of the great deep are broken up, and the windows of heaven and the gates of hell are opened.[12]

THE DANGEROUS BIBLE

On June 4, 1913, a woman was trampled to death by a horse.

The event took place during the Derby. As the racehorses rounded Tattenham corner, hooves thundering, the crowd roaring, a woman rushed out among them, her hands raised above her head. A galloping horse struck her like a battering ram, cartwheeling, crushing her. The horse died immediately: the woman in hospital four days later. She had few possessions with her: a return railway ticket; a purple, green and white scarf tied around her waist; and a membership card for the Women's Social and Political Union. She was a suffragette.

The horse was called Anmer. The horse's owner was called George Frederick Ernest Albert of Saxe-Coburg and Gotha, or George V in *koiné* English. The woman was called Emily Davison. And the night before she'd been reading her Bible.

Emily did not intend to commit suicide that day – the return ticket is evidence of that. Probably it was a stupid, naïve miscalculation: some say that she was trying to fix some kind of Suffragette pennant to the reins of the horse. But when she died, she was hailed as a martyr.

The Suffragettes were founded in 1903. They began with rallies and speeches but, after ten years of intransigence, disdain and semi-official brutality, they turned to more extreme measures: hunger strikes, arson, assault. Emily Davison was middle class, single; Oxford-educated and a committed member of her local Anglican church. She was also a jailbird. In 1909 she was arrested five times and imprisoned four. Emily Davison's extreme protests were rooted in her reading of the Bible. In an unpublished essay called 'The Real Christianity,' she argued that the teaching of the church was a horrible distortion of Scripture; that real Christianity happened when men and women were equal. She likened the persecution of the Suffragettes to that faced by the Early Church. In another piece she used Jesus' parable of the pearl of great price, to illustrate that one must be willing to pay the ultimate price for liberty

> To lay down life for friends, that is glorious, selfless, inspiring! But to re-enact the tragedy of Calvary for generations yet unborn, that is the last consummate sacrifice of the Militant.

She was a member of the Anglican Church League for Women's Suffrage. Her friends described her as someone who was 'innately religious', who 'always said very long prayers' and 'believed herself to be obeying a direct call'. Her Bible was 'always by her bedside' and her favourite saying was Benjamin Franklin's dictum – with more than a hint of the Geneva Bible – 'Rebellion against tyrants is obedience to God.'[1]

Davison never used the term martyr to describe herself, but clearly she thought in precisely those terms. In her mind, the issue of female suffrage and the outrage of women being tortured in jail was inherently bound up with her faith. Others agreed. The cover of the June 13 issue of *The Suffragette* depicted a female angel standing in front of shadowy race goers, with the legend 'Greater love hath no man than this, that he lay down his life for his friends' underneath it. In *The Suffragette* of June 27, a full-page of tributes to her had the headline 'A Christian Martyr'.

Emily was signal proof of the power of the Bible to disrupt. The Bible has always been a book which changed behaviour, which mandated, even encouraged, its readers to challenge injustice and oppression. To the totalitarian states of the twentieth century, just as it had been for the monarchies of the sixteenth, the Bible was a threat. Josef Stalin and King James I had this in common: they knew that, in the wrong hands, the Bible was subversive.

Burning books

Decree number 353 of the Soviet Commissariat for Education and Commerce, issued in 1929, states that no Bible might be printed, circulated or studied in public in any part of the Soviet Union. Importing Scripture was a criminal offence. All Bibles in the Soviet Union were to be rounded up and burnt.

Five years later in Germany, the sale of all religious literature, including Bibles, was forbidden for a period of over six months, the official reason given being that Communists were circulating their propaganda under the guise of religious publications. At the same time there was an intensification of anti-Christian propaganda in the press; this was often directed against the Bible and no right of reply was ever conceded.

The major political movements of the twentieth century were anti-biblical in their opinions. The religious texts which shaped the conflicts of the time were not the Bible, but *Mein Kampf, Das Kapital* and *Quotations from Chairman Mao Zedong.*

In some countries – notably the United States – the Bible maintained a dominant place at the heart of the culture; while in England, both the church and society were never the same after the bloodbath of the First World War. Fear of atheistic Communism lay behind the Catholic church's tacit support for some anti-democratic dictatorships.* In many parts of the world, however, the Bible was what it had always been – a document of the radical margins, a truly dangerous book.

In 1936, the Bible Society's Superintendent in Berlin – Rudolph Haupt – decided to make a point. He put up a sign pointing out to the German public that, during the previous year more copies of the Bible had been sold than of *Mein Kampf*. A little while later he was visited by the secret police who ordered the sign's removal. He slipped out of the country after that.[2]

In Nazi Germany, the children of Marcion were alive and well. The theological anti-Semitism which stretched back through Kant, Schliermacher to Martin Luther and beyond was co-opted by the thoroughly non-religious National Socialists. Nazi propagandists aimed to discredit the Bible as a predominantly Jewish book and suggested that it should be rewritten to exclude the conspicuously Jewish elements (including the teaching of St Paul.) This suggestion was taken seriously by many Germans, who occasionally asked the

---

* Many Catholics were, of course, vehemently opposed to such regimes. The Nazis incarcerated 3,647 Polish Catholic bishops and priests in concentration camps, of whom some two thousand died. And Evangelical Protestants have nothing to feel smug about; their support for South Africa and other oppressive regimes in the latter part of the twentieth century is well documented.

Bible Society's colporteurs whether they had these 'new' Bibles for sale. German Christians who found in their Bible a thoroughly anti-Nazi ideology were ruthlessly hunted. Perhaps the most well-known is Dietrich Bonhoeffer, who said that 'If the synagogues burn today, the churches will be on fire tomorrow.' When his seminary was closed down by the Nazis, he ran a 'seminary on the run', moving from village to village, working with students who were mainly operating illegally. Bonhoeffer was hanged in the Flossenberg Penal Camp in April 1945, for his involvement in the German resistance movement.

As in Germany, so in Russia, where Stalin instituted a full-out assault on the Orthodox church. Over 57,000 churches had been active in 1914; by 1941, there were around 4250 left. Only 30 of the estimated 1500 convents and monasteries remained open.[3]

It is easy, from the comfort of our society, to condemn those who stayed silent about the atrocities of the Nazi or Soviet regimes. But in that climate of terror the implications of speaking out were enormous. And, in fact, many individual Christians did, indeed, stand against the onslaught. The Pope may have given a shamefully inadequate response to the execution of Jews, but many of his followers were more active. Throughout Europe, nuns sheltered Jewish children in their convents. In Münster, that historical home of radical belief, the Catholic Bishop Cardinal von Galen preached forcefully against the murder of psychiatric patients. Both Protestant and Catholic clergy spoke out against Nazi euthanasia programmes.

One striking example of a biblically-driven community is the French Protestant village of Le Chambon-sur-Lignon, where the pastor, André Trocmé and his wife Magda led the villagers in a remarkable expression of non-violent resistance. The villagers refused to swear an oath of loyalty to Marshal Pétain, leader of the collaborationist Vichy regime. Amélie, the village bell ringer, refused to ring the bell to mark a Vichy celebration. (When visitors complained to her, she said the bell belonged to God, not Marshal Pétain.) Most of all, the village offered refuge to Jews. When a Prefect from Vichy came to 'examine' the Jews in the village – a prelude to rounding them up and shipping them to Germany – he was told that 'we make no distinction between Jews and non-Jews. It is contrary to Gospel teaching.' At the peak, five thousand Jews were hiding in the village.[4]

The Bible was dangerous to Nazi Germany and Soviet Russia, but in much of Western Europe it was ancient, toothless, decayed. Although the Revised Version and the American Standard Version had opened the issue of translation, the 'official' church drew back from any further revision.

Instead, the twentieth century is the century of the 'unofficial' Bible. The interesting thing about the new English translations of the Bible in the early twentieth century is that they are virtually all the work of individuals. We are back in the age of Luther and Tyndale, with one scholar labouring away in his study. Between 1900 and 1940 around twenty new translations of either the New Testament or the entire Bible were issued by individuals.

Some of these were the work of amateur scholars, often with an axe to grind.* Others were simply motivated by their frustration with the published editions and their desire to see the text in a more accessible language. So, you find titles like R.F. Weymouth's *The New Testament in Modern Speech* (1903), Charles B. Williams' *The New Testament, a translation in the language of the people* (1937) and S.H. Hooke's *The Basic Bible, Containing the Old and New Testaments in Basic English*. The latter aimed to translate the Bible using only a basic vocabulary of some 850 words.†

The twentieth century New Testament
One of the most interesting of these amateur attempts at translation is *The Twentieth Century New Testament* (1898–1901; revised

---

* For example, Adolph Ernst Knoch's *Concordant Version* issued in 1926. The full title is, *Concordant version the Sacred Scriptures: designed to put the English reader in possession of all the vital facts of divine revelation without a former knowledge of Greek, by means of a restored Greek text, with various readings, conforming, as far as possible, to the inspired autographs, a consistent sublinear based upon a standard English equivalent for each Greek element, and an idiomatic, emphasized English version with notes, which are linked together and correlated for the English reader by means of an English concordance and lexicon and a complementary list of the Greek elements.* I can't wait for the movie. Knoch was the editor of a magazine called *Unsearchable Riches*. He published the Bible to promote his theology. He believed that the Trinity was not biblical and that the doctrine of the soul's immortality was based on Plato rather than the Bible.

† He couldn't do it – he had to add a special Bible vocabulary of some 150 extra words.

1904), the work of Mary Higgs, Ernest de Mérindol Mallan and others. Mary Higgs was the wife of a Congregational minister in Oldham, Lancashire. Ernest de Mérindol Mallan, despite his rather exotic name, was a signal engineer from Hull. Not what you'd call traditional Bible translator material. But they identified that the ordinary working class of England were effectively ostracised by their own Scriptures. 'Though in the course of the last hundred years the Bible has been translated into the vernacular of most countries,' they wrote in their preface, 'the language of our Bible remains the English of three hundred years ago.'

They realised that they could not undertake this task, so they used a team of eighteen volunteer experts. They used the latest Greek text – as found in Westcott and Hort. They issued the book in a series of 'Tentative Editions' before a final revised edition in 1904. It's a remarkably modern, radical, collaborative approach and one which, just twenty years after the Revised Version, was bound to ruffle feathers. The text was in a single column with subheadings in bold and the books were rearranged into a chronological order: the gospels (beginning with Mark) and Acts, then James, then Thessalonians, Galatians and so on. As they stated in the preface

> It is certain that our translation will not be acceptable to those who regard any attempt to re-translate the New Testament as undesirable, if not dangerous. It is, nevertheless, hoped that, by this modern translation, the New Testament may become a living reality to many by whom the Authorized Version, with all its acknowledged beauties, is but imperfectly understood or never read.

Och aye, the Noo Testament

Between the wars, one of the most popular of these modern vernacular editions was *The Moffatt Bible*, by James Moffatt (NT 1913, Bible 1924). A brilliant scholar – he was Professor of Greek and New Testament Exegesis at Oxford – Moffatt was frustrated by the archaic translations. To ensure his version was fresh, he refrained from consulting any other version while translating. His Scottish background comes out in places, like the parable of the dishonest 'factor', the episode of Noah's barge, and the linen kilt worn by David when he

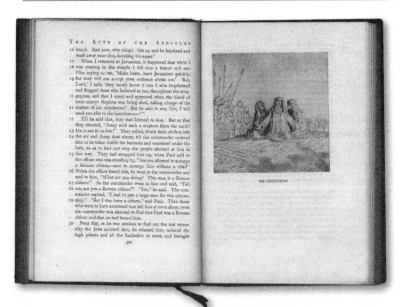

The Moffatt Bible, with illustrations by William Strang.

danced before the Lord (2 Sam. 6.14). But that's what gives the translation its vigour.[*]

It drew complaints and outrage. It was colloquial. It lacked dignity. It did, admittedly, plunge into the speculative – in the New Testament alone Moffatt adopted some thirty conjectural readings which were completely unsupported in any manuscripts. He also saw nothing wrong in altering the order of passages, so that in the New Testament, for example, John 3.22–30 appears after 2.12 and before 2.13. Sometimes, where he thought a concept could not be translated, he simply used a transliteration: John 1.1 begins 'The Logos existed in the very beginning...' In the Old Testament, he used the name 'the Eternal' to translate 'Yahweh'. In the Old Testament he used different fonts to indicate the different sources of the Pentateuch.[†] Finally, he managed to offend both Roman Catholics and Lutherans by his translation of Matthew 26.26, 'Take and eat this, it means my body.'

---

[*] And let's face it, 'barge' is a much clearer word than 'Ark'.

[†] J, E, P, D, etc. See p.33–34

Phillips

Moffatt's baton was taken up by J. B. Phillips, who published a series of New Testament translations from 1947 to 1957. They were collected together as *The New Testament in Modern English*. Phillips' translation was a result of his work as a vicar with young people in south east London during the Second World War. 'I undertook the work,' he wrote, 'simply because I found that the Authorised Version was not intelligible to them.'

He took a deliberately informal, colloquial approach. Perhaps, at times, a bit too informal. He translates John 1.1 as 'At the beginning God expressed himself' which sounds a bit unpleasant to me. Elsewhere, Phillips is rather public schoolboy-ish: upset by Jesus' apparent rudeness, he adds the word 'please' to Jesus' request for a drink in John 4.7.

Phillips aimed to explain as much as translate. In the preface to the first edition of his *Letters to Young Churches,* he offered five principles behind his translation

> 1. As far as possible the language used must be such as is commonly spoken, written and understood at the present time.
>
> 2. When necessary the translator should feel free to expand or explain, while preserving the original meaning as nearly as can be ascertained.
>
> 3. The Letters should read like letters, not theological treatises. Where the Greek is informal and colloquial, the English should be the same.
>
> 4. The translation (or in some cases, the paraphrase) should 'flow' and be easy to read. Artificial 'verses' should be discarded, though cross-headings can be introduced to divide the letters into what seem to be their natural sections.
>
> 5. Though every care must be taken to make the version accurate, the projected value of this version should lie in its 'easy-to-read' quality. For close meticulous study, existing modern versions should be consulted.

I can't imagine the AV translators signing up to any of these.

Dynamic equivalence

Phillip's approach is based on what came to be termed as dynamic equivalence – a phrase coined by the American linguist Eugene Nida, writing in the 1960s. The idea was not to provide a literal rendering, but to get the sense of the idea behind the text. As Phillips puts it, the aim was to 'produce in the hearts and minds of his readers an effect equivalent to that produced by the author upon his original readers.' Dynamic equivalence is more concerned with the meaning – it has sometimes been termed a 'thought for thought' translation and it is particularly useful when dealing with metaphors and euphemisms, which change their meaning over time.

At the other end of the spectrum is formal equivalence. This is concerned with the literal meaning: the ultimate in formal equivalence is to render the text exactly as it is written, in the same order, word-for-word.

Different types of writing require different approaches. For novels, for example, the dynamic equivalence is vital. You want the text to be readable. But in a contract or a treaty, it is absolutely vital that the correct words are used. Dynamic equivalence is all about readability; formal equivalence is all about fidelity to the original.

Having said all that, all translation is dynamic to some extent, because no translation can be one hundred per cent true to the words and concepts of another language. Modern translations adopt a variety of approachs, spanning the spectrum from the literal, word-for-word, to the ultra-informal thought-for-thought.

The Revised Standard Version

Eventually, even the official version had to take notice and it was decided to revise the Revised Version. The goal was to 'embody the best results of modern scholarship as to the meaning of the Scriptures,' but there was still an umbilical attachment to the AV, as the translators also wanted to 'preserve those qualities which have given to the King James version a supreme place in English literature'. The result was the Revised Standard Version, which appeared in several different editions, including the scholarly Oxford Annotated Bible, a Catholic version of the New Testament (1965) and the ambitious Common Bible which was an ecumenical edition, designed to appeal to Catholic, Orthodox and Protestant churches.

The RSV was a popular edition, achieving the solidity of an 'authorised' text with a more modern, readable approach. But it was not universally welcomed. When Thomas Nelson published it in the States, an irate reader wrote: 'Who is this Tom Nelson who has written a new Bible? I don't want Tom Nelson's Bible. I want the Bible the way the Apostle James wrote it.' Its ecumenical aims also opened it to accusations of liberalism. Isaiah 7.14 had 'young maiden' instead of virgin; John 3.16 read 'For God so loved the world that he gave his only Son' and not 'his only begotten Son' as in the AV. One pastor – in America – was reported to have burned a copy with a blow torch in his pulpit.* In America, the Revised Standard Version was seen as a direct challenge to the American Standard Bible, and it led to the issuing of the New American Standard Bible in 1971.

The end of this strand of 'official' publications comes with the New Revised Standard Version in 1989. This updated the language once more, and took account of the latest in critical biblical scholarship and established itself as one of the scholarly standard editions.

Fans of the AV, however, weren't giving up and they issued their own series of revisions to the AV. Mostly these were restricted to modernisations of the language. The King James II Version, issued in 1901, gives the impression, from its title, that it was issued by James II of England, before he was replaced. I doubt this is what they intended – not least because James II was Catholic. It claimed to be based on the fact that 'A pre-study of textual criticism encompassing more than a thousand hours convinced us that the best text was that used by Tyndale and the KJV scholars.' Perhaps if they'd spent a couple of hours more, they'd have realised that Tyndale and the KJV scholars actually worked from different Greek source texts.[5]

The Bible and nonviolence

The twentieth century was a century of violence, a rolling boil of continual mechanised war. The New Atheists, who see religion as the source of all evil, tend to ignore the twentieth century, when

---

* He remarked that it resembled the devil in that it was hard to burn. Perhaps he needed a bigger blowtorch.

it was not religion but race, political ideology and the crumbling of empires that ignited genocide and conflict. As Eric Hobsbawm wrote, the twentieth century was 'an era of religious wars, though the most militant and bloodthirsty religions were secular ideologies of nineteenth-century vintage.'[6]

For the first few centuries of its life, the church was committed to peace-making. The Early Church refused to serve in the army; a stance that they had to revise when, in the fourth century, Christianity became the official religion of the Roman Empire. The Reformation radicals, such as the Anabaptists, also espoused non-violence. Seventeenth century groups such as the Quakers and the Mennonites took their non-violent stand from the Bible.

In the twentieth century, amidst the carnage, the idea became more complex and more urgent. How was one to turn the other cheek in the face of fascism and communism? Hitler derided the notion of turning the other cheek as a 'Jewish doctrine'.[7]

There were those who put Jesus' ideas into practice. The most famous of these were people like Gandhi and Martin Luther King Jr. Gandhi was not a Christian, but he took his inspiration from Jesus' teaching of non-violent protest. King Jr most certainly was a Christian – despite what some right-wing websites would have you believe. A Baptist pastor from southern Alabama, he did more than anyone to destroy racial segregation in the United States.

In doing so, he held his reading of the Bible up against that of his opponents. For centuries the Bible had been used to support segregation, apartheid and slavery, via intepretations which mixed historic literalism and sheer fantasy. Slavery was justified, for example, on the grounds that it was in the Bible: the Patriarchs had slaves; some early Christians had slaves.* Separation was justified on more bizarre grounds. The Dutch Reformed Church developed a theology of separation, based on the idea that God 'willed nations to be apart'. God was a maker of separations, starting with the separating the waters from the earth, charging on through Israel's separation from its neighbours, and ending with a bizarre reinterpretation of Christ's parable of the sheep and the goats.

---

* The Patriarchs were also circumcised but, strangely, slave owners didn't seem so keen to get that done.

What is interesting, of course, is that the Bible contains the exact opposite. Far from owning slaves, Jesus called for his followers to *become* slaves. 'A slave is not greater than his master' he said (John 15.20). The Greek word used here – *doulos* – means slave, although it can mean servant. Almost all modern translations choose 'servant' rather than slave; at the times when the Bible was being translated into English, and especially in America, no-one wanted to be a 'slave'.[8] At the Synod of Dort in 1619, the Dutch Reformed Church stated the official Calvinist position: any slaves who converted to Christianity should enjoy 'equal right of liberty with other Christians'. This was vehemently rejected by Christians elsewhere. The Anglican Thomas Secker argued that 'the Scripture, far from making any Alteration in Civil Rights, expressly directs, that every Man abide in the condition wherein he is called, with great Indifference of mind concerning outwards circumstances'.[9] A preacher who later tried to persuade a congregation of slaves that Paul's letter to Philemon condemned 'the practice of running away' was met with disbelief. Half his congregation ran away from his sermon: they simply walked out.

Yet for all this oppression, slaves in America did not reject the Christian beliefs of their owners, but adopted them and reinterpreted them for themselves. Sometimes violently, as in the case of Gabriel Prosser, who, inspired by his reading of the Bible, tried to establish a black kingdom in Virginia. He was known as the 'Black Samson'. In 1831, a Baptist preacher in Virginia by the name of Nat Turner called out for a holy war against slavery. The resulting uprising claimed hundreds of lives. Turner was hanged. For other slaves, the Exodus story was foundational for the emerging African-American Christianity. 'Let my people go,' they sang. They saw in the Bible a story of liberty and rescue.

King Jr. was the descendants of slaves and he used their iconography, their Exodus-inspired glossary. His speeches are, of course, drenched in Scripture; phrases ripped from the Old Testament, mountain-tops and river-crossings and freedom. King was 'driven back to the Sermon on the Mount, with its sublime teaching on love, and to the Gandhian method of non-violent resistance'.[10] Non-violence, he believed, was not a weakness, but a strength, an expression of transformational Christian love.

Not everyone was so keen. The tub-thumping right-wing demagogue and TV evangelist Jerry Falwell claimed that 'Jesus was not a pacifist.' He must have missed that bit of Matthew.

Revelation and popular culture

But then, maybe he'd got too caught up with his readings of another book entirely. In 1999, Falwell famously declared that the Antichrist was probably alive and that 'Of course he'll be Jewish.'[11] (He later apologised to those who thought his words anti-Semitic.) He was engaging in the ever-popular hobby of end-time speculation. Because if there is one book of the Bible that has dominated the late twentieth century, it is the book that nearly got left out. Revelation, with its vivid visual imagery, its conspiracy-theory prose, its anti-Imperialist stance, fills our modern vocabulary – Armageddon, the grim reaper, Antichrist, the apocalypse, the pearly gates, number of the beast, 666, ruled with a rod of iron, Alpha and Omega, streets paved with gold – all these phrases originate in the strangest of texts.

The twentieth and twenty-first century have proved particularly fertile soil for Revelation. Partly it was the arrival of the year 2000, partly it was that, for the first time in history, mankind really did have the power to make some of those events real, to end the world in a hail of fire, but the fact is that no book is more beloved of conspiracy theorists, apocalyptic visionaries and general nutters than Revelation.

The world of Revelation-bloggers is a strange, disturbing place, where paranoia mates with real-world events to produce deformed, mutant theories: 'It is clear that the Third Horseman of the Apocalypse, Economic Chaos, is riding in the world today,' one man types, rather feverishly. 'Note that the world population officially reaches 6.8 billion near Dec. 1 2009, and Revelation 6:8 is about the Fourth Horseman, Death, so will Death ride then as a Swine Flu mutation?' another suggests. The websites are feverish with speculation: barcodes carry the numeric virus of 666, the Antichrist is Putin, Obama, Simon Cowell...

Nothing new here, of course. When William the Conqueror decided to list all his newly conquered lands in a book, many of the conquered English believed that this was the 'Book of Life' as recorded in Revelation.[12] It was the end of the world. So they named the book 'the Domesday Book' – the book of judgment.

Luther also reinterpreted Revelation to reflect the political events of his time. The 27-year old Albrecht Dürer published the text of the Book of Revelation with fifteen woodcut illustrations which made him famous. but the pictures reflect an avowedly political interpretation of the book: in one engraving the Roman emperor is dressed in a turban like a Turk – the infidel superpower of the day. In his iconic drawing of the four horsemen, the fourth horseman, death, tramples an Emperor who falls into hell. The worshippers of the beast include a cleric, a merchant, a Turk, an emperor and a queen.

In the centuries since, the protagonists of Revelation have been widely identified. The Branch Davidians identified the US Government as the smooth-talking Beast from the earth[*] but over the years Revelation-junkies have come up with many other beastly candidates: Martin Luther, various Popes, the French Revolution, Kaiser Wilhelm II, Hitler, the British Empire, the European Union, the New World Order, Bill Gates and Microsoft. The fact that it was probably Nero just spoils the fun.

The problem is that, handled incautiously, Revelation can be damaging. Toxic. Take Edgar C. Whisenant who preached that the rapture – when the faithful would be whisked away out of this world – would occur in September 1988. There would then be a period of tribulation ending in Armageddon on October 4 1995. Trusting Whisenant, some Christians sold their homes in preparation for the rapture; others even had their dogs put down to save them from suffering when their Christian masters and mistresses were suddenly take away. Whisenant's book *88 Reasons Why the Rapture Will Be in 1988* was a best-seller. 'Only if the Bible is in error am I wrong' he claimed, thus making his stupidity the Bible's fault.[†]

Today Revelation continues to inspire and frighten, nourishing our paranoia that one day all this will come crashing down, one day the world will end in fire and hail and brimstone and we'll all have to

---

[*] See page 70.

[†] More recently a man called Harold Camping has predicted that the rapture will occur on May 21, 2011. His works include *We're almost there!* and *Another Infallible Proof That God Gives That Assures The Rapture Will Occur May 21, 2011*. I have mixed feelings about this, not least because it's my birthday the next day and I'd hate to miss out on the cake.

revert to hunting like feral animals. Revelation's Willy Wonka candy store of biblical imagery looks wonderful, tastes fantastic, but spend too long in there and all your teeth start to fall out.

Dürer: Four horsemen, with an emperor-figure, falling into hell, bottom left. the picture illustrates Revelation 6.1–8. From right to left, the riders are pestilence, war, famine and death.

Apocalypse Now: Revelation in action

Revelation has fuelled a multitude of apocalyptic sects, from the Montanists of the second century to the doomed suicide sects of Heaven's Gate and Jonestown in the twentieth century. Although those who predict the date of the Second Coming have all been wrong, as Diarmaid MacCulloch puts it, 'for true apocalypticists there is no giving up hope'.[13]

Fifth Monarchy Men

The seventeenth century was one of the high-water marks of apocalypticism. Among the many sects were the Fifth Monarchy Men, who were active from 1649 to 1661. They believed that Jesus Christ – the fifth monarch – would return in 1666. When, disappointingly, the monarchy was restored in 1660, they decided to help the apocalypse along a bit. On 6 January 1661, fifty Fifth Monarchists marched on London in the name of 'King Jesus'. Their coup was crushed and the leaders executed for high treason. (1666 came and nothing happened. Well, apart from the plague. And then the fire.)

Millerites

In the nineteenth and twentieth centuries, these kind of teachings showed no signs of disappearing. The Millerites, following the teaching of their leader, William Miller, believed that the second coming would occur on October 22, 1843. (Nothing happened. This led to the non-event being given the rather depressing title of 'The Great Disappointment'). The ideological descendants of the Millerites are the Seventh-Day Adventists, and from them the Branch Davidians of Waco fame. Another group influenced by Miller's prophecies are the Jehovah's Witnesses which originated in an independent Bible study group in 1870. Their leader, Charles Taze Russell, predicted the war of Armageddon would start in 1914. (Nothing happened. But they have kept moving the date. First to 1925. Then 1975. Not sure what it is now.)

Harmonites

Many attempts have been made to found the New Jerusalem described in the Bible. Sects such as the Harmonites tried to build model, utopian communities. Fuelled by a belief that Jesus Christ was coming soon to usher in a thousand-year reign, they set up societies of communal living and celibacy. Their leader, George Rapp, predicted that the reign would begin on September 15, 1829. (Nothing happened, but they did leave some nice architecture.)

Agapemone

In England, a slightly unhinged clergyman called Henry James Prince declared that he was the herald of Christ's second coming. He set up a community near Spaxton in Somerset called *Agapemone* or 'The Abode of Love'.* Prince was married, but still took a young girl for a bride. It was supposed to be a purely spiritual union, but she became pregnant and gave birth to a baby girl. Tragically, the community viewed this girl as the devil's offspring; she grew up in the Abode as an outcast. Despite his claims of immortality, Prince died in 1899 but *Agapemone* continued until 1962 when the estate was sold.

British Israelitism

One of the weirdest strands of apocalyptic thought is British and American Israelitism, which identified Britain and the USA as the lost tribes of Israel. Among their beliefs were that the British monarch was descended from King David and the coronation stone in Westminster Abbey is actually the same stone on which Jacob laid his head when he saw his famous ladder. The founder of British Israelitism, Edward Hine, predicted that Britain would never fight a war with Germany. And also that the two nations would always preserve a strict Sabbath. (Not only did we fight two world wars, on Sundays we drive our VWs to shop at Lidl.)

Rastafarianism

Revelation is responsible for reggae. And dreadlocks. When Emperor Haile Selassie I was crowned in Addis Ababa on November 2, 1930, among the many titles he was given was 'Conquering Lion of the Tribe of Judah'. Poor Jamaicans spotted the Revelation imagery and soon street preachers like Leonard Howell started to preach that Haile Selassie was the Messiah.†
Revelation still influences the culture, religion and music of Rastas. Babylon is a common metaphor, symbolising the white political power system that has held the black race down for centuries. Even their use of cannabis has been called 'the healing of the nation', a phrase based on Revelation 22.2.

---

* The estate included the rather excellent idea of a chapel equipped with a billiard table.
† Howell himself had a Revelation-like life. He was charged with sedition by the British Government and imprisoned. In prison he wrote a tract called *The Promise Key*, which described Haile Selassie and his wife as King Alpha and Queen Omega and which referred to 'the poison 666'. When he was released, he founded a community at Pinnacle, at St. Catherine in Jamaica.

Bible smuggling

The twentieth century saw the rebirth of another time-honoured practice of the Reformation: Bible smuggling. Just as individual translators emulated Tyndale, a series of heroic individuals emulated Julian Hernandez.* Despite the ban put on by the Soviet regime, for example, there was still a hunger for the Bible. In Russia in the 1970s a Bible could command two weeks' wages on the black market.

So, a number of organisations began to smuggle Bibles across the border. Perhaps the most famous of these Bible smugglers is 'Brother Andrew' of the Open Doors organisation. He began taking Bibles across the border in 1957. In 1968 he took a vanload of Bibles into Czechoslovakia, at exactly the time when the country was invaded by Soviet tanks. Later he received a letter from a mother in the Soviet Union which thanked him for 'giving our son a Bible when he was occupying Czechoslovakia.' The smugglers were ingenious. A VW Beetle could be adapted to hold five hundred Bibles; the new motor for the pipe organ of a Roman Catholic parish in Poland had enough room in it for a Bible.

Perhaps the most spectacular project of Open Doors was Project Pearl. On June 18, 1981, one million Chinese Bibles were delivered to a beach in China on one night. The Bibles, in one-ton waterproof, floating parcels, were collected by thousands of Chinese Christians, waiting in the darkness on the beach, who took boxes of Bibles off to distribute throughout the country.

Many Chinese Christians paid dearly for their role in this operation. And the authorities made efforts to find and destroy the Bibles. One cache of boxes, which were discovered by the police and thrown into the harbour, were later retrieved – and sold – by fishermen. Elsewhere along the distribution network, a group of police found a cache of one thousand Bibles which they threw into the cesspit of the public latrine. A few days later, under cover of darkness, three Christians climbed down into the foul-smelling pit and retrieved the Bibles. They washed off the filth, dried them out, and sprayed them with perfume. Today, these 'perfumed Bibles' are still treasured by those who received them.[14]

---

* See p.170.

Project Pearl had an enormous impact on the availability of Bibles in China. Shortly after the project happened, China's Three Self Patriotic Movement announced the first official printing of Bibles inside the country. In some areas of China today it is still perilous to be a Christian. But the church continues to grow.

Project Pearl was an operation straight out of the Reformation Bible smuggling handbook – albeit on a vastly greater scale. Nowadays there are easier ways to smuggle Bibles: in the era of the internet, banning the Bible will gradually become impossible. But even so, countries like North Korea still prohibit the sale, import or ownership of a Bible.* North Korea is probably the most anti-Christian country on earth. In 1945, 13 per cent of the population of North Korea were Christian and the capital, Pyongyang, was known as the 'Jerusalem of the East'. With the establishment of the Democratic People's Republic in 1948 the church started to experience severe persecution. The government executed or arrested all of the country's religious leaders. All religious families were relocated to industrial cities on the east coast or sent to forced labour camps.

Penalties for being caught with religious materials include public execution, torture or imprisonment in gulags, where believers are forced to perform hard labour and given less than subsistence levels of food. There are fifty thousand to seventy thousand Christians currently detained in prison camps; about 15% of North Korea's four hundred thousand believers.

North Korea is just one of many countries and regions where owning, reading or distributing the Bible can get you into trouble. Yet despite all this, the church is alive and even growing. The Bible is still present, still powerful, still a threat.

The Bible in 57 flavours

The latter part of the twentieth century saw an explosion of translations. One list gives over seventy translations between 1950 and 1996.[15] Not only is every ploughboy reading the Bible, many of them are having a go at translating it as well.

---

* Ingenious methods are still found. Balloons imprinted with the text of Mark's gospel are floated across the border: when they deflate the text can be read.

Today, though, the battle is no longer over translations, although new translations continue to be made, each justifying itself in its own way. Translations don't seem to matter so much any more. There are, of course, plenty of websites which still froth at the mouth over the differences between the ESV and the NIV, but such objections appear more and more like an esoteric hobby. Translations seem less like life and death issues, and more like lifestyle choices. There are translations to suit every style of readership, ecclesiology and theology. You want a simple, pacy version? Try the CEV or the *Message*. Tradition? The AV still sells by the bucketful. A literal study version? The NRSV will do you well. Something between the extremes? The NIV, the Jerusalem, the NASB – there are a myriad of choices.

Today, the marketing men concentrate on packaging. One of the USPs of the Geneva Bible: it's all in the margins. So Bibles come specially packaged for a niche market.* Some of these have helped new readers engage with the Bible. The Youth Bible introduced young people to the Scriptures in a meaningful and relevant way. The NRSV, Jerusalem, ESV and NIV Study Bibles all help the reader interpret and explore the text. But sometimes the segmenting becomes more and more precise, laser-cutting the Christian public into ever smaller slices. A quick scan of the Bible-selling websites, those cyber-age versions of the stalls around St Paul's, reveals a bewildering array of Bibles, each with their own additives: the *Discipleship Study Bible*, the *Life Application Study Bible*, the *Transformation Study Bible*, the *Original African Heritage Study Bible*. Bibles for all stages of life: teen Bibles, kids Bibles, children's Bibles, student Bibles, parents' Bible. Women are a particular target group: there are multiple women's study Bibles; the *Woman of Color Study Bible*, the *Sanctuary for Women Bible*, the *Hugs for Women Bible*, the *Inspiring Women Every Day Bible*, the *Woman Thou Art Loosed Bible*, the *Woman Thou Art Welsh Study Bible*...†

If any of these help the people read the Bible, that is A Good Thing. But is that what's really happening? As we begin the third millennium

---

* I need to declare an interest here. I have worked on some niche Bibles. Notably *The Poverty and Justice Bible* and *The CEV Youth Bible,* as well as providing intro material for others. Just in the interests of transparency, you know.

† One of these I made up. But it would still sell.

of the Bible's life, one has to wonder whether publishers are trying to get people to read the Bible, or just consume it.

Whatever the case, as we stagger into the twenty-first century, there are no signs yet of the Bible industry slowing down. And the growth of new technology will only fuel the production. Take the New English Translation of 2005. Its acronym – the NET Bible – is a deliberate pun. This was a Bible which began life on the internet, as an open source, internet-based translation project, designed to be downloaded, freely-distributed, a kind of viral Vulgate. Only after it was launched on the web was it captured between the traditional leather covers.

Of the making of Bibles there is, it seems, no end in sight.

The people's book

Today, the Bible is the people's book in a way that it has never been in the past. In fact you could say that, in the West at least, it's been returned to the people – for the powers and authorities today don't really want it. In years gone by, there was always an established, official line on the Bible; if there is one today, it's that the Bible is just one book among many.

OK. Let them think that. Because the result is that the Bible has escaped. In many parts of the world, Tyndale's dream of ploughmen reading the Scriptures has come to fruition; where ordinary working people can read the Bible in their own language.

But one man's dream is another man's nightmare. For some the popularity of the Bible, the fact that it is so widely read, so widely available, is not a thing to be celebrated but decried.

For some people – perhaps an increasing number – the Bible is a book to be attacked rather than cherished. A book to be burnt. To be destroyed.

Attacks on the Bible come from all directions these days. The New Atheists have arrived on the scene, all wide-eyed and enthusiastic, Dawkins' disciples, his pop-science Scriptures tucked under their arms, meeting together for worship conferences, filling the comments section of the websites with their shrill voices. And opposing them at the other end of the spectrum are the Fundamentalist tribes, condemning every other version, King James Only T-Shirts, frothing, angrily, their websites filled with eye-watering 48 point headlines, day-glo green and yellow and red. In North Carolina, the Amazing Grace Baptist Church celebrates Halloween with a Bible-burning. Anything other than the King James is branded 'satanic'.[16]

Both sides are behaving in a way which the Bible emphatically doesn't. The great strength of the Bible is that there is within it room for questions, for debate. It is inclusive. Dynamic. If the story of the Bible tells us one thing, it is that it is never static. This object that we think is nailed down, fixed, is always reinventing itself; regenerating. Just like its main character, every time you shut it in a box, it bursts out again.

Because the thing about the Bible is that it contains within itself the seeds of its own regeneration. It contains within its pages permission to probe, to challenge, to question. The psalms, with their heartfelt cries to God; Job, scratching himself on the rubbish heap; Jacob, wrestling in the night with that strange, powerful figure; Paul's incendiary-blast attack on tradition; Jesus' stories and riddles. The Bible gives us permission to question, permission to debate, discuss. Permission to think for ourselves.

And boy is there a lot of thinking going on. Today, the Bible is more widely discussed than ever before. Bluff King Hal, that brutal psychopath, was worried about common people discussing the Bible in inns and taverns; what would he make of the internet? Out there, Marcion is still typing his anti-Jewish polemic, thinly veneered with Christian respectability. Montanus and his tribes are out there as well, small groups, single-figure membership, urban gnostics, reading the signs, preparing to hunker down in the face of Armageddon.

The next stage of the development in the history of the Bible is out there, as well; online. It will be on the iPads or whatever gadget comes along. And there will be more textual discoveries. Older manuscripts will be found. A teenager out on the desert will turn over a rock, or explore a cave. Something exciting will turn up.

It always does, actually. Even for those of us who are never likely to go near the desert, there are always new discoveries to be made. It amazes me when I read the Bible how often I spot something new, something I feel like I've never spotted before. I was given my first Bible when I was a kid – a children's Bible with enormous, florid illustrations. Later, on my seventh birthday I was given an AV. It's sitting in front of me, as I type, rebound in schoolbook-cover style, using some rather seventies teal green vinyl wallpaper. Tissue-thin Bible paper. Paintings by R.S. Hardy. My name on the title page. At some point, bored perhaps in a service, I coloured in the royal coat of arms in a blue biro.

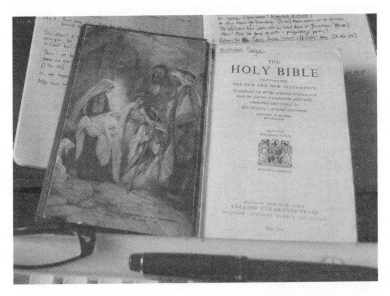

Forty-two years later I'm still reading the Bible, still discovering things.* Just today I read a verse in John's gospel that I am certain I have never read before. I must have, of course. I must have read it, passed it by on some other journey, but never noticed it. Never really stopped and looked.

It is this that gives me enormous hope about the Bible. It is this that makes the Bible so exciting. Just when you think you've got it sorted, when you've exhausted its possibilities, you turn a corner and a new view spreads out before you. A story you never noticed, a phrase you never heard, a new challenge, reminder, promise. A new idea.

---

* Still scribbling in it. Although these days I write notes in the margin, rather than colour in the coat of arms.

Let's leave the last word to one of the heroes. Tyndale. In one of his books, *Obedience of a Christian Man*, he wrote about the power of God and the power of man. The enemies of Christ could arrest Christ, try him, and execute him. They had the power to put Jesus into the tomb.

> Finally when they had done all they could and that they thought sufficient, and when Christ was in the heart of the earth and so many bills and poleaxes about him, to keep him down, and when it was past man's help: then holp God. When man could not bring him again, God's truth fetched him again.[17]

That's exactly what happens with the Bible. Every time you think it's locked away, entombed; every time the Romans or the Inquisition or the kings or the Koreans or Soviets or the Nazis think they've made the thing secure, up it jumps.

Unpredictable, you see.

Dangerous.

Appendix: Major modern versions

Since the Revised Standard Version in 1946, there has been a tsunami of translations and paraphrases, including many which are familiar to Christians today. In the descriptions of the Bibles that follow I've given each version's take on Isaiah 7.14. This is a kind of litmus test of the conservative/liberal stance of the Bible. If it's translated 'virgin', the conservatives are happy; if it's 'young woman', the liberals are happy. After 1881, with the exception of the New King James versions, all Bibles followed the eclectic Greek text.

The New English Bible (1961)

The New English Bible came into being because military chaplains realised that their soldiers simply couldn't understand a word of the AV. So in 1947 they prepared not a revision, but a completely new translation. In 1961, the New Testament sold a million copies on the day of publication. The entire Bible was issued in 1970, in post-psychedelic day-glo orange cover. It contains possibly the strangest piece of translation in any Bible ever – Joshua 15.18 – which reads: 'As she sat on the ass, she broke wind, and Caleb asked her, "What did you mean by that?"' Good question, Caleb.

Formal or dynamic?	Dynamic.
Sum it up	An eccentric English vicar: liberal, scholarly and just that little bit bonkers.
Isaiah 7.14	*Therefore the Lord himself shall give you a sign: A young woman is with child and she will bear a son, and will call him Immanuel.*

Jerusalem Bible (1966)/New Jerusalem Bible (1985)

Produced for Catholic use, but widely read because of its style. It's a very European Bible: the original Jerusalem Bible was a translation from the French, with reference to the original languages; the New Jerusalem Bible worked the other way round, translating from the original languages but referring back to the French. In 1966 the translators included J. R. R. Tolkein (he worked on the Book of Jonah). Unusually, it uses the word Yahweh for the name of God in the Old Testament. It's one of the best designed Bibles around: single column, verse numbers in the side and usually printed on cream paper. Yum.

Formal or dynamic?	Beautifully dynamic.
Sum it up	Three Michelin stars.
Isaiah 7.14	*The Lord will give you a sign in any case: It is this: the young woman is with child and will give birth to a son whom she will call Immanuel.*

The Good News Bible (1966)

Hugely popular, this is widely read in schools (at least in the UK). The New Testament first appeared as *Good News for Modern Man* in 1966. It was born out of requests from missionaries for a Bible that was friendly to non-native English speakers. It was one of the first Bibles specifically to draw on Eugene Nida's theories of dynamic equivalence and common language: 'The kind of language common to both the professor and the janitor, the business executive and the gardener, the socialite and the waiter.'[1] One of its unique features is the brilliant line drawings in the text, by the Swiss artist Annie Valloton.

Formal or dynamic?	Dynamic.
Sum it up	Ideally, it would come with crayons for colouring in.
Isaiah 7.14	*Well then, the Lord himself will give you a sign: a young woman who is pregnant will have a son and will name him 'Immanuel.'*

Living Bible (1967)

The Living Bible was created by one man – Kenneth N. Taylor – who wrote it because his children couldn't understand the AV. Taylor didn't speak either Hebrew or Greek, so he made a paraphrase of the American Standard Version of 1901. It was especially popular among youth groups in the seventies and Billy Graham gave it away for free at his events. It also made the cross-over into the Catholic world: a Catholic Living Bible was released with a foreword by Pope John Paul II. At times the language is almost shockingly vivid: Saul's response to his son Jonathan in 1 Samuel 20.30 goes 'You son of a bitch!'

Formal or dynamic?	Very dynamic.
Sum it up	It's the Bible, only wearing flares.
Isaiah 7.14	*All right then, the Lord himself will choose the sign - a child shall be born to a virgin! And she shall call him Immanuel (meaning, 'God is with us').*

New American Bible (1970)

The successor to the Douai-Rheims Bible for use in the Catholic Church, the NAB was the first American Catholic Bible to be translated from the original languages, rather than the Vulgate. As a literal translation it also suffers from a certain wooden quality. Unusually, it tried to reflect the literary qualities of the originals. According to the preface, 'Where the prose of the original flows more smoothly, as in Luke, Acts and Hebrews, it is reflected in the translation'.

Formal or dynamic?	Formal.
Sum it up	A good effort, but still too official.
Isaiah 7.14	*Therefore the Lord himself will give you this sign: the virgin shall be with child, and bear a son, and shall name him Immanuel.*

New American Standard Bible (1971)

The NASB was the work of conservative scholars and was originally designed as a reaction to the perceived liberal bias in the 1956 RSV. It is, by far, the most literal, word-for-word version, which makes it good for accurate study, but no good for reading out loud. The first version retained a Jacobean flavour, with words such as 'thee' and 'thou' for any texts which addressed God, but later revisions updated the language a bit.

Formal or dynamic?	More formal than a black tie dinner with the queen.
Sum it up	Highly accurate but at times so wooden that turning a page will give you a splinter.
Isaiah 7.14	*Therefore the Lord Himself will give you a sign: Behold, a virgin will be with child and bear a son, and she will call His name Immanuel.*

New International Version (1973)/Today's New International Version (2005)

Translated by an international committee of evangelical scholars, this is the most widely used Bible in the evangelical churches. It does betray a certain amount of evangelical bias in its translation, but it reads fairly well and is a good all-purpose Bible. The TNIV was an attempt at a revision, using more gender-inclusive language. It proved controversial and new plans have been announced for a Revised NIV in the future which will replace both versions.

Formal or dynamic?	A bit of both. A happy medium. *Comme çi, comme ça*, etc.
Sum it up	The Toyota of Bible translations. Reliable but bland.
Isaiah 7.14	*Therefore the Lord himself will give you a sign: Behold, a virgin will be with child and bear a son, and she will call his name Immanuel.*

New Century Version (1978)

The fact that this version is really only widely known as the text used for the hugely popular Youth Bible shows its origins: it was a revision of the International Children's Bible. Thus it sticks to simple language at the level a teenager could understand.

Formal or dynamic?	Dynamic.
Sum it up	Best taken with notes.
Isaiah 7.14	*The Lord himself will give you a sign: The virgin will be pregnant. She will have a son, and she will name him Immanuel.*

New King James Version (1979/1982)

Advertising itself as the first major revision to the AV since 1769, the New King James Version (NT 1979, entire Bible 1982) aimed to modernise the language and was worked on by 130 scholars. The result has been called 'a curious mixture of Elizabethan ecclesiastical style with glosses of twentieth century vocabulary and grammar.'[2] Uniquely among major modern versions, the NKJV was based on the *Textus Receptus*. Although it claimed that the 'entire text of the original King James version' was included, it didn't have the Apocrypha from the 1611 edition.

Formal or dynamic?	Very, very formal.
Sum it up	It's the AV for people who don't understand the AV.
Isaiah 7.14	*Therefore the Lord Himself will give you a sign: Behold, the virgin shall conceive and bear a Son, and shall call His name Immanuel.*

New Revised Standard Version (1989)

The successor to the RSV, the New Revised Standard Version is a scholarly standard in universities, seminaries and many kinds of theological publishing. It includes some gender-neutral language and is fairly readable. It was translated by an interdenominational committee and reviewed by an interfaith group. A good Bible for serious Bible study.

Formal or dynamic?	Quite formal, but still quite readable.
Sum it up	It's like a university lecturer: reasonable, liberal, accurate but just that little bit dull.
Isaiah 7.14	*Therefore the Lord himself will give you a sign. Look, the young woman is with child and shall bear a son, and shall name him Immanuel.*

Revised English Bible (1989)

Translated by an interfaith committee, this was the revision of the NEB. It's something of a disappointment compared to its predecessor, being more conservative and moving back towards the AV. However, it did do some radical things, notably some reordering of the text (e.g. Isaiah 41.6–7 placed immediately after Isaiah 40.20). It has also been praised for its literary style.

Formal or dynamic?	Dynamic.
Sum it up	It's like the NEB in middle-age.
Isaiah 7.14	*Because you do, the Lord of his own accord will give you a sign; it is this: A young woman is with child, and she will give birth to a son and call him Immanuel.*

Contemporary English Version (1991)

The CEV began as a result of studies into the kind of English found in newspapers, magazines and television. These studies focused on how English was read and heard. Although it is often thought of as a revision of the GNB, it's actually aimed at a lower reading age. The aim was to provide a version which could be easily listened to and understood. Bible terms were removed, or simplified The Anglicised version of the CEV won a Crystal Mark award from the Plain English Campaign

Formal or dynamic?	Dynamic.
Sum it up	Plain and simple.
Isaiah 7.14	*But the LORD will still give you proof. A virgin is pregnant; she will have a son and will name him Immanuel.*

Holman Christian Standard Bible (1999)

Why have the word Christian in your Bible? The answer may lie in the origins of this version: Holman Bible Publishers is indirectly owned by the Southern Baptist Convention, perhaps not widely renowned for their ecumenical outlook. The marketing claims that it's an 'optimal equivalence' version – i.e. between dynamic and formal, but it's slightly more literal than the NIV. Unlike most modern versions, the HCSB identifies 'supplied words' – words added to the translation which are not in the original, but which are needed to make sense in English. It puts them in square brackets, much as the 1611 AV put them in italics.

Formal or dynamic?	'Optimal' according to the marketing. (i.e. a bit of both.)
Sum it up	It's the NIV. Only older.
Isaiah 7.14	*Therefore, the Lord Himself will give you a sign: The virgin will conceive, have a son, and name him Immanuel.*

The Message (1993)

In the tradition of Moffat and Phillips, this is a vernacular paraphrase by a pastor and scholar called Eugene Peterson. It was aimed at ordinary people and succeeded fantastically – this is a remarkably vivid Bible which makes for brilliant reading. Initially it was published without verse numbers and in a single column – like a regular book. For many people – young people especially – it transformed their reading of the Bible. However, it includes a lot of Peterson's own interpretations, along with the text.

Formal or dynamic?	Any more dynamic and you'd have to put it in a cage.
Sum it up	Yee har. It's the Coca-cola of translations.
Isaiah 7.14	*So the Master is going to give you a sign anyway. Watch for this: A girl who is presently a virgin will get pregnant. She'll bear a son and name him Immanuel (God-With-Us).*

New Living Translation (1996)

In 1989 the publishers decided to revise the Living Bible, which was then twenty years old. But they ended up with a new translation. The reason? From one man's vision, they went for ninety Bible translators; from a lively paraphrase they went to a thought-for-thought translation. The result is a version which is more accurate, more reliable, but which is not half as fresh and new as the Living Bible.

Formal or dynamic?	Very dynamic.
Sum it up	It's like the Living Bible, only less fun.
Isaiah 7.14	*All right then, the Lord himself will give you the sign. Look! The virgin will conceive a child! She will give birth to a son and will call him Immanuel (which means 'God is with us').*

English Standard Version (2001)

The ESV is a modern RSV. It's a literal translation, which uses the text of the 1971 RSV as its English basis. However, changes were made where the RSV was considered too liberal. It rejected gender inclusiveness. (An approach applied to the people who worked on it: in 2008 an enormous, excellent study Bible edition was launched, but out of the 95 contributors, not one was female.) The tone of the writing is often seems quite old and even archaic.

Formal or dynamic?	Formal. With knobs on.
Sum it up	Very accurate and very dull. If it were a man (which it would be) it would be wearing a vest.
Isaiah 7.14	*Therefore the Lord himself will give you a sign. Behold, the virgin shall conceive and bear a son, and shall call his name Immanuel.*

The New English Translation (2005)

The NET Bible is a kind of open source translation project: produced on the internet, 25 scholars worked on it, and readers were encouraged to make comments and suggestions. Its translation decisions were explained in over sixty thousand footnotes. Conceived at a meeting of the Society of Biblical Literature in 1995, the initial idea was to create a reliable, entirely free version. The preface states their position: 'The Bible is God's gift to humanity – it should be free.' Since then it has also appeared in physical format.

Formal or dynamic?	Dynamic.
Sum it up	This is the future of Bible translation, my friends. (But you can still get it with a black leather cover.)
Isaiah 7.14	*For this reason the sovereign master himself will give you a confirming sign. Look, this young woman is about to conceive and will give birth to a son. You, young woman, will name him Immanuel.*

SELECT BIBLIOGRAPHY

Ackroyd, Peter, *The Life of Thomas More*, (London: Vintage, 1999)

Ackroyd, Peter R., *The Cambridge History of the Bible Volume 1: From the Beginnings to Jerome*, (Cambridge: Cambridge University Press, 1975)

Armstrong, Karen, *The Bible: The Biography*, (London: Atlantic Books, 2008)

Bauckham, Richard, *Jesus and the Eyewitnesses: The Gospels as Eyewitness Testimony*, (Grand Rapids: Eerdmans, 2006)

— *The Gospels for All Christians: Rethinking the Gospel Audiences*, (Edinburgh: T & T Clark, 1998)

Baylor, Michael G., *The Radical Reformation*, (Cambridge: Cambridge University Press, 1991)

Bigger, Stephen, *Creating the Old Testament: The Emergence of the Hebrew Bible*, (Oxford: Basil Blackwell, 1989)

Briggs, Asa and Peter Burke, *A Social History of the Media: From Gutenberg to the Internet*, (Cambridge: Polity, 2005)

Bruce, F. F., *The Books and the Parchments: Some Chapters on the Transmission of the Bible*, (London: Pickering & Inglis, 1950)

Chidester, David, *Christianity: A Global History*, (London: Penguin, 2001)

De Hamel, Christopher, *The Book: A History of the Bible*, (London: Phaidon Press, 2001)

Eusebius, *The Ecclesiastical History and the Martyrs of Palestine*, trans. Hugh Jackson Lawlor and J. E. L. Oulton (London: SPCK, 1927)

Ferrell, Lori Anne, *The Bible and the People*, (New Haven: Yale University Press, 2008)

Gamble, Harry Y., *Books and Readers in the Early Church: A History of Early Christian Texts*, (New Haven: Yale University Press, 1995)

Green, Vivian, *A New History of Christianity*, (Stroud: Sutton, 1996)

Greenslade, S. L., *The Cambridge History of the Bible: Volume 3, the West From the Reformation to the Present Day:* (Cambridge: Cambridge University Press, 1963)

Griffiths, Richard, *The Bible in the Renaissance: Essays on Biblical Commentary and Translation in the Fifteenth and Sixteenth Centuries*, (Aldershot: Ashgate, 2001)

Hampton, Christopher, *A Radical Reader: The Struggle for Change in England, 1381-1914*, (London: Penguin, 1984)

Hill, Christopher, *The English Bible and the 17th-Century Revolution*, (London: Viking, 1993)

—, *Turbulent, Seditious and Factious People: John Bunyan and His Church, 1628-88)*, (Oxford: Oxford University Press, 1989)

Holmes, Michael W., *The Apostolic Fathers: Greek Texts and English Translations*, (Grand Rapids: Baker Academic, 2007)

James, M. R, *The Apocryphal New Testament: Being the Apocryphal Gospels, Acts, Epistles and Apocalypses: With Other Narratives and Fragments*, (Oxford: Oxford University Press, 1924)

Kenyon, Frederic G., *Our Bible and the Ancient Manuscripts, A History of the Text and its Translations*, (London: Eyre & Spottiswoode, 1903)

Lambert, Malcolm, *Medieval Heresy: Popular Movements From Bogomil to Hus*, (NewYork: Holmes & Meier, 1977)

Lampe, G. W. H., *The Cambridge History of the Bible: Volume 2, the West From the Fathers to the Reformation*, (Cambridge University Press, 1969)

Lupton, Lewis Frederick, *A History of the Geneva Bible*, (London: Fauconberg Press, 1966)

MacCulloch, Diarmaid, *A History of Christianity: The First Three Thousand Years*, (London: Allen Lane, 2009)

McDonald, Lee Martin, *The Biblical Canon: Its Origin, Transmission and Authority*, (Peabody: Hendrickson, 2007)

Metzger, Bruce Manning, *The Canon of the New Testament: Its Origin, Development, and Significance*, (Oxford: Oxford University Press, 1987)

Moynahan, Brian, *If God Spare My Life: William Tyndale, the English Bible and Sir Thomas More – a Story of Martyrdom and Betrayal*, (London: Little, Brown, 2002)

Norton, David, *A History of the Bible as Literature*, (Cambridge: Cambridge University Press, 1993)

Patzia, Arthur G., *The Making of the New Testament: Origin, Collection, Text & Canon*, (Leicester: Apollos, 1995)

Pelikan, Jaroslav, *Whose Bible is it?: A History of the Scriptures Through the Ages*, (London: Penguin, 2006)

Peterson, Eugene, *Eat this Book: A Conversation in the Art of Spiritual Reading*, (London: Hodder & Stoughton, 2006)

Raven, James, *The Business of Books: Booksellers and the English Book Trade, 1450-1850*, (New Haven: Yale University Press, 2007)

Ridley, Jasper Godwin, *The Statesman and the Fanatic: Thomas Wolsey and Thomas More*, (London: Constable, 1982)

Roberts, Alexander, James Donaldson, and A. Cleveland Coxe, (eds), *The Ante-Nicene Fathers*, (I; Accordance electronic ed. 9 vols; New York: Christian Literature Company, 1885)

Roe, James M., *A History of the British and Foreign Bible Society, 1905-1954*, (London: British and Foreign Society, 1965)

Sanders, James A., *Torah and Canon*, (Philadelphia: Fortress Press, 1972)

Schulze-Wegener, Günther, *6000 Years of the Bible*, (London: Hodder & Stoughton, 1963)

Wegner, Paul D., *The Journey From Texts to Translations: The Origin and Development of the Bible*, (Grand Rapids: Baker Books, 1999)

Williams, George Huntston, *The Radical Reformation*, (Kirksville: Sixteenth Century Journal Publishers, 1992)

NOTES

The Basic Bible

1 Bigger, Stephen, *Creating the Old Testament: The Emergence of the Hebrew Bible*, (Oxford: Basil Blackwell, 1989), 25.

2 Holmes, Michael W., *The Apostolic Fathers: Greek Texts and English Translations*, (Grand Rapids: Baker Academic, 2007), 105.

3 Justin, *Dialogue with Trypho*, lxv in Roberts, Alexander, James Donaldson, and A. Cleveland Coxe, (Eds), *The Ante-Nicene Fathers*, (I; Accordance electronic ed. 9 vols; New York: Christian Literature Company, 1885)

4 Jerome, *Letter 27 to Marcella*

5 Tertullian, *Against Marcion*, IV.2 in Roberts, *The Ante-Nicene Fathers*

6 John Chrysostom, *Homilies on the Gospel of Matthew*, I.6

The Hebrew Bible

1 Sanders, James A., *Torah and Canon*, (Philadelphia: Fortress Press, 1972), 33.

2 Sanders, *Torah and Canon*, 39-40. See 'Torah' in *The Anchor Bible Dictionary*, ed. David Noel Freedman, (New York: Doubleday, 1999), VI, 606ff.

3 Shabbat 13b, Babylonian Talmud

4 Hag. ii. 1; ib. Gem. 13a

5 Hagigah 14b, Babylonian Talmud

6 Sirach 48.23; 49.8–10

7 Quoted in Sanders, *Torah and Canon*, 97.

8 Chadwick, Henry, *The Church in Ancient Society: From Galilee to Gregory the Great*, (Oxford: Oxford University Press, 2001), 27.

9 Patzia, Arthur G., *The Making of the New Testament: Origin, Collection, Text & Canon*, (Leicester: Apollos, 1995), 24.

10 M. Megillah 4.4. in Danby, Herbert, *The Mishnah, Translated From the Hebrew*, (London: Oxford University Press, 1933), 206. For more on this episode, see Bailey, Kenneth E., *Jesus Through Middle Eastern Eyes: Cultural Studies in the Gospels*, (London: SPCK, 2008), 147ff.

11 Freedman, David Noel and Pam Fox Kuhlken, *What Are the Dead Sea Scrolls and Why Do They Matter?* (Grand Rapids: Eerdmans, 2007), 27.

12 McDonald, Lee Martin, *The Biblical Canon: Its Origin, Transmission and Authority*, (Peabody: Hendrickson, 2007), 290.

13 Sanders, *Torah and Canon*, 111.

14 Bigger, *Creating the Old Testament: The Emergence of the Hebrew Bible*, 26.

The Christian Bible

1 McDonald, *The Biblical Canon: Its Origin, Transmission and Authority*, 197.

2 Justin, *Dialogue* 39 in Roberts, *The Ante-Nicene Fathers*.

3 Holmes, *The Apostolic Fathers: Greek Texts and English Translations*, 735.

4 Holmes, *The Apostolic Fathers: Greek Texts and English Translations*, 739.

5 Page, Nick, *The Longest Week: What Really Happened During Jesus' Final Days*, (London: Hodder & Stoughton, 2009), 75–79.

6 Eusebius, *The Ecclesiastical History and the Martyrs of Palestine*, trans. Hugh Jackson Lawlor and J.E.L. Oulton (London: SPCK, 1927), I, 101.

7 *Didache* 1.1. in Holmes, *The Apostolic Fathers: Greek Texts and English Translations*, 345.

8 Skeat, T. C., and Elliot, J.K., *The Collected Biblical Writings of T. C. Skeat*, (Leiden: Brill, 2004), 46.

9 Bauckham, Richard., *The Gospels for All Christians: Rethinking the Gospel Audiences*, (Edinburgh: T & T Clark, 1998), 79.

10 Bauckham, *The Gospels for All Christians: Rethinking the Gospel Audiences*, 37.

11 Bauckham, *The Gospels for All Christians: Rethinking the Gospel Audiences*, 37.

12 Grant, Robert M., *Second-Century Christianity: A Collection of Fragments*, (Louisville: Westminster John Knox Press, 2003), 46.

13 Holmes, *The Apostolic Fathers: Greek Texts and English Translations*, 467–469.

The Early Church Bible

1 The two quotes from Jesus are found in 2 Clement 4.5 and 5.2-4. *The Gospel of the Egyptians* is cited at 2 Clement 12.2. See Holmes, *The Apostolic Fathers: Greek Texts and English Translations*, 139ff..; Edwards, O. C., *A History of Preaching*, (Nashville: Abingdon Press, 2004), 16.

2 MacCulloch, Diarmaid, *A History of Christianity: The First Three Thousand Years*, (London: Allen Lane, 2009), 126

3 See Metzger, Bruce M., *The Canon of the New Testament: Its Origin, Development, and Significance*, (Oxford: Clarendon Press, 1987), 99–102.

4 Perrin, Nicholas, *Thomas: The Other Gospel*, (London: SPCK, 2007), 3. Perrin has argued convincingly that the *Gospel of Thomas* draws heavily on the *Diatesseron*.

5 *Gos. Thom.* 13.

6 Justin Martyr, *First Apology*, Chapter 66

7 Justin Martyr, *Dialogue* 100.1–2 quoted in McDonald, *The Biblical Canon: Its Origin, Transmission and Authority*, 285.

8 Justin Martyr, *First Apology*, Chapter 57

9 McDonald, *The Biblical Canon: Its Origin, Transmission and Authority*, 290.

10 Stromata 3.6, quoted in McDonald, *The Biblical Canon: Its Origin, Transmission and Authority*, 291.

11 Metzger, *The Canon of the New Testament*, 119.

12 Metzger, *The Canon of the New Testament*, 136.

13 *Hom. on Leviticus* 10.2 in Metzger, *The Canon of the New Testament*, 137.

14 *Hom. on Jeremiah* 20.3 in Metzger, *The Canon of the New Testament*, 137. See *Gos. Thom.* 82.

15 Eusebius *Ecclesiastical History*, VIII, 13

The Imperial Bible

1 The *Gesta apud Zenophilum* in Stevenson, *New Eusebius*. Also Metzger, *The Canon of the New Testament*, 108.

2 Gamble, Harry Y., *Books and Readers in the Early Church: A History of Early Christian Texts*, (New Haven: Yale University Press, 1995), 148.

3 From Musurillo, *The Acts of Christian Martyrs*, (Oxford, 1972) pp.281-93 in Metzger, *The Canon of the New Testament*, 108. See also Gamble, *Books and Readers in the Early Church*, 148–9.

4 Gamble, *Books and Readers in the Early Church*, 149.

5 From Eusebius, *Ecclesiastical History and the Martyrs of Palestine*, I, 86–87.

6 Synod of Laodicea, Canon XVI and Canon LIX in Philip Schaff and Henry Wace, Eds., *A Select Library of the Nicene and Post-Nicene Fathers of the Christian Church*, Second Series (VIII; Accordance electronic ed. 14 vols.), n.p.

7 Lampe, G. W. H., *The Cambridge History of the Bible: Volume 2, the West From the Fathers to the Reformation*, (Cambridge: Cambridge University Press, 1969), 86.

8 Tregelles, S.P., *A Lecture on the Historic Evidence of the Authorship and Transmission of the Books of the New Testament*, (London: Samuel Bagster & Son, 1852), 84–85.

9 Pelikan, Jaroslav, *Whose Bible is it?: A History of the Scriptures Through the Ages*, (London: Penguin, 2006), 116–117.

10 Ehrman, Bart D. 'The New Testament Canon of Didymus the Blind' *Vigiliae Christianae 37(1)*. 1983

11 Metzger, *The Canon of the New Testament*, 255–6.

The Translated Bible

1 Augustine, Letter 71, 403 AD

2 Lampe, *The Cambridge History of the Bible: Volume 2, the West From the Fathers to the Reformation*, 91.

3 The story is told in Bede's *Ecclesiastical History*, Book 4, Chapter 29.

The Medieval Bible

1 Riddle 24 from the *Exeter Riddle Book*. The text comes from Craig Williamson, *The Old English Riddles of the Exeter Book* (Chapel Hill: University of North Carolina Press, 1977) available here: http://www2.kenyon.edu/AngloSaxonRiddles/texts.htm

2 Finlay, Victoria, *Colour: Travels Through the Paintbox*, (London: Sceptre, 2002), 181

3 Schulze-Wegener, Günther, *6000 Years of the Bible*, (London: Hodder and Stoughton, 1963), 178–79.

4 Chidester, David, *Christianity : A Global History*, (London: Penguin, 2001), 280.

5 Chidester, *Christianity : A Global History*, 205.

6 Haldon, John F., *Warfare, State and Society in the Byzantine World, 565–1204*, (London: UCL Press, 1999), 24.

7 Chidester, *Christianity : A Global History*, 283.

8 Pelikan, *Whose Bible is it?*, 132.

9 Comba, Emilio, *History of the Waldenses of Italy*, (London: Truslove & Shirley, 1889), 15–16.

10 Rev 2.9; 3.9. O'Shea, Stephen, Th*e Perfect Heresy: The Life and Death of the Cathars*, (London: Profile Books, 2001), 213.

11 Macculloch, *A History of Christianity : The First Three Thousand Years*, 398.

12 Lampe, *The Cambridge History of the Bible: Volume 2, the West From the Fathers to the Reformation*, n.2, 152.

13 Lambert, Malcolm, *Medieval Heresy: Popular Movements From Bogomil to Hus*, (NewYork: Holmes and Meier, 1977), 175.

14 Chidester, *Christianity : A Global History*, 274.

15 Ferrell, Lori Anne, *The Bible and the People*, (New Haven; London: Yale University Press, 2008), 65.

The Reformation Bible

1 Greenslade, S. L., *The Cambridge History of the Bible: Volume 3, the West From the Reformation to the Present Day:* (Cambridge: Cambridge University Press, 1963), 43–44.

2 Greenslade, *The Cambridge History of the Bible: Volume 3, the West From the Reformation to the Present Day:* 52–53.

3 Briggs, Asa and Peter. Burke, *A Social History of the Media: From Gutenberg to the Internet*, (Cambridge: Polity, 2005), 64-65.

4 Letter comes from the translation at http://www.bible-researcher.com/luther01.html

5 Griffiths, Richard, *The Bible in the Renaissance: Essays on Biblical Commentary and Translation in the Fifteenth and Sixteenth Centuries*, (Aldershot: Ashgate, 2001), 53.

6 Griffiths, *The Bible in the Renaissance*, 51.

7 Metzger, *The Canon of the New Testament*, 242.

8 Preface to the Epistles of St. James and St. Jude (1522) in Luther, Martin, *Luther's Works*, (St. Louis: Concordia, Fortress Press: 1963), v. 35, p. 395

9 Metzger, *The Canon of the New Testament*, 245.

10 Griffiths, *The Bible in the Renaissance*, 60.

11 Griffiths, *The Bible in the Renaissance*, 65.

12 Williams, George Huntston, *The Radical Reformation*, (Kirksville: Sixteenth Century Journal Publishers, 1992), 147.

13 Baylor, Michael G., *The Radical Reformation*, (Cambridge: Cambridge University Press, 1991), 231ff.

14 De Hamel, Christopher, *The Book: A History of the Bible*, (London: Phaidon Press, 2001), 237

15 De Hamel, *The Book: A History of the Bible*, 239

The English Bible

1 Briggs and Burke, *A Social History of the Media : From Gutenberg to the Internet*, 51.

2 Quoted Norton, David, *A History of the Bible as Literature*, (Cambridge: Cambridge University Press, 1993), 207.

3 Norton, *A History of the Bible as Literature*, 205. More is possible referring to Jerome's letter 22.29.

4 Griffiths, *The Bible in the Renaissance*, 120.

5 Norton, *A History of the Bible as Literature*, 205.

6 Patterson, L. Ray, *Copyright in Historical Perspective*, (Nashville: Vanderbilt University Press, 1968), 25.

7 Strype, *Ecclesiastical Memorials; Relating Chiefly to Religion, and the Reformation of it, and the Emergencies of the Church of England, Under King Henry Viii. King Edward Vi. And Queen Mary the First.*, I.ii.65.

8 Moynahan, Brian, *If God Spare My Life : William Tyndale, the English Bible and Sir Thomas More - a Story of Martyrdom and Betrayal*, (London: Little, Brown, 2002), 102.

9 Moynahan, *If God Spare My Life*, 204.

10 Ferrell, *The Bible and the People*, 75.

11 Griffiths, *The Bible in the Renaissance*, 138.

12 Moynahan, *If God Spare My Life*, 111.

13 Green, *A New History of Christianity*, 147.

14 Lupton, Lewis Frederick, *A History of the Geneva Bible*, (London: Fauconberg Press, 1966), I,12.

15 Griffiths, *The Bible in the Renaissance*, 142.

16 Griffiths, *The Bible in the Renaissance*, 142.

The Authorised Bible

1 Quoted in Norton, *A History of the Bible as Literature*, 194.

2 Norton, *A History of the Bible as Literature*, 195.

3 Quoted in Norton, *A History of the Bible as Literature*, 199.

4 Greenslade, *The Cambridge History of the Bible: Volume 3, the West From the Reformation to the Present Day*, 167; Bush, Douglas, Bonamy Dobrée and F. P. Wilson, *English Literature in the Earlier Seventeenth Century, 1600–1660*, (Oxford: Clarendon Press, 1945), 71.

5 These comparisons from Griffiths, *The Bible in the Renaissance*, 129–31.

6 Hill, *Turbulent, Seditious and Factious People*, 169.

7 An interview with Philip Pullman revealed that he talked about 'the King James Bible and the 1662 Book of Common Prayer with the deepest affection.' *Oxford Times*, March 18, 2010, 23

8 Norton, *A History of the Bible as Literature*, 318.

9 Greenslade, *The Cambridge History of the Bible: Volume 3, the West From the Reformation to the Present Day*, 168.

The Radical Bible

1 Hampton, Christopher, *A Radical Reader: The Struggle for Change in England, 1381-1914*, (London: Penguin Books Ltd, 1984), 199.

2 Hill, Christopher, *The English Bible and the 17th-Century Revolution*, (London: Viking, 1993), 18.

3 Hill, *The English Bible and the 17th-Century Revolution*, 40.

4 Hill, *Turbulent, Seditious and Factious People*, 9.

5 Hill, *The English Bible and the 17th-Century Revolution*, 229.

6 Hill, *The English Bible and the 17th-Century Revolution*, 47.

7 Bush, Dobrée and Wilson, *English Literature in the Earlier Seventeenth Century, 1600-1660*, 72.

8 Hill, *The English Bible and the 17th-Century Revolution*, 202.

9 Raven, James, *The Business of Books: Booksellers and the English Book Trade, 1450-1850*, (New Haven: Yale University Press, 2007), 56; Cumming, H. Syer. 'On the Old Traders' Signs in St Paul's Churchyard' *Journal of the British Archaeological Association 39. 1883*

10 Roberts, William, *The Book-Hunter in London, Historical and Other Studies of Collectors and Collecting*, (London: Elliot Stock, 1895), 211-13.

11 De Hamel, *The Book: A History of the Bible*, 250.

12 Norton, *A History of the Bible as Literature*, 218.

13 Norton, *A History of the Bible as Literature*, 218.

14 Norton, *A History of the Bible as Literature*, 219-20.

15 Lewis, John, *A Complete History of the Several Translations of the Holy Bible, and New Testament, Into English: Both in Ms. and in Print: and of the Most Remarkable Editions of Them Since the Invention of Printing*, (London: Printed by H. Woodfall, for Joseph Pote, 1739), 345.

16 Hill, *Turbulent, Seditious and Factious People*, 13–14.

17 Lewis, *A Complete History of the Several Translations of the Holy Bible*, 376.

18 In Geddes, Alexander, *Proposals for printing by subscription a new translation of the Holy Bible, from corrected texts of the originals; with various readings, explanatory notes, and critical observations. (With specimens of the work.)* (London: Printed by J. Davis; and sold by R. Faulder and J. Johnson, 1788)

19 Origen, *Contra Celsus*, quoted Gamble, *Books and Readers in the Early Church*, 1.

20 See Peterson, Eugene, *Eat this Book: A Conversation in the Art of Spiritual Reading*, (London: Hodder & Stoughton, 2006), 147-150.

The Global Bible

1 De Hamel, *The Book: A History of the Bible*, 260.

2 De Hamel, *The Book: A History of the Bible*, 261.

3 Roe, James M., *A History of the British and Foreign Bible Society, 1905-1954*, (London: British and Foreign Society, 1965), 9 Only one language – Fante – came from tropical Africa, and two languages – Malay and Formosan – from the Far East.

4 He's another link to Burford, actually, having invested in a Burford paper mill. Gretton, R. H., *The Burford Records: A Study in Minor Town Government*, (Oxford: The Clarendon Press, 1920), 477.

5 Roe, James M., *A History of the British and Foreign Bible Society, 1905-1954*, 2

6 Roe, *A History of the British and Foreign Bible Society, 1905-1954*, 51–52.

7 Roe, *A History of the British and Foreign Bible Society, 1905-1954*, 84.

8 Roe, *A History of the British and Foreign Bible Society, 1905-1954*, 80.

9 Wegner, *The Journey From Texts to Translations: The Origin and Development of the Bible*, (Grand Rapids: Baker Books, 1999), 316.

10 Quoted in Norton, *A History of the Bible as Literature*, 315.

11 Quoted in Norton, *A History of the Bible as Literature*, 317.

12 T.H. Darlow, 'Deep Calleth unto Deep' in Roe, *A History of the British and Foreign Bible Society, 1905-1954*, 210-11.

The Dangerous Bible

1 From Gullickson, Gay L. 'Emily Wilding Davison: secular martyr?' *Social Research* 75 (2). Summer 2008

2 Roe, *A History of the British and Foreign Bible Society, 1905-1954*, 271-72.

3 Green, *A New History of Christianity*, 307.

4 On Christian resistance to the Nazis, see Glover, Jonathan, *Humanity: a Moral History of the Twentieth Century* (London: Pimlico, 2001), 382–393.

5 Wegner, *The Journey From Texts to Translations*, 328. Tyndale used Erasmus' *Greek New Testament* for his source text, whereas the scholars of the Authorised Version used 'fewer than twenty five late manuscripts of the New Testament and these were carelessly used.' Jack P. Lewis quoted in Wegner *The Journey From Texts to Translations*, 311.

6 Quoted in Ferguson, Niall, *The War of the World: History's Age of Hatred*, (London: Penguin, 2007), xxxviii.

7 Chidester, David, *Christianity: A Global History*, (London: Penguin, 2001), 547.

8 '"Servant" for "slave" is largely confined to Biblical transl. and early American times.' See 'δουλος,' in Danker, Fredrick William (ed.) *A Greek - English Lexicon of the New Testament and other Early Christian Literature*, Electronic text hypertexted and prepared by OakTree Software, Inc.

9 Chidester, *Christianity: A Global History*, 436.

10 Chidester, *Christianity: A Global History*, 565.

11 'Antichrist Is Alive, and a Male Jew, Falwell Contends', *New York Times*, Jan 16, 1999.

12 Rev 3.5; 13.8; 17.8; 20.12, 15; 21.27; 22.19

13 MacCulloch, Diarmaid, *A History of Christianity*, 905

14 http://www.opendoorsuk.org.uk/press/articles/archives/000811.php

15 Wegner, *The Journey From Texts to Translations*, 394–395.

16 'North Carolina church plans Halloween Bible burning', *Daily Telegraph*, 16 Oct 2009

17 Tyndale, William, The Obedience of a Christian Man, (London: Penguin, 2000), 5.

Appendix 1: Major Modern Versions

1 Nida, Eugene A., *Good News for Everyone: How to Use the Good News Bible (Today's English Version)*, (London: Fount Paperbacks, 1977), 12.

2 Wegner, *The Journey From Texts to Translations*, 330.

INDEX

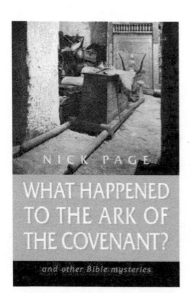

What Happened to the Ark of the Covenant?

And Other Bible Mysteries

Nick Page

This book looks at more than 30 mysteries of the Bible. From frequently asked questions like 'Where is the Ark of the Covenant?' and 'Where was Jesus born?' to less common ones such as 'Did Jesus own a house?'

Light-hearted but thoroughly researched, fun and informative, entertaining and enlightening, Nick Page combines good humour and good scholarship to create a book of biblical history that is like no other.

So, if you've ever wondered 'Just how tall was Zacchaeus?' or 'What was the date of the crucifixion?' or 'Was Jesus an only child?' then this is the book for you.

978-1-85078-751-8

The Big Story

What Actually Happens in the Bible

Nick Page

What actually happens in the Bible? How do the individual stories fit in? And how does the whole Bible come together?

The Big Story is about what happens in God's amazing book. From the creation of the universe to the end of the world, this retells the whole biblical narrative in fifty bite-size chunks. This is the ultimate family saga and the best of all blockbusters.

Fully illustrated, peppered with explanatory information and written with Nick's trademark humour and insight, this is the Bible as you have never read it before.

978-1-85078-726-6